PRINCESSES

BEHAVING

BADLY

Princesses
Behaving
BADLY

REAL STORIES
FROM HISTORY—
WITHOUT THE
FAIRY-TALE ENDINGS

BY LINDA RODRIGUEZ MCROBBIE

QUIRK BOOKS

PHILADELPHIA

Library of Congress Cataloging in Publication Number: 2012953988

ISBN: 978-1-68369-025-2

Printed in Singapore
Typeset in IM Fell and Bembo

Cover design by Doogie Horner
Cover illustration by Sara Kipin
Interior illustrations by Douglas Smith
Production management by John J. McGurk

Quirk Books
215 Church Street
Philadelphia, PA 19106
quirkbooks.com
10 9 8 7 6 5 4 3

Contents

Once Upon a Time: An Introduction   9

WARRIORS
Princesses who fought their own battles

1. Alfhild, the Princess Who Turned Pirate   15
2. Pingyang, the Princess Who Led an Army   20
   SEVEN WARRIOR QUEENS OF ANTIQUITY   25
3. Olga of Kiev, the Princess Who Slaughtered
   Her Way to Sainthood   32
4. Khutulun, the Princess Who Ruled the Wrestling Mat   37
5. Lakshmibai, the Princess Who Led a Rebellion
   (with Her Son Strapped to Her Back)   41

USURPERS
Princesses who grabbed power in a man's world

6. Hatshepsut, the Princess Who Ruled Egypt as a King   51
   A FAMILY AFFAIR: A WORD ABOUT ROYAL INCEST   56
7. Wu Zetian, the Princess who Became Emperor of China   58
   WEI'S WAY   64
8. Njinga of Ndongo, the Princess Who Kept Male
   Concubines in Drag   66

SCHEMERS
Princesses who plotted and planned

9. Justa Grata Honoria, the Princess Who Nearly Wrecked the
   Roman Empire   75

10. Isabella of France, the "She-Wolf" Princess   79

THE SORCERESS PRINCESSES   85

11. Roxolana, the Princess Who Went from Sex Slave to Sultana   92

12. Catherine Radziwill, the Stalker Princess   97

13. Stephanie von Hohenlohe, the Princess Who Partied for Hitler   105

SURVIVORS
Princesses who made controversial
and questionable choices

14. Lucrezia, the Renaissance Mafia Princess   113

15. Malinche, the Princess Who Served
Her Country's Conquerors   120

THE WAR BOOTY PRINCESS   126

16. Sophia Dorothea, the Prisoner Princess   127

MARRIAGE OR INSANE ASYLUM?   134

17. Sarah Winnemucca, the Princess Accused of Collaborating   136

18. Sofka Dolgorouky, the Princess Who Turned Communist   144

PARTIERS
Princesses who loved to live it up

19. Christina, the Cross-Dressing Princess   155

20. Caraboo, the Phony Princess Who Hoodwinked England   162

SIX WAYS TO FAKE PRINCESSHOOD   170

21. Charlotte of Prussia, the Princess Who Threw a Sex Party   182

22. Clara Ward, the Princess Who Ran Off with a Gypsy…
and a Waiter…and a Station Manager   188

THE DOLLAR PRINCESSES   196

23. Gloria von Thurn und Taxis, the Punk Princess
Who Went Corporate   200

PRINCESS EXCESS   206

FLOOZIES
Princesses notorious for their sexy exploits

24. Caroline of Brunswick–Wolfenbüttel, the Princess
Who Didn't Wash 213
 DEATH AND THE VICTORIAN AGE 221
25. Pauline Bonaparte, the Exhibitionist Princess 223
26. Margaret, the Princess Who Caused a Bank Robbery 232
 THREE PRINCESSES WHO CHUCKED THEIR CROWNS FOR LOVE 241

MADWOMEN
Princesses who were likely mad, or close to it

27. Anna of Saxony, the Princess Who Foamed at the Mouth 245
 THREE MAD PRINCESSES (AND ONE WHO PROBABLY WASN'T) 250
28. Elisabeth of Austria, the Princess Who Wore a Meat Mask 258
 BEWARE THE BLACK DWARF 265
29. Charlotte of Belgium, the Princess Who Scared the Pope 266
 ROYAL HOTLINE TO HEAVEN 272
30. Franziska, the Amnesiac Who Became the Lost
Romanov Princess 273
 FAMOUS LAST WORDS 282

Selected Bibliography 287
Index 298
Acknowledgments 302

Once Upon a Time: An Introduction

"EVERY GIRL PRETENDS SHE IS
A PRINCESS AT ONE POINT."
Lindy, from Alex Finn's Beastly

Every little girl? Not quite.

When I was growing up, I didn't want to be a princess. I wasn't a tomboy or anything; I just wasn't into them. Horses, yes, especially the unicorn or winged or, best of all, winged unicorn kind. But then again, when I was a little girl, the Disney princess wasn't the glittery pastel-colored juggernaut it is today. You could be a little girl and not limit your dress-up choices to Belle, Ariel, or Cinderella (or Mulan or Merida, if you're feeling feisty).

Nowadays, princess obsession is the default setting for many little girls. In 2000 Disney decided to market the doe-eyed denizens of its feature films by their primary identifying characteristic: their princess titles. And thus was born the princess plague. Princesses are now *the* biggest industry for the pre-tween set. In 2012 the Disney Princess media franchise was the best-selling of its kind in North America, outselling *Star Wars* and Sesame Street and earning more than $4.6 billion worldwide. Add to that all the collateral stuff—*The Princess and the Popstar* Barbies, the Melissa & Doug Decorate Your Own Princess Mirror sets, countless pink-spangled princess T-shirts—and you've got what social commentators and worried parents are calling the "Princess Industrial Complex."

In her fascinating book *Cinderella Ate My Daughter* (Harper, 2011), Peggy Orenstein examines the obsession with bundling girls into "pink and pretty" princess costumes. Orenstein, among many others, worries that princess play presents unrealistic expectations of feminine beauty, is overly restrictive (pink ball gown, or purple?), and is turning little girls into budding narcissists. So do I. Though no direct evidence supports claims that the ubiquitous princess culture harms girls' self-esteem, it seems to me that the phenomenon smacks of an unjustified sense of entitlement, a kind of fake power derived not from good decision-making skills or leadership or intelligence but physical attractiveness, wealth, and relationships with strong male characters. "Princess" is a title that establishes bizarre expectations of how one should be treated, of what has value, and of what women will or should achieve in their lives.

Obviously, most little girls don't grow up believing that life is all dress-up heels, fairy godmothers, and Prince Charmings. But the princess fantasy is one that we don't ever really give up. Witness the fascination with Kate Middleton, the pretty girl-next-door commoner who married Britain's dashing Prince William in April 2011. Though she's technically not a princess—her official title is Duchess of Cambridge—Catherine's story has all the hallmarks of a fairy tale. The royal wedding even looked like a cartoon—I almost expected to see twittering bluebirds carrying Kate's train.

Sweetly two-dimensional "Princess Kate" was the image that tabloids the world over traded on, despite the grim reality of what happened to the last British princess given the fairy-tale treatment. Blonde blue-eyed Diana *was* Cinderella, a similarity not lost on media then or now. Diana's real story, however—her marriage of convenience, her husband's infidelity, rumors of her own unfaithfulness, struggles with fame and eating disorders, her courtship of the British press, and her eventual death after being chased by paparazzi—is distinctly *not* the happy fairy tale everyone hoped for.

Perhaps the best way to make sure that the fairy tale doesn't become the expectation is to talk about real princesses and to stop turning their lives into fairy tales. Some real princesses were women who found themselves in circumstances they couldn't control. Sophia Dorothea of Celle, for example, was forced to marry a man she called "pig snout," a man who violently assaulted her, cheated on her, and, after she retaliated by having her own affair, locked her in a castle for more than three decades until her death. Others, like Anna of Saxony, were genuinely mentally unstable—a limited gene pool can be just as corrupting as absolute power. Pretty Grimm.

But some princesses found ways to shape their own destinies. Empress Wu of China showed that princesses can be just as Machiavellian as any prince. Some, like Sarah Winnemucca, used their titles (both real and imagined) to draw attention to a higher cause. Others were just out for a good time, like the American Clara Ward, a so-called Dollar Princess who left her Prince Not-So-Charming to run off with a gypsy violinist. And more than a few weren't even princesses at all, like Caraboo or Franziska, the Polish factory worker who claimed to be the lost Romanov princess Anastasia.

Historical princesses have been capable of great things as well as horrible things; they've made stupid decisions and bad mistakes, loved the wrong people or too many people or not enough people. They are women who lied, murdered, used sex as a weapon, or dressed like a man to hold on to power. They weren't afraid to get a little dirt, or blood, on their hands. These women were human, but the word *princess*, along with its myriad connotations, often glosses over that humanity.

For each of the women described in the following pages, I've tried to strip away the myth and portray something as close as possible to the real person. But history is only as accurate as those who record it, and that goes double when the subject is a woman. I've made every effort to track down stories from the most reliable sources, but, as with any reconstructing of the past, some of the tales must be chalked up to rumor, gossip, and assumption.

Nevertheless, here are the stories of real princesses and real women. They may begin once upon a time, but they don't always end happily ever after.

Warriors

PRINCESSES WHO
FOUGHT THEIR OWN
BATTLES

Alfhild

The Princess Who Turned Pirate

CA. 5TH CENTURY
THE ICY WATERS OF THE BALTIC SEA

*P*rincess Alfhild had a choice to make. On the one hand, a really awesome guy had finally managed to bypass her father's deadly defenses and call on her without being beheaded or poisoned. She could marry this brave young man and enjoy the life of domestic bliss that women of her era were supposed to aspire to. Or she could give up royal life and become a pirate.

Guess which path she chose?

Daddy's Girl

The only daughter of the fiercely protective fifth-century Goth king Siward, little Alfhild was raised to be modest, almost pathologically so. She was supposedly so modest that she kept her face "muffled in a robe" lest the sight of her incredible beauty provoke any nearby men to go mad with lust.

Alfhild had good reason to be so dedicated to preserving her chastity. Her story appears in the *Gesta Danorum* (Deeds of the Danes), a twelfth-century multivolume work in Latin by historian Saxo Grammaticus. If Saxo is to be believed, virginity was pretty much the only currency a woman had. But covering her face was just one of the measures taken to keep her untouched by a man. According to Saxo, King Siward did what any father of a pretty teenage daughter would do if he could:

> [He] banished her into very close keeping, and gave her a viper and a snake to rear, wishing to defend her chastity by the protection of these reptiles when they came to grow up. For it would have been hard to pry into her chamber when it was barred by so dangerous a bolt. He also enacted that if any man tried to enter it, and failed, he must straightway yield his head to be taken off and impaled on a stake. The terror which was thus attached to wantonness chastened the heated spirits of the young men.

There was, however, one young man whose "heated spirits" were inflamed by these strictures, who thought "that peril of the attempt only made it nobler." His name was Alf, and he was the son of the Danish king Sigar. One day Alf burst into Alfhild's chamber. Clad in a bloody animal hide (to drive the reptiles insane, *obviously*), he killed the viper by tossing a red-hot piece of steel down its gullet. The snake he dispatched by more traditional means: a spear to the throat.

Though impressed by how the rash young Dane had destroyed his reptilian defenses, Siward would accept him only if Alfhild "made a free and decided choice" in his favor. Alfhild was definitely charmed by the brave suitor who'd just killed her delightful pets; her mother, however, was not. She told Alfhild to "search her mind" and not to be "captivated by charming looks" or forget to "judge his virtue."

Swayed by her mother's wise counsel, Alfhild decided that Alf was not the man for her. Instead, she decided to trade her modesty for men's clothing and go to sea as a rampaging pirate, leading a crew of lady buccaneers. As you do.

HELLO, SAILOR

Why Alfhild decided to become a pirate is unclear. Saxo makes no attempt to explain her reasons, nor does he say why the "many maidens who were of the same mind" and accompanied her were of the same mind. Despite her unconventional decision, Alfhild's story was typical of historical lore of the period in one important way: the overprotection of chastity, to the exclusion of both fun and safety, speaks to the realities and values of ancient Scandinavia. And it's certainly of a piece with other shield-maiden stories, romantic tales of virgin warrior women who put down needlework and took up arms.

Although he does little to explain her motivation, Saxo took pains to note that Alfhild, though unusual in her adoption of "the life of a warlike rover," wasn't entirely unique. Other women, he claimed, "abhorred dainty living" and traded their natural "softness and light-mindedness" for swords and weapons. They "unsexed" themselves, "devoting those hands to the lance which they should rather have applied to the loom. They assailed men with their spears whom they could have melted with their looks, they thought of death and not of dalliance." Women, according to Saxo, should be off doing lady things and keeping their pretty faces hidden so as not to inflame the passions of unsuspecting men. That men's unbridled passion was hazardous enough to drive women to take up a weapon doesn't seem to have crossed his mind.

In any case, Alfhild was a raging success as a pirate. Given that becoming a pirate wasn't simply a matter of picking up a cutlass and slapping on an eyepatch, exactly how or why she succeeded is lost to the ages. Saxo is rather stingy with the details. But despite his prudish misgivings on the subject of women warriors, he concedes that Alfhild "did deeds beyond the valor of woman" (*harrumph*). She led her lady mateys to great riches, eventually becoming captain of yet another crew, this time of male pirates who were entranced by her beauty and devoted to her badassness. In time, Alfhild amassed a fleet of ships that preyed on vessels cruising the waters off Finland.

But the good times were about to come to an end. Alfhild hadn't reckoned on one thing: the doggedness of her rejected snake-slaying suitor. Alf had never given up on the beautiful, modest maiden and pursued her on "many toilsome voyages," over ice-locked seas and through several of his own pirate battles. While sailing the coasts of Finland, one day he and his crew came upon a flotilla of pirate ships. His men were against attacking such a large fleet with their few vessels, but Alf would have none of it, claiming that "it would be shameful if anyone should report to Alfhild that his desire to advance could be checked by a few ships in the path." Oh, the irony.

As the sea battle raged on, the Danes, between being massacred, wondered where "their enemies got such grace of bodily beauty and such supple limbs." Alf, along with his comrade-in-arms Borgar, stormed one of the enemy ships and made for the stern, "slaughtering all that withstood him." But when Borgar knocked the helmet off the nearest pirate, Alf saw to his astonishment that it was none other than the beautiful Alfhild, "the woman whom he had sought over land and sea in the face of so many dangers."

At that moment, Alf realized "that he must fight with kisses and not with arms; that the cruel spears must be put away, and the enemy handled with gentler dealings." Those gentler dealings included getting Alfhild out of those sweaty sailor's clothes and into Alf's warm bed. And so the plundering days were over—for Alfhild at least.

The language Saxo uses to describe Alfhild's return to princess life is particularly telling: he writes that Alf "took hold of her eagerly," "made her change her man's apparel," and "afterwards begot on her a daughter." What Alfhild wanted, and how she felt about giving up her roving adventures, is unknown, probably because Saxo didn't really care; the words he chose make it clear that Alfhild did not have a choice. After that, history (or Saxo, at least) has nothing more to say about her.

ONCE UPON A PRINCESS PIRATE

Saxo's tale of the modest princess-turned-pirate may or may not be true. After all, the *Gesta Danorum* is a "history" that includes giants, witches, and dragons alongside real-life heroes and rulers. Still, Alfhild's life as a woman warrior is likely based in a real tradition, and whether true or not, her story (and others in Saxo's rich tapestry of historical lore) was claimed to be instructive by later scholars and historians in understanding early and middle Scandinavian culture.

But what exactly did it teach future generations, those children who would have listened to the tale all snuggled up around the fire on one of those endless Scandinavian winter nights? It's hard to say. To the modern reader, it's disappointing to see Alfhild's exploits subdued by man and marriage. Why couldn't she have been a wife *and* a mother *and* a pirate? But before judging the story by a yardstick of twenty-first-century feminist values, let's remember that Saxo was recording his version of Danish history for a Christian audience living some 700 years after Alfhild's lifetime.

In Saxo's hands, Alfhild's saga, itself based on centuries-old pagan oral tradition, reinforces Christian gender norms. Alfhild is modest and chaste but also handy with an axe and a sword, in keeping with shield-maiden folklore. Alf must somehow overcome her fierceness to be worthy of her. And of course everything works out in the end, because Alfhild gives up the life of a "warlike rover" to settle down to her role of wife and mother. Saxo makes it clear how he feels about such women-in-arms—in fact, he spends more time lamenting them than he does describing Alfhild's life.

So, in its way, the story of Alfhild is as much a didactic fairy tale as Cinderella or Snow White. It just has more swashbuckling . . . and snakes.

Pingyang

The Princess Who Led an Army

CA. 600–623
TANG DYNASTY CHINA

Y ou don't take down a corrupt emperor all on your own. As a general's daughter, Pingyang knew this well. So when her father and her brother were struggling to combat the emperor's army, she didn't wait around to become war booty. She raised and commanded her own army of more than 70,000. With her help, her father was able to take the imperial throne and start a dynasty regarded as a golden age in imperial China.

And did we mention she did all that before the age of 20?

LIKE FATHER, LIKE DAUGHTER

Pingyang was the daughter of General Li Yuan, a garrison commander in seventh-century China who controlled a substantial army. Li Yuan didn't exactly *want* to be a rebel leader—he was a distant cousin of the reigning emperor—but he was influential, powerful, and ambitious. And for that reason he eventually found himself in the sights of the paranoid emperor of the Sui dynasty, Yangdi.

Yangdi remains, even today, one of the great mustachio-twirling villains of Chinese history. He murdered his own father to secure the throne, and once there, squandered his country's money and military might on failed expeditions to conquer foreign lands. He also used what was left of the treasury to finance expensive building projects for his own glory. Now broke, he raised taxes. But no one could pay them—Yangdi had conscripted all the able-bodied men for his army, leaving too few behind to farm and earn money. In 613–14, his overburdened people began to revolt—just starving peasants at first, but the rebellion soon spread to opportunistic nobles and government officials. Terrified, Yangdi began to imprison or execute anyone he found suspicious.

Yangdi had long been wary of Li Yuan, and with good reason. Sure, it was concerning that Li Yuan was an ambitious general with a strong army. But more worryingly, Li Yuan supposedly sported a birthmark in the shape of a dragon under his left armpit, an obvious sign he was destined to be emperor. Yangdi's suspicions were further confirmed in 615, when a popular street ballad making the rounds foretold that the next emperor would be named Li. Since Li was one of China's most common surnames, the prediction could have meant just about anybody, but Yangdi was pretty sure he knew which Li posed the greatest threat.

In 617 Yangdi gave the order to imprison Li Yuan, on the pretext that the general had been caught having sex with not one but two of Yangdi's concubines, a capital offense. But Yangdi was forced to rescind the command when he fell under the threat of rebels and needed help. Li Yuan, of course, saw which way the wind was blowing and realized he had two choices: seize the moment and rebel openly or be crushed in the emperor's panic. He chose rebellion.

Aided by the neighboring eastern Turks, Li Yuan pulled together an army of more than 30,000. He sent secret messages to his son Li Shimin and son-in-law Cao Shao (Pingyang's husband), informing them of his plans. That made things for Pingyang and her husband a bit tricky—they were living at the emperor's court, where Cao Shao was head of the imperial guards. Cao Shao told his wife of his plans to sneak away and join her father's rebel army, but he worried she would be in danger after he left. There was no doubt she would be; Yangdi was more than capable of holding Pingyang hostage or harming her to get back at her father and husband. But Pingyang wasn't the type to faint or fret or wait around to be tossed in a dungeon. She told her husband she could take care of herself, and a few fraught days after he left the palace, she did just that.

Pingyang made her way to her family's estate in the province of Hu. There, she found the people starving—not only was war afoot, but a severe drought had brought widespread famine. So Pingyang opened the food stores to the hungry masses, an act that forever endeared her to them. It also indebted them to her, a clever move for a woman who would soon need to raise her own army.

The Army of the Lady

Just a few months later, Pingyang's father's forces and those of her brother were embroiled in a bloody conflict with the emperor's army. Realizing that survival depended on superior numbers, Pingyang wanted to augment their troops with her own.

She started recruiting soldiers from among the people she'd just saved from starvation, enlisting the fittest and ablest to join her so-called Army of the Lady. Then she cast a wider net, reportedly ordering a young servant to try to convince a local highway robber and his merry band to join her cause. She then sent out other servants to track down additional bandits and ask them to join her as well. Why these brigands agreed is unclear, but Pingyang did have the benefit of being on the side that seemed likely to win. She made alliances with the largest and most capable of the disparate rebel groups operating in Hu. She even convinced imperial allies to desert Yangdi, including the emperor's prime minister and a general with more than 10,000 troops under his command. Within months, Pingyang had amassed more than 70,000 troops under the banner of the Army of the Lady; they swept through the countryside and went on to take the capital of Hu.

Pingyang's keen public relations instincts served her well as a general. She made her soldiers swear an oath not to pillage or loot the villages they captured. Even more surprising, after their victories, the troops distributed food to the territories' inhabitants. As the story goes, people saw the Army of the Lady as liberators, rather than just another horde of ravening locusts. Her ranks continued to swell.

The Army of the Lady's escapades in Hu forced the emperor to send troops to deal with this brave woman warrior. She roundly defeated them, enabling her brother's and father's forces to take down the bulk of the emperor's army. Less than a year after she had fled the court to join the rebellion, Pingyang, along with her father, her brother, and her husband, marched with their forces on the imperial palace in Daxingcheng. The emperor didn't stand a chance. Gazing in the mirror as his country burned around him, he reportedly said to his empress, "Such a fine head. Who will be the one to hack it off?" Yangdi fled south before the approaching armies, abandoning his palace and his throne. In the end, he wasn't beheaded—he was strangled in a bathhouse by his own advisors in 618.

Li Yuan swept into the palace and became the new emperor, establishing himself as the first leader of the Tang dynasty—still regarded as the high-water mark of imperial China—and taking the name Emperor Gaozu, or "High Progenitor." One of his first acts was to honor Pingyang as princess and bestow on her the status of marshal, a rank that came with its own military aides and staff.

Barely five years later, Pingyang died. The details remain unknown; she was only 23 years old, so the likeliest prospects are illness, death in childbirth, or, given that this is imperial China, assassination. When her father planned an elaborate funeral, complete with military honors, for the daughter whose courage and bravery had helped bring him the empire, his court asked why he would bestow such an honor on a woman. Li Yuan responded, "She was no ordinary woman."

In Pingyang's time, Chinese women of all ranks enjoyed a bit more respect and freedom than women in other contemporary societies; emperors' wives, for example, were often their husbands' acknowledged political advisors. But Pingyang *was* unique. In her day, women might exert control from behind the scenes, but jumping on a horse to command an army was extraordinary. Had she lived, she might have someday been empress in her own right.

As it was, her father abdicated the throne in 626, just three years after Pingyang's death, and her brother became Emperor Taizong. Although punctuated by a series of rebellions and civil conflict, the Tang is regarded as the last of the great Chinese dynasties, a golden era of military might and beautiful poetry. Pingyang was the PR-savvy warrior princess who helped make it happen.

Seven Warrior Queens
of Antiquity

These horse-punching, armor-wearing women who sipped wine from the skulls of vanquished foes and rode on fire-breathing steeds were tough as nails. These are ladies you do not want to cross.

Fu Hao

In 1976, Chinese archeologists uncovered the remarkably well preserved and unlooted tomb of Fu Hao, the consort of King Wu Ding of the Shang dynasty; she'd died around 1200 BCE.

Much of what is known about Fu Hao came from oracle bones found in her tomb. On these fragments, ancient Chinese diviners inscribed questions to the gods. The bones were then heated until they cracked; diviners interpreted the patterns for answers and then inscribed what they read onto the same bone. It was probably about as accurate a form of divination as augury (i.e., reading bird entrails), but it did afford modern archeologists a glimpse into what people of earlier times were worried about. Many of the questions about Fu Hao were pretty standard, such as whether her impending childbirth would be easy or whether that toothache would go away. (The answer to both: probably not.) But other questions weren't so usual, even for one of the king's three main wives: whether she'd be victorious in battle, for example, or when would be the best time for a specific sacrifice. Fu Hao wasn't just Wu Ding's wife; she was also his shaman and commander of his military forces. She conducted important religious rituals, including human and animal sacrifices, and led the Shang armies to victory against neighboring tribes. How highly Fu

Hao was esteemed is perhaps best indicated by the grand fashion in which she was sent to the afterlife. Buried with her were 468 bronze objects, including many weapons; 755 jade objects; and a stunning 6,900 pieces of cowry shell, a form of currency often buried with the dead for use in the afterlife. She was also kept company by 16 human sacrifices, including an armed man and six dogs, one of which was buried directly underneath her coffin.

ARACHIDAMIA

Women in third-century-BCE Sparta were all-around badasses. But Queen Arachidamia, wife of Eudamidas I, was among the toughest.

About 272 BCE, the mercurial military genius Pyrrhus of Epirus was persuaded to lay siege to Sparta by a jealous lord who had been passed over for the throne. Pyrrhus's armies were better equipped and far greater in number, so the Spartan Senate decided to gather the women and children and send them to safety in nearby Crete. According to the classical historian Plutarch, that decision didn't sit well with Arachidamia. She marched into the Senate, sword in hand, and declared that the women were going to stay in Sparta to face the Epirians alongside the men.

Part of the Spartan defense plan was to dig a deep trench parallel to Pyrrhus's camp. Arachidamia organized the women and children to help with the digging, completing a third of the trench themselves. Once the fighting began, these battle-hardened broads stayed to fight and nurse the wounded. Pyrrhus was forced to flee before the Spartans' snarling rage (and, it must be said, an infusion of fresh reinforcements from Macedonia).

BOUDICCA

Boudicca was wife to the chief of the Iceni tribe in East England. While her husband was alive, the Romans, who had spent the last 40 or so years trying to maintain their slippery grip on Britannia, considered him an ally and left the area alone. But after his death, they reconsidered the pact. They already held southern England, why not shoot for the whole thing?

First, the Romans tried to claim Boudicca's lands; when those weren't forthcoming, they stripped her naked, whipped her, and raped her two teenage daughters. Enraged, Boudicca raised an army of Iceni and allied tribes in AD 60. At the vanguard of what was claimed to be 120,000 warriors, both men and women, she must have made for a terrifying sight. According to Cassius Dio, a second-century Roman chronicler, she was incredibly tall and graced with curly red hair that tumbled to her hips, a sharp eye, and a "harsh" voice.

A fierce leader "possessed of greater intelligence than often belongs to women," Boudicca led her rebel forces on a path of destruction through the countryside. They destroyed the Roman Ninth Legion and sacked the capital at Colchester, and when they made it to Londinium—the commercial settlement that would later become London—they burned it to the ground. Over the course of the rebellion, thousands were killed.

In her final battle, Boudicca gave what sounds like a pregame pep talk that could rival Henry IV at Agincourt, William Wallace in *Braveheart*, or that guy in *Varsity Blues*. She rallied her troops from atop a chariot, declaring that the gods were on their side and that she, a mere woman, was prepared to die for her freedom. "Let us show them that they are hares and foxes trying to rule over dogs and wolves!" she cried.

And then her forces were destroyed, ending a tremendous run of violence and righteous rebellion. The fierce Boudicca was laid to rest, having died of illness or self-administered poison to avoid capture.

TOMYRIS

Queen Tomyris was the fourth-century ruler of the Massagetai, a nomadic people in what is now Iran. According to Herodotus, they were a warrior race, handy with a bow and arrow and good on a horse. A few more interesting details from Herodotus: they used weapons made out of gold (which sounds incredibly impractical); their wives were held in common by all tribesmen; and when a man reached old age, his relatives would ritually sacrifice and eat him.

Tomyris became their queen after the death of her husband, the king. Cyrus the Great, ruler of the Persians, thought her time of mourning would be the ideal opportunity to make a play for her kingdom. He sent an emissary to her court, pretending to be in the market for a wife, but canny Tomyris knew that wasn't what he really wanted.

After she called him on it, Cyrus set artifice aside and launched an invasion. At first, things did not go well for Tomyris: clever Cyrus divided his army, leaving some troops behind to act as bait. Led by the queen's son, the Massagetai attacked the camp, slaughtered the troops, and promptly drank all of their enemy's wine. Cyrus's soldiers then returned and massacred the drunken Massagetai, taking Tomyris's son hostage.

Tomyris gave Cyrus an ultimatum: either turn over her son and leave peacefully or face the full wrath of the Massagetai. If Cyrus refused, Tomyris wrote, "I swear by the sun, the sovereign lord of the Massagetai, bloodthirsty as you are, I will give you your fill of blood."

Cyrus, of course, wasn't about to give up. So Tomyris mustered all the warriors in her kingdom and led them into battle against the Persians. It was a fiercely pitched struggle, but eventually the Persians fell, Cyrus included. When she found his body among the fallen, Tomyris decapitated it and dipped his head in blood, making good on her threat. Legend has it that she also kept his skull as a drinking cup.

SIKELGAITA

In 1058, when the Norman Conquest hacked its way to northern Italy, the Lombard princess Sikelgaita was married off to the chief conqueror, Robert "the Weasel" Guiscard. These unions were pretty standard practice: conquest may have been won on the point of a sword, but it was often cemented in front of the altar.

Though Sikelgaita could have become just another pawn in first her family's and then her husband's political maneuvering, she didn't. In fact, she was awesome enough to merit a mention 100 years later in the writings of another royal from a rival empire. According to Anna Komnena, a twelfth-century Byzantine princess and historian, Sikelgaita disapproved of the Normans' campaign against the Byzantines in 1081. Robert had already taken much of southern Italy, including Salerno, and Sikelgaita tried to persuade him not to press his luck with the neighboring superpower. But after Robert made up his mind to ignore her advice, Sikelgaita decided to do more than her wifely duty called for. Donning armor ("she was indeed a formidable size"), she marched with her husband to Brindisi, on the coast of Italy, and crossed the Adriatic with him to face the Byzantines on their own turf.

Robert and his Normans were no match for the Byzantines. Terrified for their lives, Robert's men began to retreat, which pissed off Sikelgaita mightily. Glaring "fiercely" at them, she shouted, "How far will ye run? Halt! Be men!" (Maybe not quite in those Homeric words, but something like them in her own dialect, according to Komnena.) The story continues: "As they continued to run, she grasped a long spear and charged at full gallop against them. It brought them back to their senses and they went back to fight."

And they won, at least in the short term. Within two years, Robert was forced to return to Italy and defend his ally the pope against the grabby Holy Roman Emperor. But two years after that, Sikelgaita returned to Byzantium with her husband, ready to rally the troops. This time, her pep talks weren't enough, and to make matters worse, her husband died of a fever in the middle of staging their comeback. The Normans never really regained the lands they had lost to the Byzantines.

When Robert was on his deathbed in 1085, Sikelgaita was involved in some more bold behavior, this time of a more questionable nature. Supposedly, she tried to poison Robert's son by his first wife, paving the way for her own son to rule. Her scheme was found out by her dying husband, and she was forced to provide an antidote. (Also supposedly, she then poisoned Robert, if just to hasten his death.)

Sikelgaita worked out her differences with Robert's first son, and her own child was allowed to become a duke. She lived out her years as a powerful duchess until her death, in 1090.

Queen Durgavati

That Queen Durgavati resisted the Mughal conquest of her lands is impressive enough. But that she did so *with an arrow stuck in her eye* is even more so.

Born in 1524 in what is now north-central India, Durgavati was a descendant of the Chandel kings, a 300-year-old line of rulers. Her marriage to a prince of the Gondwana kingdom united two independent dynasties. When her husband died in 1545, Durgavati's infant son was too young to rule, so, like many queens before and since, she became his regent. For the next two decades, Durgavati's rule was marked by both an expansion of her nation's economic wealth and her brave resistance to the invasion threats of the neighbouring Malwa and Bengal states.

But in 1564, Durgavati faced an enemy even greater and more implacable: the Mughal emperor Akbar, who wanted to add the Gondwana lands to his own. First, Akbar sent a message saying that should Durgavati agree to become his vassal and pay him tribute, he would leave her kingdom unharmed. Durgavati refused, declaring that it would be better to die in freedom than to live as a slave to this foreign king. So Akbar sent an army in an effort to either affect the latter or hasten the former.

Durgavati responded with an army of her own, leading the charge with bow and arrow. After heavy losses and the wounding of her son, things looked bleak. And then Durgavati was struck by an arrow through the eye. Undaunted and fueled by battle lust, she broke off the shaft and kept on fighting with the arrowhead still embedded in her eye. But she was hit again, this time in the neck. Afraid of being captured, she commanded her elephant handler to kill her. He refused, and so she grabbed his dagger and took her own life.

The battle was lost, and so was the kingdom.

AMINA OF ZARIA

The eldest daughter of the ruling queen, Amina was the best rider and archer in sixteenth-century Hausaland, the fertile area between Lake Chad and the Niger River in what is now north-central Nigeria. This "pink-heeled" princess, as legends describe her, defended her lands against invasions by other African tribes who had recently converted to Islam.

A wicked archer who could pick off targets in even the farthest hills, Amina rode a horse named Demon that was said to snort fire. With her armies of more than 20,000 men and women, Amina retook lands that invaders had captured and beyond, claiming territory as far as the source of the Niger River. To protect her states, she built a series of fortresses, the remnants of which still exist. In each village she conquered, she took a lover, discarding him when she moved on to the next town.

When she wasn't making war or taking lovers, Amina forged trade routes through the Sahara. She reigned as queen for 34 years and is still remembered today thanks to the Nigerian schools and other institutions that bear her name.

Olga of Kiev

The Princess Who Slaughtered Her Way to Sainthood

CA. 890-969
KIEVAN RUS (NOW KNOWN AS UKRAINE)

P rincess Olga of Kiev was married to a greedy man. Greedy and, it appears, none too bright. His name was Igor, and he was the unpopular ruler of Kievan Rus, the proto-Russian tenth-century kingdom that took its name from the capital city of Kiev. Igor's subjects resented his military campaign against the Derevlian tribe, a Slavic kingdom to the west, and the subsequent drain on their resources. And if Igor was unpopular with his own people, imagine how much less the Derevlians liked him. Especially after he violently subjugated them and forced them to pay an annual tribute not just once, as was customary (and implied by the word *annual*), but twice.

In 945 Igor demanded still more from the Derevlians: more money, more furs, more honey. Prince Mal, their leader, cautioned his comrades: "If a wolf comes among the sheep, he will take away the whole flock one by one, unless he be killed. If we do not thus kill him now, he will destroy us all." So kill Igor they did, in spectacularly gruesome fashion: they captured him, tied him between two trees, and ripped him in half. Igor's death left Olga a widow with a three-year-old son, Sviatoslav, barely tall enough to reach the throne, much less sit on it.

Next it was the Derevlians' turn to get greedy. Emboldened by their execution of the tyrant, they thought, "See, we have killed the Prince of Russia. Let us take his wife Olga for our Prince Mal, and then we shall obtain possession of Sviatoslav, and work our will upon him."

It was a good plan and it might have worked, except they hadn't reckoned on one thing: Olga.

BLOODY REVENGE

The story of how Olga handled her Derevlian problem appears in *The Tales of Bygone Years*, also called the "Russian Primary Chronicle," a collection of myths and stories that date from the founding of the proto-Russian state. It goes like this:

After they killed her husband, the Derevlians sent 20 of their top men to negotiate with Olga. Olga greeted them graciously and asked why they'd come. Their answer: with her husband dead, how did she feel about marrying Prince Mal? Olga could not have seemed more reasonable. "Your proposal is pleasing to me; indeed, my husband cannot rise again from the dead," she told them. She then asked the men to return the next day so that she could honor them in the presence of her court. That night, Olga had her men dig a large ditch in front of her castle. When the envoys returned, they were dumped in the pit and buried alive. Before her men shoveled dirt over them, Princess Olga leaned over the edge and asked if this particular honor was to their taste. And she was far from finished.

Her next move was to send word back to the Derevlians, requesting their noblest and most distinguished men to come to her court and accompany her back to their kingdom so that she could join their prince. If not shown this honor, she warned, her people would not let her go. The duped Derevlians complied, and Olga received the noblemen kindly, directing them to a bathhouse where they could wash after the long journey. Once the visitors were inside, she ordered the doors locked and then set the building on fire. Round two.

Apparently, no one was telling the Derevlians that every man they'd sent so far had been murdered. So they weren't suspicious when Olga sent yet another message. This one claimed that she was coming, and it directed the Derevlians to "prepare great quantities of mead" in the city where her husband's body was buried, so that she could "weep over his grave and hold a funeral feast for him." She arrived with a small retinue of soldiers. When the Derevlians asked where all their noble and best men were, she lied and said they were on the way. In the meantime, she suggested they all get down to feasting and drinking. The Derevlians did so, and with gusto; once they were drunk enough, Olga gave the word. Her men fell upon the drunken Derevlians and slaughtered 5,000 of them.

But she wasn't done yet.

Olga returned to Kiev and readied her "large and valiant army" to attack the surviving Derevlians. Her soldiers cut a devastating swath through the countryside; after the Derevlians' cities fell to her bloodthirsty horde, the vanquished retreated behind the walls of their principal city, Izkorosten. Olga and her army spent a year trying to take the city by force, but without success. Finally, she devised another plan.

Olga sent a message to the besieged people, asking, "Why do you persist in holding out? All your cities have surrendered to me and submitted to tribute, so that the inhabitants now cultivate their fields and their lands in peace. But you had rather die of hunger, without submitting to tribute." The Derevlians responded that they'd be happy to give her tribute, but they knew she was still bent on revenge.

Not so, replied Olga. "Since I have already avenged the misfortune of my husband twice on the occasions when your messengers came to

Kiev, and a third time when I held a funeral feast for him, I do not desire further revenge but am anxious to receive a small tribute. After I have made peace with you, I shall return home again." It was indeed a small tribute she requested: three sparrows and three doves from everyone in the city. The people gladly handed over the birds and rejoiced.

But Olga *still* wasn't done.

Once night fell, Olga had her soldiers tie cloths dipped in sulfur to the feet of each bird. The winged incendiaries were released, flew straight home, and set every house on fire. She ordered her soldiers to kill or capture anyone who escaped.

Only then was Olga done.

An Unorthodox Saint

The Tales of Bygone Years was written centuries after Olga's death, and it's unclear if the account of her bloody revenge is factual. The story echoes several Viking myths, which seem particularly fascinated with the gory revenge of angry widows. Moreover, if the timing is accurate, Olga would have been a mature mom of about 55 when she went to war. Other sources do corroborate parts of the story, specifically Igor's grisly murder and the equally gruesome military retribution that followed.

But Olga *was* a real person, though little is known about her life before the events in her revenge story. What is certain is that she was a member by marriage of the Riurikid dynasty, which was founded in 862 by the Viking warlord Riurik and which ruled Kievan Rus until the 1500s. When Olga came to power, Kievan Rus was still just a loose federation of Vikings, Slavs, and other pagan tribes. After exacting her revenge, she acted as regent for her son with efficiency and strength for at least two decades. She was the first Kievan ruler to introduce the use of currency, and her administrative innovations resulted in a more unified nation, with embassies and ambassadors across Europe and the Mediterranean.

She was also the first of her dynasty to convert to Eastern Orthodox Christianity, which opened up new commercial and diplomatic possibilities with Christian Byzantine, Moravian, and Bulgarian neighbors. Her baptism in Constantinople in 954/55 is another legendary example of her cunning. The story goes that Constantine VII was so enamored of her that he proposed marriage. But Olga wanted only to trade with Byzantium, not give Constantine an excuse to rule Kievan Rus, so she pointed out that marriage would be impossible because she wasn't a Christian. If he were willing to perform the baptism himself, however, then she would reconsider; the ceremony was arranged. Afterward, when Constantine reiterated his proposal, Olga replied, "How can you marry me, after yourself baptizing me and calling me your daughter? For among Christians that is unlawful, as you yourself must know."

Olga's conversion to Christianity made her a religious minority in her own country, and it eventually made her a saint. Though her efforts to establish the Orthodox church as the religious authority in Kievan Rus did not succeed in her lifetime, she's still regarded as the grandmother of the church in Russia and Ukraine.

Olga's brutal revenge story is rooted in her pagan past. In the years after her death, she was revered by the faithful for her piety. Later church biographers would claim that "although she was a woman in body, she possessed a man's courage," bestowing the "compliment" that she was as "radiant among infidels like a pearl in the dung." The whitewashing of her record succeeded—these days it's Saint Olga the Ukrainians remember. In 1997, an Eastern Orthodox monastic order called the Order of Princess Olga was formed, devoted to the bloody saint of Kievan Rus.

Khutulun

The Princess Who Ruled the Wrestling Mat

CA. 1260–CA. 1306
CENTRAL ASIA

P rincess Khutulun's parents were getting nervous. It wasn't just that their little girl was a bit of a tomboy; most women in thirteenth-century Mongol tribes were capable of playing rough. What was worrying was that Khutulun was approaching 20 years old, practically a spinster, and still wasn't married. She refused to wed anyone who couldn't beat her at her favorite sport—wrestling. And so far, no one could. Even worse, the nasty rumors about why she remained single were starting to tarnish her father's reputation.

A bold prince who fit all the specs had come forward to accept Khutulun's challenge; he was so cocksure of winning that he put a herd of 1,000 horses on the line. Khutulun's anxious parents pressured her to let him win. But would she go to the mat, even for the sake of her kingdom?

Ready to Rumble

Khutulun had battle in her blood. Born around 1260, she was the daughter and favorite child of Qaidu Khan, a fierce regional ruler in Central Asia. She was also the niece of Khubilai Khan, the great-great-granddaughter of Genghis Khan, and the only girl in a family of 14 boys. That she took up wrestling is no surprise. But that she turned out to be unbelievably good at it, so good that no man in the kingdom could best her? That was a problem.

Some chroniclers describe Khutulun as "beautiful," although that might've been a bit of artistic license—she was a big-boned, broad-shouldered girl who, from an early age, was taught to ride and to shoot with bow and arrow. In Mongol tribes, both sexes learned to defend their flocks of sheep, and a bow made an ideal weapon for children and women because it required precision rather than great strength to wield. Unlike other Mongolian girls, however, Khutulun also learned to wrestle. She proved to be exceptional at all of it, which endeared her to her father tremendously. As she grew up, her father came to lean on her for strength, support, advice, and battle prowess.

Khutulun's skills were remarkable enough to attract the attention of outsiders like Marco Polo, the nomadic Venetian merchant whose travel chronicles gave birth to the West's fascination with the East. But in Mongolian royal tradition, she may not have been so unusual. Besides their skill at archery, Mongolian royal women commanded armies, raced horses, and ruled vast territories. Genghis Khan considered his daughters superior leaders compared to his sons, and he awarded them kingdoms that they defended tooth and nail (oftentimes against their male siblings).

Khutulun was clearly an inheritor of Mongolian X-chromosomal martial strength. When at her father's side in battle—which was pretty often since Qaidu was perpetually at war with Khubilai Khan's forces—

she was terrifying. Marco Polo reports that at the right moment, she would "make a dash at the host of the enemy, and seize some man thereout as deftly as a hawk pounces on a bird, and carry him to her father."

Stories of Khutulun's battlefield prowess were passed around contemporary chroniclers as lurid, tantalizing tales of war-mad Mongols. But among the tribes, it was Khutulun's wrestling skills that made her a legend. She was unbeatable. Mongols frequently bet horses on wrestling matches, and she reportedly amassed more than 10,000 by winning all her bouts. And as Marco Polo noted, Khutulun, a veritable "giantess," refused to marry unless her prospective groom could beat her in the ring.

Meet Your Match

By 1280, enemies of Khutulun's family were spreading rumors that the reason she refused to marry was because she was not only her father's favorite, but his lover as well. Then along came that eligible young prince (and his wager of 1,000 horses) to try his luck. He was quite the catch, according to Marco Polo, "a noble young gallant, the son of a rich and puissant king, a man of prowess and valiance and great strength of body," not to mention "handsome, fearless and strong in every way." Seeing a way out of an uncomfortable predicament, Khutulun's parents pressured her to throw the match.

At first it looked like she would. Polo, history's favorite tourist, witnessed the event and attests that "they grappled each other by the arms and wrestled this way and that, but for a long time, neither could get the better of the other." But the match was over when Khutulun threw her opponent "right valiantly onto the palace pavement. . . . And when he found himself thus thrown, and her standing over him, great indeed was his shame and discomfiture." Khutulun now had no prince, and another thousand horses to feed.

Eventually, and probably to her parents' great relief, Khutulun did marry. But it wasn't to a man who beat her on the wrestling mat—it was, gossips claimed, true love. Little is known about the man who finally tamed her heart, other than that she chose him of her own volition. But not even marriage could bring this princess to the mat. She still fought alongside her father, venturing ever deeper into Mongolia and China on punishing military campaigns. When Qaidu died of battle wounds in 1301, there was even talk of Khutulun succeeding him as khan.

That didn't fly with the rest of her family, especially all those brothers. "You should mind your scissors and needles!" one of them said, according to a contemporary Persian historian. What happened to her next is unclear—her detractors claim that she spent the years after her father's death "stirring up sedition and strife" in support of her brother's candidacy for the khan. By 1306 she was dead, either killed in battle or assassinated by a rival sibling.

Khutulun's death signaled a change in Mongolia and the empire that Genghis Khan had built. She was the last of the wild warrior-women leaders of the tribes. One theory posits that as women began to fall away from leadership, the ruling of the empire was left to increasingly indolent men. As a result, the Mongol empire stagnated and disintegrated. Maybe.

Khutulun's legend might have been forgotten if not for an exotic tale titled "Turandot," published in a volume of fables by French scholar François Pétis de la Croix in 1710. Pétis de la Croix came across her story while researching his biography of Genghis Khan, and he transformed the brutish wrestling princess into the beautiful 19-year-old daughter of a fictional Chinese emperor who refused to marry unless her suitor could prove himself her intellectual equal. In 1761, the story became *Turandotte*, a play by Italian playwright Carlo Gozzi, featuring a "tigerish woman" whose pride is her undoing. *Turandotte* became Giacomo Puccini's *Turandot*, the opera he was working on when he died in 1924 (it was completed by a colleague).

In Mongolian culture, Khutulun is remembered by the sport in which she so excelled. These days when Mongolian men wrestle, they wear a sort of long-sleeved vest that is open in the front to prove to their opponents they don't have breasts. It's a tribute to the woman wrestler who was never defeated.

Lakshmibai

The Princess Who Led a Rebellion (with Her Son Strapped to Her Back)

1834–June 17, 1858
Jhansi, north-Central India

Rani Lakshmibai of Jhansi died in the heat of battle with the reins of her horse in her teeth and a sword in each hand. Or maybe she was turning to cut down the soldier who'd just shot her in the back. Or maybe she was only wounded and survived long enough to distribute her jewelry to her men and have them build her funeral pyre. Accounts vary. However death came, Lakshmibai did die and in death became a legend, a symbol of India's struggle against colonial oppression.

But the truth is, she didn't set out to be a rebel. She was the young widow of a maharaja in the state of Jhansi when the Indians rebelled against the British East India Company in 1857, and her intent was to hold on until the British regained control. But when the British labeled her a sympathizer at best and a rebellious whore at worst, Rani Lakshmibai decided to show them just how rebellious she could be.

Becoming Rani

Before she was Rani Lakshmibai (*rani* means "princess" or "queen" in Hindi), she was just Bithur Manu, a little Brahmin girl who'd lost her mother when she was very small. Growing up in the luxurious court of the deposed chief minister of the defunct Maratha Empire, Manu played only with boys, and so she did the things they did. She learned to read and write and was taught to ride horses and elephants, use a sword, and fly a kite. She was said to be exceptionally brave. Once, when a rampaging elephant was loose in her city, Manu leapt onto its trunk and calmed the beast before it could do any more damage. It's unclear how much of this tomboy tale is true—the elephant probably is not—but little Manu was destined for greatness.

In 1842, she was married to a childless widower, the much older maharaja of a city-state in north-central India that had sworn allegiance to the British East India Company (EIC). Traditional sources claim that she was only 8 years old at the time, not an uncommon marrying age for Indian royalty in the nineteenth century. The union gave her a new name, Lakshmibai, put an end to her carefree childhood, and tied her to Jhansi, a hot, dry place where the wicked dust storms were called "the devil's breath."

By the time Lakshmibai was 14, her marriage was consummated; by 17, she was pregnant. But the birth of her son and the maharaja's heir brought only short-lived happiness—the boy died at just 3 months old, followed soon after by her devastated husband.

So in November 1853, Rani Lakshmibai was a teenaged widow. A *vulnerable* widow, the British probably thought. Just before his death, the old maharaja had tried to keep the EIC from seizing Jhansi lands by adopting a 5-year-old boy and naming him as heir; administration of the state would be vested in Lakshmibai until the child came of age. But Lord Dalhousie, governor general of the EIC, refused to recognize either Lakshmibai or the boy as rightful rulers. In early 1854, the EIC annexed Jhansi, claiming it would be better for the inhabitants if they were under direct company rule. Rani Lakshmibai was given a life pension and allowed to remain in the palace. She demanded the governor general reconsider, writing letters pointing out various aspects of British and Indian law that upheld her claim. Dalhousie refused, and Jhansi was swallowed up by the EIC.

On the Offense

British presence in India would have been ludicrous if not for the money the country brought in and the pretensions of empire it afforded. The EIC had ruled since around 1773 through a combination of outright landownership, mostly acquired through wars and annexation, and by using existing royal families as puppet administrators. But India was hot and full of diseases to which the colonials were unaccustomed. Local populations chafed under the restrictions placed on their autonomy as well as British residents' general disregard for local religious institutions, laws, and customs. It was only a matter of time before things got nasty.

In May 1857, Indian sepoys (native troops recruited by the EIC) decided they'd had enough. The spark that lit the powder keg was the decision by EIC army commanders to use greased-cartridge rifles. It was common practice to bite open the cartridges to release the gunpowder, meaning that the soldiers would probably inadvertently consume some of the grease. In a ridiculous oversight, the grease in question was made from cow or pig fat, angering both the Hindus, whose religion regards the cow as a sacred animal and the pig as disgusting, and the Muslims, whose faith explicitly disallows the consumption of pork products. The grease was replaced, but the damage was done—several sepoys refused to use the cartridges.

On May 10, after the protesting sepoys were court-martialed and sentenced to hard labor, revolt began in the city of Meerut. The British were slaughtered as they left church; looting, rape, murder, and arson swept through the city. Chaos thundered into nearby Delhi, where the last Mughal emperor gave his support to the rebellion and nominated his own (inexperienced) son to command the military forces.

Within a month, revolutionary fire spread to Jhansi, where British administrators had not exactly endeared themselves to the local population after taking control four years earlier. First, they'd lifted the ban on the slaughter of cows, an outrage to the Hindu population. Then they demanded that revenues earmarked for a Hindu temple be remitted to the East India Company. Finally, they forced Lakshmibai to pay some of her husband's state debts out of her private pension and cut her off from funds left by the late maharaja for the couple's adopted son. The rani's appeals on behalf of her people went unanswered, and by the time rebellion reached Jhansi, anger had long been building.

The simmering resentment exploded into the June 8, 1857, massacre of 61 English men, women, and children who'd taken refuge at the fort in Jhansi before surrendering to rebel forces. Contrary to later reports, Lakshmibai seems not to have taken part in that uprising—she was besieged in her palace by mutineers at the time.

When the insurgents left Jhansi later that month, the remains of British authority left with them. The rani took control and began to deal with the defense of her lands by enlisting troops, casting cannons, and making weapons. Popular legend claims that Lakshmibai trained her own regiment of female soldiers. Whether or not that's true (most likely not), the military wasn't created to fight the British. Rather, her army was defending Jhansi from neighboring rajs looking to exploit the power vacuum and build their own empires. In September and October of 1857, the rani successfully fended off assaults from two would-be emperors.

In fact, though Rani Lakshmibai had more than enough reason to cast her lot with the rebels, throughout that summer and into autumn she repeatedly affirmed her allegiance to the absent British authority. When, for example, the mutineers who'd besieged the English at the fort demanded she provide them with weapons and money, Lakshmibai agreed but wrote to the British explaining her actions and asking for help and protection against her neighbors, appeals that were never answered. Even when asked by the warden of the local jail if she'd fight against the British, Lakshmibai replied that she would return Jhansi to English rule as soon as they returned. The British, however, didn't believe her.

In the months after the rebellion broke out, Lakshmibai was declared a rebel by British forces, slandered in the press and in official company documents. She was branded a "licentious" woman, a "jezebel," and a whore responsible for that horrifying massacre at the fort. The British wanted someone to blame, and Rani Lakshmibai was a convenient scapegoat.

By winter 1858, the unorganized rebellion was dying in the face of British counterinsurgency; most of northern India was back under colonial rule. At the end of February, British forces were moving to take back Jhansi, and they intended to do so with force. After months of pleading for aid and declaring herself their loyal friend, Lakshmibai came to realize that if she were caught by the British, she would likely be tried as a rebel and hanged. But if she sided with the rebels, at least she could die fighting. So as the army marched ever closer, Rani Lakshmibai finally became what the British claimed she was.

Rebel with a Cause

On March 23, the British siege of Jhansi began. Lakshmibai oversaw the defense of her city against cannon fire; when walls crumbled, she directed that they be rebuilt. On March 30, another rebel leader (and childhood friend of the rani) came to her defense with 20,000 troops. Hope was extinguished, however, when the army of raw recruits was defeated and the British broke through city walls. Contemporary accounts say the streets "ran with blood" as the Jhansi forces fought in hand-to-hand combat. The palace was captured, but as the British readied their final assault, their general received word that Lakshmibai had escaped. And with a contingent of soldiers, to boot.

The British assault devastated Jhansi's defenses, but more problematically, the fort's water supply had gone dry. Flight was Lakshmibai's only option. Dressed as a soldier and with her adopted son in tow (either strapped to her back or tucked in her lap), she took off on horseback into the night. The British cavalry was hot on her heels. An officer came within snatching distance, but Lakshmibai succeeded in striking him down with her sword. (This is probably the genesis of the folk-art images of Lakshmibai plunging into battle with her son strapped to her back, which, were it true, would be a very questionable parenting decision.)

Lakshmibai now had a price on her head. She joined the other rebels at Kalpi, a city some 90 miles east of Jhansi, but to her great chagrin and the everlasting lament of the people in the region, she was not given command of the rebel army. That honor went to the childhood friend who'd failed to save Jhansi even when his army outnumbered the British five to one.

The city of Kunch fell to the British, and then Kalpi capitulated, with Rani Lakshmibai barely escaping. The rebels decided to make one last stand at Gwalior, traditionally a region that supported the British but whose troops had been won over to the rebel cause. Confident that Gwalior would be the site of victory, rebel leaders started celebrating before the battle had even begun. But not Rani Lakshmibai. While her compatriots ate and prayed and sang, she inspected the troops from horseback, armed with sword and pistol.

When the British arrived on June 17, 1858, Lakshmibai and her forces were waiting for them at the gates. Dressed in full battle gear, with sword drawn, the rani of Jhansi plunged into battle and, all accounts agree, faced death bravely.

The exact circumstances of her demise are unclear. One story says that when she was cut down, she was fighting with two swords, one in each hand, the reins of her horse gripped in her teeth. Another says she was shot in the back, turned to fire on her assassin, and was run through with a sword. Still other accounts claim she was fatally wounded but managed to stay alive long enough to instruct her soldiers to build her funeral pyre; before she dragged herself to it to be burned alive, she distributed her gold jewelry among her troops. However it happened, Rani Lakshmibai's death signaled the end of the rebellion. The road to Gwalior was taken by the British, and the city itself soon fell. The revolt was over.

Despite defeat, the rebellion could claim one important victory—the end of rule by the East India Company. By August 1858, the dust had cleared and the EIC was officially dissolved. But the British experiment in India was far from over. Queen Victoria assumed the title Empress of India, and her government took control of the country as the British Raj. It wasn't until 1947 that the country gained its independence, remaining a dominion of the British crown until 1950.

Throughout India's struggle for independence, Rani Lakshmibai's legend was an inspiration. Her story is still taught in schools, and she even stars in an eponymous series of comic books; she is a hero, a political symbol, the Indian Joan of Arc. Even Sir Hugh Rose, who faced this "bravest of the rebel leaders" in battle, had to admit: "The best man on the side of the enemy was the Rani of Jhansi."

Usurpers

PRINCESSES WHO
GRABBED POWER IN
A MAN'S WORLD

Hatshepsut

The Princess Who Ruled Egypt as a King

Ca. 1508-1458 BCE
Ancient Egypt

*H*atshepsut must have known a thing or two about public relations. How else could an overweight, balding, middle-aged princess transform herself into a svelte, athletic, divinely conceived king? It's lucky that the men who tried to chisel her from history didn't do a very good job. Otherwise, we probably wouldn't know anything about ancient Egypt's most successful and longest-serving female ruler, one of only three women in as many millennia to seize the title and power of pharaoh.

Hatshepsut was born during the New Kingdom period, ancient Egypt's golden age. She was the eldest daughter of the Eighteenth Dynasty ruler Tuthmosis I, a great military leader, and his consort, Queen Ahmose. According to her own (probably less than honest) claims, Hatshepsut was her father's favorite child and the person he wanted to ascend to the throne after his death. Unfortunately for her, Dad didn't make his wishes explicit. So when he died, a prince was located among the sons born to the women of the pharaoh's harem.

The leading candidate was Prince Tuthmosis, the son of a minor concubine, who was willing to marry Hatshepsut, his half-sister, to solidify his claim to the throne (see "A Family Affair," page 56, for more on royal incest throughout the ages). Unchallenged, he became Tuthmosis II, and his wife/half sister became queen.

But Tuthmosis II died unexpectedly only three years later (CT scans of his remains indicate the cause was heart disease). Once again, a dynastic struggle loomed—Hatshepsut had borne only a girl, and so another prince from the mistress pack was pushed forward. Though just a baby, Tuthmosis III became the new pharaoh.

Hatshepsut, now dowager queen, stepped in to rule as regent until the boy (technically her stepson *and* nephew, mind you) was old enough to assume power. This was pretty much standard procedure in Egypt at the time; mothers often ruled in place of their infant sons, and wives took over while their husbands were at war. For about two years, Hatshepsut played the role of dutiful regent, recognizing Tuthmosis III as pharaoh. Then something strange happened: Hatshepsut shoved aside the toddler pharaoh and crowned herself king.

Female Pharaoh

Boldly naming herself king required more than a little cunning to pull off. It was a move that took balls (literally), because divine order required that a pharaoh be male. So how'd she do it? With a three-pronged strategy. First, Hatshepsut claimed that her father had appointed her as his successor, which also reinforced the idea that she was the result of a true blue-blooded union, not just the random offspring of a minor concubine (*ahem*, Tuthmosis III). Second, Hatshepsut claimed that she was conceived when Amun, pharaoh of all the gods, had disguised himself as her father and had sex with her mother. Hatshepsut began referring to herself as "God's Wife of Amun," which doesn't entirely make sense but does imply that she was really royal *and* the daughter/wife of the godliest of gods. Her final, and perhaps most politically astute, move was to kick out all existing courtiers and then to stock the palace with supporters beholden to her.

Hatshepsut kept plenty busy outside the palace walls as well, embarking on a prodigious propaganda campaign. To cement her image as pharaoh, she was often depicted as a man; in official carvings and statues, she was shown with the slim, athletic, masculine build of the ideal ruler, wearing a cobra-shaped headdress and false beard, both pharaonic attributes. Of seemingly no consequence was that by this time she was well on her way to becoming a portly middle-aged woman cursed with the familial overbite and "huge pendulous breasts" (so say the archeologists who found her mummy).

Hatshepsut's reign was remarkable, an era marked by prosperity and peace. Foremost among her accomplishments was reestablishing trade networks with neighboring kingdoms. Her focus was clearly on enrichment rather than expansion: though she did enjoy some early martial success, she ordered her armies to embark on lucrative trading expeditions rather than mounting costly and risky military campaigns.

Hatshepsut also spent some of Egypt's significant wealth on an ambitious architectural binge. She put her subjects to work constructing massive obelisks, built or renovated temples throughout the kingdom, and commissioned hundreds of statues of herself, all so that posterity would remember her well. As she had written on an obelisk at Karnak: "Now my heart turns this way and that, as I think what the people will say. Those who see my monuments in years to come, and who shall speak of what I have done."

Which is really rather ironic, not to mention sad, given what happened next.

Hatshepsut died, apparently from complications from diabetes, about 1458 BCE, which meant it was finally time for the rightful ruler, Tuthmosis III, to take over. T-III, now in his mid-twenties, was more than ready to rock. He proved himself to be a skilled and acquisitive military commander, the Napoleon of ancient Egypt. He led 17 campaigns into the region we now call the Middle East; one of his most notable victories is still taught in military academies today.

When his own successful reign began drawing to a close, the aging Tuthmosis III decided to wage another sort of war: the eradication of any trace of his aunt/stepmother's reign. He had stonemasons chisel her name off her many monuments, cover the text on her obelisks with stone, knock down or deface her statues, and destroy painted images of her. She was even left off the official lists of Egyptian pharaohs. And it worked, at least for a couple of millennia. Though Hatshepsut was briefly mentioned in a biography of Egyptian kings written in 300 BCE, it wasn't until AD 1822, when hieroglyphics were first deciphered, that anyone had a clue she'd ever ruled.

So why did Tuthmosis III attempt to erase Hatshepsut from history? At first glance, his efforts look like more than mere spite. Ancient Egyptian culture worshipped death, or, to put it more accurately, life after death, hence the obsession with mummification. They believed that a person's spirit could survive if enough images of that person were left behind. So chiseling Hatshepsut's name off the walls and eradicating her image from statues was more than just a symbolic effort to get rid of her memory. It was an attempt to make sure she stayed dead.

Or maybe not. Egyptologists have long been divided on just how Tuthmosis III really felt about Hatshepsut. On the one hand, she had ruled in his place, and he reacted by destroying or claiming everything she'd ever made. Which helps explain why earlier historians felt obliged to cast her as the wicked stepmother, declaring her "vain, ambitious and unscrupulous" and "of a most virile character." On the other hand, consider that Hatshepsut didn't have Tuthmosis III killed, which was certainly an option. And instead of hiding him away, she allowed him to receive military training. That was a potentially dangerous decision, because it could have easily allowed him to amass loyal followers and gain strength to back up his right to rule. Tuthmosis also seems to have held his stepmother-aunt in some regard. He didn't destroy her body, which would have been the logical place to start had he really wanted to sabotage her afterlife. Moreover, his revisionist efforts didn't begin until decades after her death, meaning that he had either very long simmering resentment or other reasons altogether.

Modern Egyptologists believe that Tuthmosis acted out of not anger or resentment but rather political expediency. By all accounts a rational, clear-headed ruler, T-III simply wanted to subsume Hatshepsut's glorious reign into his own. That's why he left untouched certain images of her as queen regent. Tuthmosis was probably also worried about the succession of his son, Amenhotep II: rewriting history was one way of discouraging rival claims to the throne and ensuring that Tuthmosis's line remained in charge.

Even if Tuthmosis's attack on Hatshepsut's memory was nothing personal, it was something of a fatal blow. It has taken more than 150 years to piece together a satisfying biography of the princess who became pharaoh, and gaps still puzzle and confound. Fortunately, Tuthmosis's crew of statue-chiselers didn't get everything. One of three sarcophagi Hatshepsut made for herself was unearthed in 1903 (it was empty), and the stones that covered the inscriptions on her obelisks had helped preserve them.

Hatshepsut's mummy was found in the early part of the twentieth century; it had been unceremoniously dumped on the floor of an obscure tomb in the Valley of the Kings and robbed of its jewelry by looters. For more than two decades archeologists were unable to connect this sad pile of bones, bereft of golden afterlife accessories, to the woman who had ruled Egypt. It wasn't until 2007 that scientists were able to definitively claim that this was the body of the mysterious female pharaoh.

Still, the discovery of her mummy can't explain why Hatshepsut did what she did—why she shoved aside the rightful ruler, crowned herself pharaoh, and embarked on a prodigious campaign of propaganda to legitimize her claim. Dynastic crisis, a thirst for power, political wrangling, a need to assert authority, a hunger for glory—all are possibilities that historians have batted around. None are truly satisfying. At the end of the day, all we really know is that Hatshepsut was a remarkable woman: one who assumed supreme executive power, and did so without apology.

A Family Affair:
A Word about Royal Incest

Most cultures have incest taboos, but throughout history many royal families have been exempt. Why?

First and foremost, the practice is a way of ensuring that power stays within the same family. Brother–sister and even parent–child marriages were not uncommon in ancient Egypt, Incan Peru, or nineteenth-century Thailand and were a crafty way to keep sovereignty concentrated within a single family.

Second, some cultures believed that incest reflected the behavior of their gods. Emulating the practice strengthened the link between divinity and earthly rulers. In the early 1800s, for example, the chiefs of Hawaii encouraged a marriage between Princess Nahi'ena'ena and her brother, King Kamehameha III, citing a precedent among the old deities. That didn't go over so well with the newly arrived Christian missionaries, and instead the princess was married off to someone else, though she and her brother continued to have a sexual relationship until her death in 1836.

Third, incest set royalty apart, giving them license to do something no one else could. If you were a dutiful Catholic monarch, you could even get papal dispensation to allow your consanguineous marriage, making it acceptable in the eyes of God and man. The average Joe, meanwhile, can't even skip Sunday mass without putting his immortal soul in jeopardy.

But let's not forget that there's one very good reason why marriage between close relations is a bad, and almost universally reviled, idea: the lack of genetic variation between sexual partners can cause a match-up of harmful recessive genes, leading to significant congenital defects. The famous

Egyptian pharaoh Tutankhamun's partially cleft palate and clubfoot can probably be attributed to his parents being full siblings. Like King Tut, children of the royal houses of Europe were also victims of the need to consolidate and retain power. Marriage between cousins, even first cousins, was fully within bounds well into the twentieth century, with such unfortunate consequences as mental illness and hemophilia.

The Spanish Hapsburgs offer a cautionary tale of the problems that can come from incest. The family ruled Spain for nearly 200 years, all the while encouraging ever-closer relations to wed. The line came to a spectacular end with Charles II, the son of an uncle and his niece who were themselves mildly inbred. Charles was born mentally and physically disabled, afflicted by a tongue so large he couldn't speak until the age of 4 and a body so weak he didn't walk until 8. Later in life, he exhibited signs of mania, demanding, for example, that the bodies of his dead relatives be exhumed so he could look at them. Charles died without an heir in 1700, just five days before his 39th birthday. That he'd lived so long was a shock to most of Europe; the coroner who examined his body reportedly claimed that it "contained not a single drop of blood, his heart looked like the size of a grain of pepper, his lungs were corroded, his intestines were putrid and gangrenous, he had a single testicle which was as black as carbon and his head was full of water."

Wu Zetian

The Princess Who Became Emperor of China

FEBRUARY 17, 624-DECEMBER 16, 705
TANG DYNASTY CHINA

*W*u Zetian had "a heart like a serpent and a nature like that of a wolf," "favored evil sycophants and destroyed good and loyal officials," and "killed her sister, butchered her elder brothers, murdered the ruler, poisoned her mother. She is hated by gods and men alike."

Or so people said. Teasing out the real story from the tangle of official histories, which tend to be heavily weighted against female rulers, is tricky. In these accounts, she comes off as sadistic, cruel, and power hungry. But she managed to accomplish what no other woman did in the 3,000-year history of imperial China: rule in her own right. That she had to kill a few people to do it—including, allegedly, her own week-old daughter—was the price of power.

True Wu

Perhaps the most horrifying story about Wu was how she became empress. A minor princess of the Tang dynasty, Wu was a royal concubine who had long plotted to move up the ranks. When she had a baby girl by Emperor Gaozong—not her first child with him—she saw her chance. As was custom, the current empress came down to Wu's apartments to coo over the new child. After Empress Wang left, Wu quickly smothered the baby. When Gaozong arrived to visit, he found his daughter dead in the crib, with a distraught and weeping Wu claiming that Wang must have killed her. Gaozong believed the lie, and the empress was packed off to a deep, dank dungeon, soon to be joined by another of Wu's rivals: the emperor's second-favorite concubine. As if that wasn't bad enough, once Wu became empress, she went down to the prison to punish her former nemeses. She had them beaten with a hundred lashes, their hands and feet chopped off, their arms and legs broken, and then ordered the women—who were *still alive*—dumped into a vat of wine to drown. As she watched them struggling vainly, she cackled, "Now these two witches can get drunk to their bones."

If true, that is the kind of evil even a horror movie franchise wouldn't touch. But though Wu did have a murderous, Machiavellian-before-Machiavelli streak, it's also true that her demonization by historians was fueled by a lot of false propaganda. Many thought Wu disrupted the Confucian order of things just by being a woman, and even more so by first ruling through her husband and then usurping the throne from her own sons. Folks didn't look too kindly on such behavior, and if you're going to write a cautionary tale, why not throw in all the infanticide and grisly murder you can?

To understand how Wu came to power, and why she did what she did, you have to understand that Tang dynasty China was a viper pit. A glorious viper pit—the height of Chinese ancient civilization, a golden age of poetry and legal enlightenment, and all sorts of great stuff (and which owed its existence to Princess Pingyang; see chapter 2)—but a viper pit nonetheless. Inconvenient people were "invited" to commit suicide, and often helped along if they failed to comply. Murder, especially among relatives, wasn't uncommon. Even more often, citizens brought false charges against political rivals in the hopes their enemies would be executed. If some historical texts are to be believed, the palace halls must have run red with the blood of the executed, the assassinated, and the conveniently suicidal.

Before she was slaughtering rivals, Wu was the daughter of a governor and a lady; she was a princess, but just barely. And though as a teenager she was a concubine in the imperial household, she was really little more than a maid, chiefly employed to change the emperor's bed linens. Though Wu appears to have been endowed with remarkable physical beauty as well as intelligence, such attributes would not have been enough to get her into the royal bed she turned down so faithfully. Still, Emperor Taizong did notice her, calling her his "Fair Flatterer," after a popular song. According to some sources, Wu would perform a certain sexual act (exactly what has been lost to history) that other ladies would not, earning her additional affections from the old ruler.

Taizong's death in 649 seems to have led directly to Wu hooking up with his son, Gaozong, who also had taken a shine to the concubine princess. According to the official dynastic history, Gaozong first noticed Wu, now in her twenties, when she was nursing his sick father on his deathbed. Other reports claimed that Wu offered Gaozong a bowl of water to wash his hands after he went to the bathroom. When he inadvertently flicked water in her face, marring her white makeup, she said, "I accept Heaven's favor of rain and mist," apparently a naughty poetic reference to sex and some really interesting foreplay. However they met, the two were definitely intimate before the old emperor was dead. (In true Tang imperial fashion, Gaozong's way to the throne was cleared by the fortuitous deaths and executions of four of his brothers.)

Confucian law declared that relations between a son and his father's concubine constituted incest, so Wu and Gaozong's budding relationship was kept secret. Moreover, custom dictated that after the emperor's death, Wu had to shave her head and be committed to a convent, although she spent only a few months sequestered (and didn't cut off her hair). Evidently, Gaozong liked her enough to knock her up and *then* spring her from the nunnery to serve as one of his concubines.

Wu soon became the emperor's favorite, through a combination of sexy insect-inspired eyebrows, duplicitous cunning, and near-constant pregnancy. One contemporary wrote, "Lady Wu, with her lovely eyebrows arched like the antennae of a butterfly, yields to no woman, but coyly hides her face behind her long sleeve and applies herself to slandering others, knowing her vixen charms hold the power to bewitch the emperor." Meanwhile, in her first five years in Gaozong's harem, Wu produced three, possibly four, children, and there's nothing so appealing to an emperor as fertility.

It was around this time that Wu supposedly smothered her own child and did away with her rivals in remarkably grisly fashion. The infanticide is probably untrue, given Wu's later reluctance to harm her own children *directly* (exile was her preferred method for dealing with disobedient offspring). It's quite possible the baby died of natural causes, and Wu took the opportunity to blame her rival for the death. Either way, that wasn't what brought down Empress Wang—it was her inability to produce a male heir. Ultimately, Gaozong (likely prompted by Wu) claimed that his wife, along with his second-favored concubine, was plotting to poison him. Sentencing them both to prison was the perfect pretext for making room for baby-making Wu.

Madam Emperor

Wu and Gaozong appeared to have ruled "jointly," although some historians claim she was the real power. By 660 she was a fixture in the throne room, observing all of her husband's audiences and offering advice and pronouncements from behind a screen. After Gaozong suffered a series of strokes that left him half blind and unable to walk or speak, Wu assumed his official duties, and the screen was taken down.

Upon Gaozong's death in 683, Wu became empress dowager, a title that usually indicates it's time to leave the stage. But Wu's final act was yet to come. With her son nominally on the throne (after, it should be noted, the deaths of his two older brothers, at least one of which was indirectly ascribed to Wu), Wu now held the real power. And when this son proved to be less malleable than she'd hoped, she had him exiled to a distant province and replaced with another son. (Not for nothing did she also have the Chinese word *prince* changed to be made up of the characters meaning "one who keeps a peaceful mouth.")

Four years after Gaozong's death, Wu was done trying to rule through her sons. After a carefully cultivated campaign of prophecy, public relations, and propaganda, she declared herself "Sage Mother, Holy Sovereign," giving herself extraordinary power. But even that wasn't enough. Three years later, in 690, she shrugged off the "Sage Mother" mantle and declared herself emperor.

Wu ruled through a combination of public relations shrewdness and secret-police terror. By declaring herself emperor, she effectively ended the Tang dynasty and started her own, the Zhou, angering the remaining imperial family members. To silence her critics, she had them all exiled or executed. She had always relied heavily on informants, creating an atmosphere of distrust and fear. She'd had copper "suggestion boxes" posted in cities, allowing people to anonymously report information on rivals, and invited anyone with useful information to travel to the palace on her dime. The fruits of that information could be deadly; between 684 and 693, Wu went through 46 chief ministers, half of whom were murdered or committed suicide. After outliving his usefulness, her supposed lover, the Rasputin-like leader of a Buddhist cult, was beaten to death on her command. Even her own relatives lived in mortal fear they'd become "inconvenient."

According to Chinese chroniclers in later centuries, Wu was also free with her sexual favors, supposedly forming her own male harem at the advanced age of 66. She reportedly entertained a string of inappropriate lovers, including a well-endowed peddler, a pair of smooth-cheeked singing brothers, and her own nephew. (Take all that with a big grain of salt, though—the easiest way to slander a woman in any era is to call her a slut.)

But Wu also ruled effectively, benignly, and even wisely over a nation of 50 million. Her subjects didn't see her as a dangerous monster or a tyrant; she united the kingdom at a time when it appeared to be disintegrating. Not only did she manage to keep the empire together and end the predations of the Tartars, who were ripping apart the northern border, she also expanded its territory, doing so with remarkably few wars.

Under Wu, as both empress and emperor, taxes decreased, financial waste and military expenditure were reduced, retirees got pensions, and salaries of deserving officials rose. She introduced the system of entrance examinations for bureaucratic service, a huge step toward meritocracy and away from nepotism. She passed legislation allowing children to mourn the death of *both* parents, not just the father, as had been custom and law. Under her rule, Chinese generals helped Korea oust their Japanese overlords and unite under a new king. The Japanese were so impressed that they started copying everything the Tang did, right down to building their capital city in imitation of China's capital.

FORCED RETIREMENT

Wu ruled for 15 years as emperor before anyone got up the nerve and resources to challenge her. In 705, a faction of Tang loyalists, headed by Wu's exiled son, suggested that it was time for her to abdicate the throne. When Wu didn't take the hint, her pair of singing lovers was found murdered, their bodies placed in her rooms. When she still didn't take the hint, a knife was held to her throat and she was forced to "retire."

Wu died later that year—of natural causes, surprisingly—after ruling ably and peacefully for the better part of 50 years. She had used the same tools as emperors had for many a generation before her: execution, banishment, terror. But such behavior has been deemed unbecoming of a woman, and Wu has gotten short shrift.

How later rulers felt about Wu is clear by how they chose to remember—or in this case *not* remember—her. Chinese tradition at the time dictated that rulers be buried in sumptuous tombs marked with huge memorial tablets. Usually, the tablets were covered with details of all the great and glorious deeds the ruler had done and how he would be missed. Not so with Wu. Her tablet remained blank, a mute testament to women who accomplished much, but about whom no one had a good word to say.

Wei's Way

Empress Wu Zetian wasn't the only crafty woman in imperial China. In 684, Wu had her son Li Xian kicked off the throne and exiled to a remote outpost. He brought along his wife, Princess Wei, and lucky for him he did: if it weren't for Wei's constant goading and admonitions, Li Xian probably would have committed suicide while in exile.

It likely wasn't out of love for her husband that Wei talked him down—she simply was not about to let the chance to become empress pass by twice. When, in 705, the opportunity finally came again, she seized it. A group of Tang family loyalists took Li Xian as their leader and deposed Emperor Wu; Li Xian became Emperor Zhongzong, and he and his wife, Empress Wei, made their way back to the palace.

Now sitting pretty on the throne, Empress Wei had an affair with Wu's nephew Sansi, who was having an affair with the emperor's old private secretary. This wicked threesome made a fortune selling official posts, but the power still wasn't enough. Wei and Sansi, who by that time had been elevated to a high ministerial post, proposed that the imperial daughter, Princess Anle, be named heir apparent. Not so fast, cried the legitimate crown prince, Li Chongjun, who marched on the palace but was repelled after his own troops turned on their commanders.

Despite the setback, Wei and Anle weren't cowed. Three years later, they finally pulled off their own coup, killing Emperor Zhongzong with a poisoned cake and installing a more malleable son, Li Chongmao, on the throne. Inspired by Wu, they planned to rule through him while preparing to install Anle on the throne as China's second female emperor. Unfortunately for them, Wu Zetian's daughter Princess Taiping got wind of the plan first and went to battle on behalf of her brother Ruizong. Anle's head was lopped off while she was putting on eye makeup.

But as usual, things weren't exactly what they seemed. Ruizong knew full well that his sister, Princess Taiping, was only biding her time until she could make her own attempt to steal the crown. So he got crafty. First, he named his son Xuanzong to be his successor and abdicated the throne; then he had Xuanzong move on Taiping, based on the claim that she was about to try to depose him. After several of her men were killed, Taiping fled to a Buddhist monastery, where she was "allowed" to kill herself.

The real surprise is that the Tang dynasty would continue for another 200 years, shocking given its members' murderous (and suicidal) tendencies to kill themselves and each other.

Njinga of Ndongo

The Princess Who Kept Male Concubines in Drag

CA. 1581-DECEMBER 17, 1663
SOUTHWESTERN AFRICA
(PRESENT-DAY ANGOLA)

T he year was 1621. Princess Njinga was charged by her half
brother Mbandi, ruler of the West African kingdom of Ndongo,
to meet with Portuguese officials. For decades, the two powers
had been fighting an on-and-off war, with the Europeans trying to seize
more territory and resources. Now a treaty seemed possible. But when
Njinga met with the Portuguese governor, she was faced with a blatant
power play intended to humiliate her. While the governor lounged com-

fortably like a king on a throne, Njinga was not even offered a chair.

The princess was having none of this nonsense. At her gesture, one of her maidservants got down on hands and knees. Njinga then sat on the woman's back and addressed the governor as an equal. The negotiations were successful, and the peace treaty was signed. And just a few years later, Njinga would be sitting on a throne of her own—and it wouldn't be made of maidservants.

Politics as Usual

Njinga was the eldest daughter of the ruler of the Ndongo kingdom, a loose federation of Mbundu-speaking tribes in what is now the Central African state of Angola. At the time of her birth, the country was roughly 100 years into a complicated relationship with the Portuguese; the colonizers had arrived in the area in 1483 and been working hard to enslave or convert the population ever since.

This situation didn't exactly sit well with the people of Ndongo, though not entirely for the reasons you might think. A slave trade already existed between Ndongo and Kongo, its neighbor to the north, largely in war captives; by the 1500s, the two countries shared this trade with the Portuguese. But the Europeans were always angling for a bigger piece of the pie. The Ndongo nation fought several wars with Portuguese forces over independence and control of the slave trade and profitable salt and silver mines. Of course, that didn't mean that Africans and Europeans were always at odds. If, say, the king of Kongo was getting a little grabby in their territory, Ndongo rulers called on the Portuguese as allies.

But in 1575, the Portuguese upped the tension by establishing a colony at the city of Luanda, located between the two kingdoms' territories, and started to stir up dissension among some of the disaffected factions nominally under Ndongo rule. Njinga's father, Ngola Kilajua (*ngola* means "king"; the word was later taken by the Portuguese as the name of Angola), went to war against them, kicking off a protracted and bloody dispute.

Princess Njinga was born into this uncertain landscape of shifting alliances and near-constant conflict. Stories about her childhood read like something out of *Girls' Own Adventure*. She was a tomboy who could hold a spear like a warrior and preferred climbing trees to doing more traditional girl things. She also didn't take any crap—she once beat her half brother Mbandi bloody after he stole her beaded necklace, humiliating him in front of the entire village.

The mythos about Njinga tells us that she grew into a strong, proud, decisive princess, the kind who was born to rule. But when her father died in 1617, her gender precluded her from ascending to the throne. It was Mbandi who became king, but only after murdering another brother as well as Njinga's infant son. As you might imagine, Mbandi was neither a benevolent nor a sensible ruler. One story claims that when Njinga spoke out against his plans to pit his spear-armed warriors in open battle against the cannon-armed Portuguese, he had her forcibly sterilized. The Portuguese also knew his faults and pressed their advantage, sending missionaries and soldiers farther into Ndongo territory.

So in 1621, Princess Njinga was sent by her cowardly, villainous sibling to meet with the Portuguese governor and negotiate the end of hostilities. Njinga forced the governor to meet her eye to eye, both figuratively and literally. The treaty was signed, the Portuguese recognized the sovereignty of the Mbundu-speaking people, and all it cost was the return of a few European captives.

Three years later, Mbandi was dead and Njinga took the throne with the backing of a grateful people. She reengaged the Portuguese after they broke the peace treaty (surprise!) and relocated her subjects to a more defensible location in the highlands. From there, Njinga directed a guerilla war that left the invaders demoralized and weakened, holding them off for four decades. After her death, the kingdom disintegrated. Yet, even as Ndongo became Angola under Portuguese rule, her people still remembered her. In 1860, a Scottish missionary recorded meeting an Angolan man who told him, "In Angola, every living, breathing thing, down to the last blade of grass in your path, still remembers our great queen."

NJINGA WARRIOR

So now you've heard the lore. The reality is messier . . . and bloodier. Rather than deferring to her brother until her country needed her,

Njinga had in fact been looking for a path to the throne since her father's death. Because Ndongo precedent disallowed women rulers, she publicly supported Mbandi while busily amassing supporters and justifications for her own claim to the throne.

When Njinga met with the governor in 1621, she really did use her maidservant as a chair. But that gutsy move may have been motivated more by her own political ambitions than by a desire to represent her people: Njinga wanted the Portuguese to reinforce her claim to the throne. Given the political realities of colonized Central Africa, the best way to accomplish that goal was to share a religion with the invaders, so Njinga was baptized as a Christian in 1622. She took as her new Christian name Anna de Sousa, the name of the governor's wife.

Mbandi's death was the opening Njinga needed; pretty much everyone agrees that she created that opportunity herself by poisoning him. Her apologists later claimed that she'd done so only because he was an awful ruler and she was desperate to protect her people. But as ambitious as she was, Njinga was not the popular choice for ruler, owing to her gender and the pervasive suspicion that she'd killed Mbandi. So she initially stepped up as regent for Mbandi's 8-year-old son. Within two years, however, she had her nephew murdered and assumed power.

Njinga's power grab precipitated an internal war, prompting her to call on the Portuguese for support. Unfortunately for her, they sided with a rival faction whose male heir was more malleable to their own agenda. Njinga renounced Christianity and made it her life's mission—for a while at least—to thwart Portuguese efforts to monopolize the slave trade. She even began to offer sanctuary to slaves who escaped Portuguese coastal plantations, in the process swelling the ranks of her supporters.

This succession war led to one of the more grisly aspects of Njinga's reign: her alliance of convenience with the Imbangala, marauding bands of mercenaries. In probably the first documented instances of African child soldiers, the Imbangala descended upon villages with a bloody ferocity, enslaving children and killing everyone else before moving on to the next town. Starting in 1628, Njinga not only employed Imbangala soldiers but, to keep them loyal, also claimed that she *was* Imbangala. (It's unlikely that she was ever initiated formally into the tribe, a gruesome ritual that involved the murder of a child.) Two decades later, she symbolically attempted to distance herself from their bloody rites by reconverting to Christianity, which had the added benefit of allowing her to call on the Portuguese to support her plans for hereditary succession.

Woman King

With Njinga's tenuous grasp on the throne as the backdrop, some of her stranger actions as ruler make more sense—especially what she did to cast herself as the *king* of the Mbundu-speaking people. For one thing, she took several husbands at a time, as many as 50 or 60, and called them "concubines." They were forced to wear women's clothing and sleep in the same room as her ladies-in-waiting, though if they touched the women with any sexual intent, they were immediately executed. This unusual situation likely engendered the Marquis de Sade's claim that Njinga immolated her lovers after spending one night with them, a practice that seems spectacularly wasteful.

Though she probably didn't burn her lovers alive, Njinga's gender-bending habits asserted her identity as king, as did her martial prowess. She led her troops skillfully in battle and had her ladies-in-waiting equipped and trained as soldiers to serve as her personal bodyguards. It's even alleged that she cut off a man's head in a ritual sacrifice and drank his blood directly from his neck. Given how long she ruled, her efforts to cast herself as king seem to have worked.

But eventually, Njinga was forced by the Portuguese and internal factions arrayed against her to decamp to the highlands; her Ndongo lands were given over to a puppet king in service to the foreign powers. Her retreat was a strategic one, however, offering more freedom to engage the Portuguese in the kind of battle her warriors could win: guerilla warfare.

Njinga also took territory as far as 500 miles inland, using war captives to fuel her slave trade. Within a few years, she conquered the kingdom of Matamba and made it her base, turning it into one of the most important and wealthiest states in Central Africa. By 1640, she was the region's most powerful African king. She ruled much of the land formerly belonging to the Ngola puppet king and controlled a commercial slave trade circuit that sold upward of 13,000 enslaved Africans a year.

But in 1650, after nearly 25 years of warfare, Njinga again found it politically palatable to make friends with the Portuguese. Her Dutch allies, who'd long supported her efforts to harass the Portuguese, had left the region in 1648; not only that, Njinga was getting older and had begun worrying about who would take over after she was gone. An alliance with her old friends/foes promised some measure of security. So she reconverted to Christianity, introduced Portuguese missionaries and ambassadors into her court, adopted European dress, and reestablished trade with the Portuguese slavers. All was made official in a peace treaty in 1656.

Njinga died in 1663, at age 82; her death prompted a struggle for succession that led to the disintegration of the Ndongo-Matamba kingdom. She had held it together by sheer force of will, and no one else could do that. In the 350 years since her death, Njinga has been rehabilitated into the heroine of colonial resistance who rejected the yoke of foreign rule. She was never more important as a symbol than during Angola's struggle for freedom in the twentieth century, which culminated in independence in 1975. Although the details of her mythology aren't exactly accurate, there's one point her legend does get right: Njinga was a warrior who forced the colonials to deal with her as an equal.

Schemers

PRINCESSES
WHO PLOTTED
AND PLANNED

Justa Grata Honoria

The Princess Who Nearly Wrecked the Roman Empire

Ca. 417-452
The Roman Empire

When Roman princess Justa Grata Honoria found herself about to be packed off to some backwater to be the docile wife of a yes-man in service to her brother, Emperor Valentinian III, she sat down to write a letter. To Attila the Hun. Seeking help from Rome's worst enemy didn't endear her to the emperor. And it didn't exactly solve her problem, either. But if the emperor thought his sister would take de facto banishment gracefully, he'd obviously forgotten who she was.

Practicing Patience

Honoria was the daughter of strong-willed Galla Placidia Augusta, herself the daughter of the late Roman emperor Theodosius I, and Galla's second husband, Constantinius III, emperor of the Western Roman Empire. About 424, Constantinius died, leaving Galla with two young children, 7-year-old Honoria and 6-year-old Valentinian, and a crisis of succession on her hands. By this time the Roman Empire was in deep trouble. External pressure from raiding barbarian hordes was fueling internal political combustion; the empire was already split in two and ruled by coemperors. Honoria grew up in an atmosphere of intrigue and uncertainty, witnessing her mother manipulate and bully those around her.

Eventually, Galla's faction prevailed, and Valentinian III was crowned emperor of the western half of the empire. Honoria was forced to live out her days in the dull but strategically important city of Ravenna. By order of her brother the emperor, she was forced into a life of Christian celibacy, a political rather than a pious decision, given that any man she married could lay claim to the empire. Adding insult to injury, Valentinian III was a "worthless man of pleasure," according to one classicist, and by no means her intellectual equal. For Honoria, consignment to days of quiet desperation in a dead-end Roman village probably felt like a life sentence without parole. The situation became even less tolerable when Valentinian married and had two daughters, who quickly began to eclipse Honoria in political importance.

In 449, Honoria's frustration reached a breaking point. Now 31 years old—about the same age as her mother when her second husband died—she became romantically involved with a man named Eugenius, steward of her estates. According to some less-than-kind, and probably less-than-accurate, biographers, Honoria plotted with Eugenius to murder her brother and seize the throne. It's likely this accusation was a meritless effort on the part of a few Christian historians to cast Honoria as a ruthless grasper; how such a scheme could have succeeded is unclear. But engaging in unapproved sex with an imperial princess was considered high treason, and when the relationship was found out, Eugenius was executed.

Hey, Hun

Honoria was sentenced to a kind of living death: her lover murdered, she was banished to Constantinople, capital of the Eastern Roman Empire, and betrothed to a boring Roman senator loyal to her brother. Unsurprisingly, Honoria was not pleased. And that was when she pulled out her stationery set and started writing. Her plan was to hitch her wagon to a man with a track record of success.

Leader of the Huns since murdering his brother in 445, Attila was the most threatening of the barbarian invaders who had been eating away at the Roman Empire. The Western Roman Empire, under Honoria's brother, was ready to fight him, but the East—where Honoria now resided—was somewhat more obsequious. They'd already tried, unsuccessfully, to pay off the Hun to avoid an invasion. Taking her cue from the eastern court, Honoria asked Attila to "avenge her marriage," as fifth-century historian John of Antioch put it; her letter, conveyed by her trusty eunuch Hyacinthus, was accompanied by money and a ring.

Attila eagerly agreed. This was his big chance to take a bite out of the Roman Empire and do it without too much trouble. Whatever Honoria promised him is unknown, but Attila claimed that she offered her hand in marriage. Producing the ring as evidence, he demanded half the Western Roman Empire as dowry from Theodosius II, the emperor of the eastern portion. Taken aback, Theodosius sent a messenger to coemperor Valentinian advising him to placate the Hun and hand over his sister.

Valentinian would have none of it; giving up Honoria meant giving the Hun a claim to the throne. Torturing Hyacinthus into a confession, Valentinian learned the full story of Honoria's treasonous plans. After lopping off the eunuch's head, he then took aim at his sister's. Only the intercession of their mother, still the real power behind Valentinian's throne, kept it firmly attached to her neck. As penance, however, Honoria was stripped of her Augusta title, forcibly hitched to the senator, and exiled from both courts.

Attila, meanwhile, dispatched an embassy to Valentinian's court, declaring Honoria innocent of all treason, insisting that her imperial title be restored, and, oh yes, demanding that they hand her over as his rightful bride. He was rebuffed—she *was* married after all. But that didn't stop him from trying again in 452, using the marriage claim as a pretense to invade Italy. Though he didn't manage to conquer Rome, he left a lot of the countryside in ruins while trying.

What happened to Honoria after this disastrous episode is unclear. By 455, just six years after the unfortunate affair with Eugenius, she dropped off the radar, probably dead (whether of natural causes or by order of the emperor is up for debate). What is known is that, having fallen out of power and out of favor, she did not live happily ever after.

Neither did the Roman Empire. Honoria, it seems, inspired other princesses to try to get out of bad marriages by inviting barbarians over for a bit of tea and sympathy. In 455, for example, Licinia Eudoxia, forced to marry the successor of her murdered husband, Valentinian, took a cue from Honoria and invited the Vandal king Gaiseric to lay waste to Rome. Gaiseric did so with gusto, sacking the city and taking Licinia and her two daughters as willing "hostages." Ultimately, Attila's repeated attacks, which lasted until his death in 453, Gaiseric's invasion, the predations of other barbarians, and internal struggles led to the hacking off of the empire's gangrenous western half. In 476, when the last western Roman emperor was deposed by a Germanic prince, the great superstate was downsized to the much more manageable Byzantine Empire in the east.

And Honoria is remembered as the treacherous princess who held open the door for the invading barbarians.

Isabella of France

The "She-Wolf" Princess

1295–1358
CIVIL-WAR-TORN ENGLAND

French princess Isabella was only 12 years old in 1308 when she sailed into the court of English king Edward II as his wife. And he, the 24-year-old freshly crowned monarch, was very much in love . . . just not with her.

The person Edward *was* in love with was a young knight named Piers Gaveston. That Edward had a lover wasn't shocking, nor was it a big problem that his lover was a man. The problem, as the English court saw it, was how "immoderately" Edward loved the glamorous, arrogant Gaveston—enough to risk his entire kingdom and the lives of thousands of soldiers. When Gaveston was around, Edward was worse than useless, barely able to hold a conversation, much less govern. When Gaveston wasn't around, Edward was a wreck.

Three's a Crowd

While Edward and Isabella were married in France, Gaveston stayed in England with his own child bride, Edward's 15-year-old niece. Less than a month later, Isabella witnessed firsthand just how deep the man's hooks went into her husband's heart. During the ceremony at Westminster Abbey investing Isabella with the title of queen, it was Gaveston who held the crown. At the coronation feast afterward, he sat next to the king under tapestries that depicted not the emblems of Edward and Isabella but the arms of Edward and Gaveston. And just to turn the dagger a bit more, Edward handed over the wedding gifts from Isabella's father—jewels, warhorses, the whole lot—to his one true love.

Isabella's uncles, who had attended the coronation, returned to France in a frothy rage. Which was bad news, given that France and England were perpetually squabbling and barely maintaining an uneasy truce. England was already embroiled in a conflict with Scotland and didn't need another front to open up. England's powerful magnates—the lords and earls who really ruled the land—decided that Gaveston was too great a distraction for the king and needed to be removed. But attempts to exile the king's favorite proved futile. Edward would send Gaveston away and then, a few months later, call him back.

Their frustration with Edward reached a boiling point in 1312; civil war was in the making. Edward and Gaveston traveled the countryside, trying to keep ahead of the lords baying for the latter's blood, but they couldn't run for long—England is only so big. On May 19, Gaveston surrendered to the king's enemies at Scarborough Castle, where Edward had left him ensconced with a battalion. Just over a month later, Gaveston was executed, brutally and without a trial. The king swore he'd have his revenge.

Isabella, meanwhile, was biding her time. She'd become an adult while following Edward and Gaveston around the country; at the time of Gaveston's execution, she was pregnant with her husband's son and heir. On November 12, 1312, the 17-year-old queen gave birth to a healthy baby boy. She'd done her duty to crown and husband, and her position was secure. She had also accumulated enough political acumen to manage her useless husband and try to keep the nation from civil war. Edward and his warring lords patched things up long enough to sign a peace treaty, which got them through the first few months of 1313 without killing one another. With Isabella's mediation, the lords swore fealty to Edward once again, but it was a tenuous peace. The Scots were hammering England's defenses to the north, and Edward's most powerful earl (and the man responsible in part for Gaveston's murder), a man named Lancaster, refused to aid him. Worse, Lancaster was actively plotting against Edward while England was left rudderless, without a real leader.

Isabella remained at Edward's side, his confidante and advisor. That is, until about 1318, when Edward again became infatuated with a young man in his company. Unlike the foppish Gaveston, Hugh Despenser was shrewd, cruel, and paranoid. He used the royal relationship to seize his rivals' lands and treasuries. As Despenser hoarded more gold and more land, more and more lords began defecting to Lancaster's side. Isabella worked to maintain peace between her husband, his magnates, and an irate France, but they all demanded that Despenser be exiled. In July 1321, Edward gave the order; ever the sly one, Despenser went only as far as the English Channel, where he and his father turned to pirating merchant ships while awaiting word from Edward. Meanwhile, the king's struggles with Lancaster came to a head. Lancaster found himself on the losing side of the battle; he was arrested and executed as a traitor. Edward had his revenge.

Trumped

Edward may have won a battle, but he was about to lose the war. Triumphant after Lancaster's death, he hastily called the Despensers back to England and made Hugh his chief advisor. Ever the opportunist, Hugh then started to make moves on Isabella's property and that of her children. Bad decision.

Hell hath no fury like a woman whose children's birthright is in danger. Now a seasoned political manipulator, Isabella waited for just the right moment to act, and in 1325 opportunity finally landed in her lap. By then, England's relationship with France had frayed over land that both claimed to rule. It was decided that Isabella was ideally suited to work out a solution with her relatives back home. So the queen (who had likely planted the idea with Edward and Despenser) made her way back to France, where she spent several restorative months in the bosom of her family. Six months after landing in Calais, she was followed by her son, 12-year-old Prince Edward, on the pretext that relations between France and England would be softened if he were made duke of Aquitaine. And just like that, 27-year-old Isabella held the trump card: the heir to the English throne.

Within weeks, Isabella showed her hand. "I feel that marriage is a joining together of man and woman . . . and someone has come between my husband and myself trying to break this bond," she said in a statement. "I protest that I will not return until this intruder is removed." Edward was gobsmacked. "On her departure, she did not seem to anyone to be offended," he supposedly remarked. Isabella's plan was ingenious and subtle. Her husband was a useless king, but she couldn't say so without looking like a traitor. So she cleverly shifted the blame to Despenser and cast herself as the dutiful wronged wife. Isabella also knew that Edward was unlikely to be a worthy leader even if Despenser were removed. Lucky, then, that she happened to have an alternative ready to roll and under her control: her son, the prince.

Isabella had spent the last six months getting all her ducks in a row. Not only did she have France on her side, she had also won the loyalty of a faction of disaffected Englishmen to legitimize her rebellion. They were led by Roger Mortimer, one of the nobles who had led the revolt against Edward. Two years earlier, Mortimer had made a daring escape from the Tower of London and turned up in the French court. He and Isabella met up in Paris; he became not only her captain, but her lover as well.

To get her son on the throne, Isabella needed military might, so she and Mortimer engineered a marriage between young Edward and the daughter of a French count. In late September 1326, Isabella and Mortimer set sail for England with her daughter-in-law's dowry—700 soldiers—along with a pack of mercenaries paid for by Isabella's brother, the king of France. Isabella was, without a doubt, at the head of this operation; one fourteenth-century image shows her leading the troops while clad in shiny armor. Popular support for her as a romantic, righteous figurehead had been growing since word of her rebellion spread; that support, and her ranks, continued to swell after she returned to English soil. Edward had fallen out of favor not only with his lords and magnates but also among his people, who had suffered famine and war while he was occupied with avenging his lover's death.

The end came swiftly. On November 16, the king and his companion were caught trying to make it across open country in Wales. Hugh Despenser was brought before the queen and her lords and sentenced to death. He was dragged through the streets, stripped naked, and hauled 50 feet in the air by his neck. He was then disemboweled while alive and castrated—punishment, it was rumored, for his intimate relationship with the king. As if all that wasn't enough, he was beheaded, too.

The king was confined to Monmouth Castle as a prisoner of Henry of Lancaster, brother of the rebellious earl whom Edward had executed four years before. But Isabella and Mortimer still had one problem: with Despenser gone, the dynamic duo no longer had reason to challenge Edward's fitness to rule. So, clever Isabella argued that, by fleeing to Wales, Edward had abandoned England and his right to rule it. Prince Edward was, therefore, the rightful king. The relieved bishops and lords of England agreed. Now all that remained was to convince Edward to resign the throne in favor of his son. Faced with overwhelming opposition, he agreed, and Prince Edward, just 14 years old, became King Edward III on February 1, 1327. Isabella, as the mother of the underage ruler, and Mortimer, as leader of the deposing army, now held authority in England.

Murder, She Wrote

The situation was unprecedented—it was the first time the country had ever had a living ex-king. And there was also the issue of Isabella's marriage: Edward may have been an ex-king, but he was not her ex-husband. With Despenser gone, she had no legitimate reason not to return to him. Moreover, Edward's very existence posed a threat to the new regime, especially since it appeared he wasn't completely without supporters. Indeed, by September 1327, three plots to free him had been foiled. So the queen and her captain hit upon a more traditional means of ridding themselves of this troublesome ex-king: murder.

The story is probably apocryphal, but later chroniclers morbidly insist that Edward II was murdered by the violent application of a red-hot poker up his backside. However death occured, on the night of September 21, 1327, the 43-year-old relatively robust former king conveniently died. He was buried with all the ceremony accorded to a dead monarch, his wife and son weeping and kneeling before his gilded hearse.

But young King Edward III, it seems, had learned a trick or two at his mother's knee. Though Isabella and Mortimer were content to run things in England indefinitely, Edward wasn't about to sit idly by and watch them do it. In late 1330, just three years after Isabella and Mortimer seized power, the 18-year-old king outflanked them. Mortimer was arrested as a traitor by a group of nobles loyal to the crown; he was hung on November 29, 1330. Isabella had but one choice: accept the death of her lover and an enforced retirement, surrendering her vast estates to her son. Ever the realist, she did so within a week of Mortimer's execution. Isabella lived the rest of her life in quiet obedience to her son, dying in 1358. The "She-Wolf of France," as she came to be called, was buried as she requested: with a silver vase containing the heart of her husband, the man she'd kicked off the throne and probably murdered.

The Sorceress Princesses

Being close to the English throne was a dangerous place for a woman, even if you weren't trying to maneuver the monarchy away from your husband. Not only can bad behavior bring your fairy-tale life crashing down around you, just the *accusation* could cost you your freedom . . . or your head.

The charge of witchcraft was a popular one. Most people in medieval England believed in witches, sorcery, and the Devil as much as they believed in Jesus, God, and the Holy Spirit. They believed, without question, that there were perverted individuals who made pacts with Satan, sacrificed babies, copulated with demonic beasts at Black Masses, had animal familiars, and flew on broomsticks. The pointy hat? Well, that was optional.

Witchcraft was heresy, a crime that, given the power of the church, endangered one's mortal body as well as one's immortal soul: often, the punishment was execution. That made the accusation of witchcraft, which could be difficult to disprove, a handy way to neutralize a woman who'd grown inconvenient or too big for her britches. Between the kings Henry IV and Henry VIII, roughly 150 years of civil instability, no fewer than four royal women were brought down by charges of dabbling in the dark arts. Here are their stories.

JOAN OF NAVARRE

The French second wife of Henry IV, Joan of Navarre was among the first European princesses to be accused of sorcery. Joan married Henry in 1403, several years after he'd deposed Richard II to take the throne; both she and Henry had children from their previous marriages, and at first this medieval Brady Bunch seemed to get along just fine.

But in 1419, six years after Henry IV's death, Joan was accused of using witchcraft to try to poison her stepson, the young Henry V. No matter that, by most accounts, Joan had a pretty good relationship with young Henry and little reason to want him dead. Nevertheless, her confessor, the duplicitous Friar Randolph, claimed that Joan had told him she imagined "the king's death in the most horrible manner that could be devised," and she was supposedly using a wax figure of him to bring it about. She was put under house arrest at Pevensey Castle and denied access to revenue from her dowry; she was released in 1422 (the year that Henry V died of dysentery, not sorcery).

In reality, the charges were likely punishment for Joan supposedly trying to help her French son from her first marriage to escape prison after his capture by her adopted country's forces at the Battle of Agincourt in 1415. Confused? So were everyone's loyalties. England was in a fog of civil unrest, frequent coups, increasing church power, and unrelenting superstition. In that climate, it was easy to use a charge like witchcraft for political ends.

Eleanor Cobham,
Duchess of Gloucester

Twenty years later, another royal Englishwoman was charged with sorcery. Eleanor Cobham was the second wife of Humphrey, duke of Gloucester, who was the brother of the late Henry V and uncle of the young Henry VI. The only thing that stood between Eleanor and the throne was a damp disappointment of a monarch no one really liked—if Henry VI were out of the picture, then the duke would become king and Eleanor queen. In 1441, rumors flew that people near the 20-year-old King Henry were practitioners of the "Black Art" and had been conspiring to kill him with "incantations and witchcraft." Even worse, the Devil had appeared in a church in Essex not long before. Clearly, something evil was afoot.

What happened may have been wicked, but it had more to do with politics than sorcery. Roger Bolingbroke, an Oxford priest, physician, and astrologer, and Thomas Southwell, a canon of St. Stephen's, Westminster, were arrested and accused of plotting to kill the king by means of necromancy. In Bolingbroke's possession was found a wax figure of the monarch, which authorities claimed was being slowly melted to bring about the deterioration of the king's health. Both men were tossed in the Tower of London in July 1441. Bolingbroke, under "examination" (read: torture), revealed that he had been instructed by the duchess of Gloucester, who he claimed wanted to use magic to murder the king. Eleanor soon found herself facing charges of witchcraft, a burning offense, and treason, a hanging one. She tried to flee but was caught and brought before the religious authorities, most of whom were her enemies.

At the trial, Eleanor's two supposed accomplices were joined by a third, Margery Jourdemayne, dramatically called the "Witch of Eye," from whom it was alleged that Eleanor begged love potions to ensnare the affections of the duke of Gloucester. Faced with the evidence against her, Eleanor admitted to dabbling in sorcery; she claimed the drugs she obtained from the Witch of Eye were to help her conceive a child but denied plotting against the king.

All four were found guilty. The Witch of Eye was burned alive at a market in London; Bolingbroke was hanged, beheaded, and quartered; and lucky Southwell died in prison, probably by his own hand. Eleanor was spared death after the king interceded. Stripped of her title, she was forced to walk through London barefoot, bearing a heavy candle, to the altar of St. Paul's Cathedral and then to two more London churches to do the same penance. It was winter; the filthy ground cut her feet, and crowds along the way jeered at her. She was then made a prisoner in a castle in Wales, where she stayed until her death 18 years later. Her husband abandoned her to her fate, knowing he could do nothing to save her. There can be no doubt that Gloucester's political enemies had a part in engineering her downfall. Eleanor hadn't made many friends in her climb to the top of the social ladder, and Gloucester had lost some of his own because of both his marriage to her and his efforts to increase his wealth by diminishing that of others. Losing his wife in such a spectacularly public fashion meant the loss of Gloucester's influence in the affairs of the king; he was fully discredited by her shame and would never again play a major role in England's politics.

Meanwhile, Eleanor would go down in history as an ambitious sorceress. In Shakespeare's *Henry VI, Part 2*, Gloucester pleads with his wife to "banish the canker of ambitious thoughts," but haughty Eleanor cannot. When she and her accomplices raise a spirit to tell them the future, they are caught by Gloucester's political rivals and arrested. Gloucester, who hears about her crimes from her accusers, banishes her from his "bed and company/And give her as prey to law and shame/That hath dishonour'd Gloucester's honest name."

Jacquetta of Luxembourg and Elizabeth Woodville

Twenty years after Eleanor was forced to take those penitential steps, more accusations of witchcraft popped up on the other side of the family tree. In 1432, 17-year-old Jacquetta of Luxembourg married John, duke of Bedford, a 43-year-old widower who was also the younger brother of Henry V and the duke of Gloucester. Three years later Bedford died, leaving Jacquetta a young and wealthy widow; she remarried within two years, to Sir Richard Woodville, a minor knight.

Despite her new marriage, Jacquetta was still the dowager duchess Bedford, and she remained tangentially involved in court intrigues. She certainly would have witnessed the downfall of the only other living duchess, Eleanor. So Jacquetta would have at least been wary of anything that looked like sorcery, knowing as she did how quickly fortunes in the court of England could change. And wow, did they.

In 1461, Edward IV deposed the mentally ill Henry VI, with the help of the earl of Warwick. Three years later, Jacquetta's daughter, the beautiful Elizabeth Woodville, was secretly married to Edward IV, and the Woodville fortunes seemed to be cemented. But in 1469, civil war threatened to throw everything into turmoil.

Edward was facing insurrection from his former ally, Warwick. Fearing the increasing influence of the Woodville clan, Warwick executed Jacquetta's husband and son and charged her with witchcraft. Witnesses came forward claiming that Jacquetta had made tiny lead effigies of the king and queen. Gossips claimed that she and her kin could have achieved so much only through witchcraft, and that the little figures were part of Jacquetta's black magic to pull off the match.

Jacquetta was ultimately cleared of all charges, but the taint of sorcery remained on her and her daughter and grandchildren. After Edward died in 1483, his youngest brother, Richard III, declared that Edward's children with Elizabeth had no right to the throne. His justification was that not only was Edward contracted to marry another woman before Elizabeth, making Edward a bigamist and their children bastards, but also that the union between Elizabeth and Edward was brought about by magic. Elizabeth's two sons, the 12-year-old heir to the throne and his 9-year-old brother, were locked in the Tower of London and never seen again.

ANNE BOLEYN

Joan, Eleanor, and Jacquetta all suffered under the accusations of sorcery, but at least they got to keep their heads. Anne Boleyn wasn't so lucky.

Anne came to the English court in 1522, at age 21, after having come of age in France. Despite her English heritage, she was totally French—pretty, witty, clever, expertly flirtatious, and devastatingly fashionable. Henry had already made her sister his mistress, but Anne was different; she toyed with him, talked back, and refused to sleep with him (at least for a little while). They became lovers of the everything-but-actual-sex sort. Henry, meanwhile, was dealing with the usual royal problem of a wife, Catherine of Aragon, who had not yet produced a male heir; he believed that Anne could, if only she'd give him a chance to knock her up.

For six years, their relationship was an open secret in the court. Everyone knew that Henry was looking for a way out of his marriage; that the Boleyns were rocketing through the social stratosphere; and that it was Anne who ruled the court and Henry's heart. But it wasn't until 1533 that Henry's advisors hit upon a clever but dangerous way of getting him his divorce. If the Catholic pope wouldn't grant him one, then why not divorce the pope? Henry's decision to usurp the power of the Roman Catholic church not only got him excommunicated, it also gave the nation a new state religion, the Church of England, as well as a new queen. With Catherine out of the picture, Henry and Anne had a hasty shotgun wedding, and, already six months pregnant, Anne got her crown.

That year, Anne delivered a healthy baby girl, Elizabeth (the future Elizabeth I). But all of her subsequent pregnancies ended in tragedy; she miscarried a boy who, according to popular lore, was a deformed "monster," and then another boy. Anne just couldn't give Henry what he desperately needed, and the couple quarreled constantly. Anne was jealous, she made scenes, and Henry was already starting to size up other court ladies, presumably keeping a weather eye out for birthing hips. His roving gaze hit upon Jane Seymour, one of Anne's ladies-in-waiting, a somewhat unsparkling woman who came from a big family and could be expected to breed well.

Henry had found his next queen, but a second divorce was out of the question, so his advisors devised another solution. In 1536, on the evidence of one possibly homosexual and definitely tortured minstrel who claimed he'd slept with her, Anne was charged with adultery; among the five men accused of having sexual relations with her was her own brother. She was also charged with treason and conspiracy to kill the king, supposedly having chatted about which of her lovers she'd marry after Henry was dead.

Contrary to lore, Anne was not formally charged with witchcraft, but the public accusations made it easier to convict her. Witchcraft explained the miscarriage of a child at a time when people believed congenital defects were Satan's work and the fault of the mother. It also absolved Henry from guilt, because he could claim Anne had bewitched him into divorcing Catherine. That Anne was rumored to have an extra digit on one hand and a mysterious mole on her neck were touted as proof of her dalliances with the Devil.

Anne was found guilty on all counts by the presiding judge, her own uncle. She was beheaded at the Tower of London on May 19, 1536. She went to her death denying all charges and still professing love for the king who'd abandoned her. Before mounting the scaffold, she seemed resigned to her fate and joked with the executioner that killing her would be easy. "I have only a little neck," she said with a laugh, placing her hands around her small white throat.

Roxolana

The Princess Who Went from Sex Slave to Sultana

CA. 1502–APRIL 1558
THE OTTOMAN EMPIRE

*I*n 1536 Suleiman, the sultan of the Ottoman Empire, had only two people he could trust. One was Ibrahim Pasha, his grand vizier and longtime friend. The other was his wife, Roxolana. She was Ukrainian and a former sex slave who survived the tiger pit of the harem to become sultana. After the grand vizier was found dead, his throat sliced open, Roxolana became Suleiman's sole advisor and confidante. Guess who was behind Pasha's murder.

Harem Scare 'Em

When Roxolana came to the sultan's court about 1520, the *hasseki* (chief concubine) was a beautiful Circassian woman named Gulbahar who had already borne the sultan a son. Almost immediately Roxolana, then about 17 years old, managed to claw her way up from her status as a servant to become one of the sultan's favorites. She became his only favorite by losing a fight.

Gulbahar and Roxolana hated each other from the beginning and the rivalry only intensified after the birth of Roxolana's son. Tensions came to a head one day when Gulbahar called Roxolana a "traitor" and "sold meat" (trust us, a really rude thing to say). Infuriated, Roxolana greased up for a catfight. When it was over, Roxolana's hair was torn out, her face covered in scratches; she was in no condition to see the sultan.

Which may have been her plan all along. When an envoy came to bring Roxolana to her lover's apartments, she refused, sending word that she didn't want to offend Suleiman's magnificence with her battered appearance, no matter how desperately she wanted to see him. Alarmed, the sultan demanded her to come; once he saw the damage, he sent Gulbahar packing to an outpost of the Ottoman Empire—and just like that, Roxolana became first lady of the harem.

The sultan was so enamored of her that he became nearly monogamous (pretty much as good as it gets with emperors). Once, when he was presented with a gift of beautiful women, Roxolana made such a fuss that he was forced to return them. She reportedly even convinced him to marry off the most attractive members of the harem, arguing that their beauty was going to waste. Roxolana enjoyed other signs of his favor, too. For example, she bore Suleiman one daughter and four sons in rapid succession, in contravention to the age-old "one concubine, one son" principle meant to minimize a woman's influence and reduce fighting over the throne.

Her meteoric rise was all the more remarkable for her humble origins. The name Roxolana (or Roxelane) means "the Russian woman" and was probably given to her by the court; it's not strictly accurate, because Roxolana was from Polish-controlled western Ukraine. Though her real name is lost to us, making it difficult to track her origins, it's generally accepted that Roxolana was born between 1502 and 1505, possibly the daughter of a priest; one persistent rumor claimed that she was the illegitimate daughter of Sigismund I of Poland, but that was probably just an attempt to gussy up her origins. Whatever her heritage, at age 15 she was abducted by Crimean Tatars during a raid and forced to walk to Caffa, the biggest slave market in the Black Sea region. There, legend has it that the future grand vizier Ibrahim Pasha picked her out as a present for Prince Suleiman (just a bit ironic, given Pasha's fate).

So what was it about this young slave that ensnared the sultan so completely? After all, she entered the harem at the lowest level and found herself in competition with 300 other women, all of whom were attractive, interesting, or talented in some way. According to one ambassador, Roxolana was no beauty—she was short and a little fat, though she was elegant and modest, graced with fair skin and red hair. Suleiman's initial attraction was probably based on her personality; she was pleasant and witty, played the guitar, and made him feel good. The name the Turks knew her by was Hurrem, meaning "joyful" or "laughing one." Of course, detractors claimed that she held the sultan's affection through love potions and sorcery; the Turkish public called her *ziadi*, or "witch." She certainly was crafty. For example, when a fire destroyed the Old Seraglio, the palace where she and the other concubines lived, she demanded to be installed in the new palace with the sultan, giving her the advantage over rivals.

Once there, Roxolana never left. In either 1533 or 1534, not long after she moved in, the sultan married his red-haired concubine in a sumptuous ceremony outfitted with everything a good royal wedding should have: music, dancing, feasting, swings, giraffes. The marriage was a very big deal. As a contemporary reported, "There is great talk about the marriage and none can say what it means." That was because Suleiman was the first sultan to marry a concubine in three centuries; moreover, Roxolana was the first slave concubine in the history of the Ottoman Empire to be freed and made a legal wife.

As sultana, Roxolana enjoyed more latitude than other women who'd come before her (mothers of sultans, for example), often taking care of matters of state when the sultan was away. To combat public opinion that she was a witch, she worked hard to foster a reputation as a charitable woman, doing good works and funding the construction of magnificent and useful buildings.

MURDER MOST CONVENIENT

But all her privileges could easily disappear if Roxolana didn't keep a tight grip on her power. She hadn't fought her way out of the anonymity of the harem just to become the sultan's trophy-wife broodmare. And that was why she set her sights on taking down the grand vizier. He was the only other person the sultan trusted, the only person at court with as much power as she had; plus she just didn't like him. Ibrahim Pasha was no shrinking violet—this was a man who, when a poet slandered him in public, ordered the unfortunate man paraded around the city on a donkey and then strangled to death.

Roxolana made sure the sultan heard all the court gossip about the vizier and knew how much she disliked him. Ibrahim, meanwhile, didn't do himself any favors at court: he was becoming increasingly arrogant and seemed to be making decisions without the sultan's permission. Whispers that he was plotting against Suleiman were growing louder (perhaps because Roxolana was shouting them into her husband's ear). On March 15, 1536, Ibrahim's battered corpse was found in his bloodstained bedroom. He'd been executed by the sinister deaf-mute assassins the sultan kept around for just such a purpose.

By the 1550s, Roxolana was a power unto herself, but even she needed allies. She soon formed a political faction with Rüstem Pasha, her daughter's like-minded husband and the new grand vizier. On the opposite side was 37-year-old Prince Mustafa, Suleiman's heir and son of the disgraced concubine Gulbahar. Though he governed a distant outpost of the empire, Mustafa was his father's son in strength of mind, character, and ambition. He was also popular, whereas Roxolana's sons were not.

Roxolana knew that if Mustafa took the throne, she'd be either killed or sent back to the Old Seraglio, home to second-string wives and used concubines. She also knew that for Mustafa to clear a path to the throne, he'd need to have her sons murdered. She had only one option:

make sure he never got the chance.

Popular legend claims that Roxolana first tried to dispatch Mustafa herself, sending a gift of poisoned clothing. When that failed, she used her influence to get the sultan to do her dirty work for her. In 1553 Mustafa was executed by his father on the pretext that he was planning to assassinate the sultan and usurp the throne. In the minds of the Turkish public and politicians, Roxolana and Rüstem Pasha were responsible for trumping up the charges and turning the sultan against his son; some even claimed that Roxolana used witchcraft to poison her husband's affections. Rüstem Pasha took the fall—he was stripped of his title on the day Mustafa was executed. The demotion was only temporary, however; Roxolana's insistent urging brought him back to his old position two years later.

Love Conquers All

Concubines in the Ottoman Empire lived, bore children, and died by the thousands without anyone ever knowing their names. Roxolana's charm must have been great, indeed, for her to sway the sultan into making an honest woman out of her.

But all wasn't due to her craftiness and scheming. At the heart of the story is something a bit wonderful—love. Suleiman loved Roxolana dearly, and for the most part faithfully, for the better part of four decades. His deep devotion is evident not only in how he treated her but also in what he wrote to and about her. One of his poems reveals the depth of his feelings: "My intimate companion, my one and all/sovereign of all beauties, my sultan./ My life, the gift I own, my be-all,/my elixir of Paradise, my Eden."

Roxolana seems to have loved her husband back in equal measure. During his frequent absences, she wrote him constantly, sparing no detail of her days, the children's health, and life at court. She wrote, "My Lord, your absence has kindled a fire in me that does not abate."

When Roxolana died in 1558 (of causes unknown), Suleiman was heartbroken. He built her a beautiful mausoleum, making her the first harem woman to be buried in such grandeur. The sultan died eight years later, suffering from gout, arthritis, an ulcer on his leg, and a blood feud for the throne between his two remaining sons.

Catherine Radziwill

The Stalker Princess

MARCH 30, 1858-MAY 12, 1941
GERMANY AND SOUTH AFRICA

O ver a few weeks in 1884, fashionable Europeans were shocked and scandalized, as well as highly amused, by the letters of one Count Paul Vasili published in a French magazine. The "count" was supposedly a diplomat at the Berlin court of Kaiser Wilhelm I, though everyone knew the name was a pseudonym.

Whoever he was, he appeared to have access to all the most important people, whom he ruthlessly skewered, calling them out by name and revealing their every fault. On Empress Augusta: "She is intriguing, false, and affected. She has no dignity and notion of propriety. . . . She surrounds herself with courtiers and favorites who are the first to speak ill of their Imperial mistress." And the court: "Adultery flourishes like a plant in its chosen soil. . . . Virtue is among the number of things regarded as useless. As to love, one meets with it rarely. In Berlin society, they take and quit each other according to their fancy." About Berlin's well-to-do *Frauen*: "The high-class Berlin woman neither reads, works, nor has any occupation. She passes her time in chattering, dressing and undressing, and seeking who will help her in these things. She has neither a serious idea in her head, not a worthy thought in her heart. . . . She is wanting in grace, education, and tact." In short, Berlin was a tar pit of intolerance, provincial manners, sexual intrigue, gossip, and dissolution. The letters proved so popular that they were reprinted in a book called, appropriately enough, *Berlin Society*.

Not surprisingly, Berlin society wasn't pleased. The royal court, seat of the German Empire, was only about 15 years old, and the city itself only lately raised from a unsophisticated, dirt-road backwater. Its inhabitants were a bit touchy about that fact, and to see themselves mocked by someone who'd been allowed into the inner circle was just too much. The real writer, however, was not a diplomat at all but one of their own— 26-year-old Princess Catherine Radziwill.

Biting the Hand That Feeds

Born Countess Ekaterina Adamevna Rzewuska, the daughter of an exiled Polish noble in what is now Ukraine, Catherine grew up in a castle haunted since the days when a family member decided to brick his mother alive in the tower in order to get his inheritance. At age 15, Catherine was married off to Prince Adam Karl Wilhelm Radziwill, a 28-year-old Polish exile living in Berlin. It was a quick and drab ceremony. In 1873 Catherine, who'd spent time in Paris and St. Petersburg, made her entrance into Berlin society; she was not impressed.

Catherine always had an acerbic wit, which she now used to show her disdain for the kaiser's newly established court; one British ambassador noted that she was feared in court for her "mordant tongue."

Encouraged by her aunt (widow of the French writer Honoré de Balzac), Catherine turned her sharp observations into words, first through letters and then later in the scathing and anonymous *Berlin Society*.

Gossip was all well and good, but what Catherine was really passionate about was politics, a sphere that, as a woman, she could never fully inhabit. When not pregnant (she had five children by age 22), she spent her days listening to speeches at the German Parliament. Her thwarted political ambitions turned her toward journalism, and before long people began to suspect that it was her "mordant tongue" behind *Berlin Society*. In 1885 she and her husband were forced to decamp for St. Petersburg, though Catherine didn't mind; she obviously hated Berlin and felt much more Russian in spirit, a reflection of her mother's heritage. She never fully acknowledged her expulsion from court, only later claiming that Empress Augusta didn't like her because she was guilty of the "inexcusable crime of having written a book, a most innocent book by the way." That book was by no means the last Catherine would write, nor would it be the final example of her writing to get her into trouble.

Rhodes Scholar

The next few years were not kind to the princess—her efforts to become an influential political matchmaker in St. Petersburg yielded little fruit, and the ascension of Tsar Nicholas II, who had no time for her, rendered her even less useful. As her marriage was breaking down and her children were leaving the nest, Catherine devoted her attention to political journalism. But without the support of the tsar, she lacked the one thing that had made her more than just another witty writer: access. What Catherine needed was another political situation into which she could insinuate herself.

In February 1896, she found the perfect circumstance while at a dinner party in London. That night, she was seated next to Cecil Rhodes, a British-born South African statesman (namesake of Rhodesia and founder of the Rhodes scholarship). The former prime minister of the British Cape colony was at a career low. Only a month earlier, he'd been forced to resign after the disastrous Jameson Raid, a failed attempt to invade and overthrow the government of the Boer republic of Transvaal. The raid was led by Dr. Leander Jameson, Rhodes's right-hand man, and had Rhodes's approval.

Rhodes soon forgot Catherine almost completely, but she sure remembered him. In 1897, about a year and a half after their meeting, she wrote to him declaring that she had at first been suspicious of him but now realized his greatness. Moreover, she was "blessed or cursed with the gift of second sight" and had visions of harm coming to him within six months. She enclosed a gold charm and begged him to wear it. Rhodes, it appears, was favorably impressed—the letter was kept, and so was the amulet. She wrote him again a year and a half later, this time asking for investment advice. He wrote back, advising her to invest in the Mashonaland Railway.

At this point, Catherine was living alone in Paris; depressed and increasingly poor, she turned a bit stalker, at least according to Rhodes's secretary at the time, Philip Jourdan. In his memoirs, Jourdan recounts how Rhodes was trying to book passage to Africa but had to cancel and rebook several times. Catherine, too, was making frequent trips to the travel agent to learn Rhodes's plans and remake hers accordingly. So no one was at all surprised when Rhodes finally did set sail for South Africa in July 1899 and Catherine floated into the first-class dining room.

At 41 years old, Catherine was still pretty; she was also connected, intelligent, and versed in politics. And to the embarrassment of the dinner table, she showed herself to be extremely candid about her reasons for traveling to South Africa—she reportedly declared that her husband, whom she was divorcing, was a terrible brute and she was desperate to leave Europe. Jourdan claimed that she once fainted into Rhodes's arms, wholly undone by her terrible plight (no other passengers saw this bizarre behavior, mind you). Rhodes was at least charmed enough to offer a standing invitation to his home when they reached their destination.

If Catherine's goal was to gain Rhodes's romantic affections, as Jourdan claimed, she was barking up the wrong tree. Rhodes was either a confirmed bachelor or a closeted homosexual. Initially, at least, she seemed to have a different objective in mind: political influence and access. Through Rhodes, she met several South African politicians; as a princess, she was an immediate sensation in Cape Town, a fixture at all the most important social events and a regular visitor to Parliament. Rhodes's aides called her "Princess Razzledazzle" for all her intrigues and attempts at political maneuvering. Within a few months, however, she had worn out her welcome, especially after Rhodes heard tell that she was saying they were having an affair, even that they were engaged. Catherine was indeed spreading bizarre and untrue stories, and her reasons for doing so remain unclear though may have had to do with gaining political credibility. Unfortunately for her, the plan backfired.

In the meantime, the shifting political landscape turned dangerous with the advent of the Boer War. With Rhodes under siege in the town of Kimberly for four months, Catherine contacted Dutch leaders of the Afrikaner Bond party, with the intention of creating a broader Anglo-African Party and reconciling the political elite to Rhodes. She even started a newspaper called *Greater Britain*, devoted to his defense. Catherine's behavior had crossed the line into weird; she wanted to be the one who orchestrated the rise of Rhodes to the role of prime minister of a federated South African state. Rhodes, however, did not want "the old Princess" in his corner, nor did he want her around, period. But no matter how far he ran, she pursued him with undaunted zeal.

Catherine probably kept up her gambit because by that time she was broke. In March 1900, she wrote asking Rhodes to act as her financial guarantor. He never responded in writing, though he later said that he instructed his attorney to inform her that he would pay her outstanding hotel bill if she agreed to leave the country. In April Catherine did leave, but only for a little while. After a short stay in London, during which she penned newspaper articles pushing for Rhodes's political rebirth, she again boarded a ship bound for Cape Town in June. At some point in the next few months, relations between Rhodes and Catherine erupted into all-out war, with some historians claiming it started when she began blackmailing the object of her unusual affection.

What did she have on Rhodes? Likely the so-called missing telegrams, documents related to the failed Jameson Raid that were supposedly evidence that the British secretary of state for the colonies had foreknowledge of the raid and worked out the plan with Rhodes. How Catherine got hold of the telegrams is a bit of a mystery, but it's plausible she had stolen them during one of her unattended visits to Rhodes's office. Whatever the documents were, she had them and he wanted them—the two reportedly had a "violent quarrel" over them. Authorities subsequently searched her room but turned up nothing.

Catherine's behavior took an even more overtly criminal turn in 1901, when, desperate for money, she began forging Rhodes's name on promissory notes to the tune of £24,000. When denied at a bank, she turned to a less reputable moneylender: a loan shark. Lies compounded upon lies, and over the next ten weeks, Catherine got in over her head so deeply that little could be done to extricate her. When a Mr. Tom Louw brought action against both Catherine and Rhodes for nonpayment, Catherine's crimes came to light. Neither defendant showed up at the hearing; the case was postponed, and Catherine was arrested on 24 counts of fraud and forgery. She was released a week later after mysteriously finding bail money. The trial was set for February 1902.

PRINCESS ON TRIAL

Now it was Catherine's turn to be the victim of blackmail—Rhodes's camp offered to pay off the forged checks if she returned the papers. Catherine refused; she seemed to be most concerned with escaping South Africa. "If I don't go tomorrow, I shall be put in the street or in prison. Suicide is better a thousand times," she wrote to a former friend. So Rhodes decided to pursue a different tack: public humiliation. He traveled back to South Africa to appear in court to discredit "that woman." Catherine repeatedly postponed her court appearance, pleading illness. In her absence, the checks were declared to be forgeries, and Rhodes was vindicated. But because it was a civil matter, Catherine went unpunished.

And she would have escaped unscathed had she not gone and done something completely crazy: she sued Rhodes for a £2,000 bill. He responded by turning her case over to criminal prosecution. Unless she could prove that Rhodes had signed the checks, she was jail bound. Catherine decided to wage a bizarre campaign against her accuser. She paced in the road outside Rhodes's cottage, tormenting the man who, by all accounts, was rapidly dying of heart disease. If she was deliberately trying to kill him, it worked: Rhodes died on March 26, at only 49 years old.

A month later, Catherine stood trial. The whole thing was a farce: she called no witnesses, had no defense, and seemed disinclined to help her lawyers come up with one. She appeared confused under questioning, and her answers often provoked laughter from the audience. Two days later, having already been convicted by the court of public opinion, Catherine was found guilty of fraud and forgery and sentenced to two years in prison. "If that is justice," she said, "I pity those who are administered by people having such a peculiar idea of it."

Catherine served 16 months in a South African prison. Her own lawyer, who by this time had turned against her, claimed she was released early because she'd made life so difficult for the guards and staff (the real reason: ill health). No documents relating to the Jameson Raid were ever found in her possession.

Royal Tell-All

When Catherine's daughter heard that her mother had been sentenced to prison, she declared that "she regretted the sentence had not been harder." Only Catherine's half brother believed in her innocence; the rest of her family abandoned her. She emerged from prison nearly destitute. She married again in 1911, this time to a businessman named Charles Emile-Kolb, a brief union about which little is known.

Around this time, Catherine moved back to St. Petersburg and the bosom of her old court. She managed to live off her writing, publishing books purporting to reveal the inside scoop on European royalty, including *Secrets of Dethroned Royalty, Royal Marriage Market of Europe, Confessions of the Czarina,* and, most intriguingly, *Black Dwarf of Vienna and Other Weird Stories.*

But the princess was not quite done with the bizarre public episodes. In 1913 she resumed her old nom de plume, Count Paul Vasili, and in a book titled *Behind the Veil of the Russian Court,* she let slip the one secret the Russian court had tried so hard to hide: that the young tsarevich suffered from hemophilia. Catherine was immediately found out and deported (which might've been for the best, given that the Bolshevik Revolution was about to cut a mighty swath through the aristocracy). She moved to Stockholm, continued to write prodigiously, and embarked on a lecture tour. In April 1917, she traveled to America to give a talk on Russian royalty and the revolution but was held at Ellis Island and ordered to explain her "career in South Africa." She eventually made it to Manhattan, where she tried to earn a living as a writer. More often, however, she was the subject of news items, such as the time she showed up at a lecture to denounce as a hoax the Protocols of Zion, a supposed Jewish plot for world domination, or when she was turned out of a hotel because she couldn't pay her bill.

So although her title earned her headlines, it didn't always earn her bylines. Over the next decade, Catherine lived hand to mouth, sometimes working as a telephone switchboard operator while trying to sell wordy articles offering her royal perspective on world events. In 1932, she wrote her second autobiography, *It Really Happened*, detailing her life in Europe and the United States and leaving out everything about South Africa. In it, she describes her life as a broke princess living in a New York tenement and befriending the local hooker with a heart of gold, a little dying girl, a haggard old woman who turns out to be dollars-stuffed-in-the-mattress rich, and a boy abused by his drunken father whom Catherine takes under her wing. As one biographer noted, "The title seems to have been a misnomer; it is unlikely that much of what she describes ever really occurred."

At some point in her adventures, Catherine converted to Catholicism and became a U.S. citizen. She later said, "I really became an American in heart. I cannot conceive of living anywhere else"—and she never did. She died in New York on May 12, 1941, at age 84. Her family had never forgiven her, in life or in death.

Stephanie von Hohenlohe

The Princess Who Partied for Hitler

SEPTEMBER 16, 1891-JUNE 13, 1972
SOCIAL CIRCLES ACROSS EUROPE
AND AMERICA

I n 1938 Princess Stephanie von Hohenlohe arrived in Manhattan with a visitor's visa and 106 pieces of luggage. The picture of a glittering socialite, she was greeted by the press—and by the FBI. Stephanie's wit and charm endeared her to nearly everyone she met—everyone, that is, except Allied intelligence. They thought Adolf Hitler's own "dear Princess" was a devious "gold digger," a blackmailer, and an amoral Nazi agent. But getting her out of the country, well, that would be tough.

Princess Partier Schmoozer Spy

Born into a middle-class family in Vienna in 1891, Stephanie clawed her way into the aristocracy armed with little more than a fine profile, an ability to flirt, and a useful manipulative streak. In 1914 she married an Austro-Hungarian prince, despite being two months pregnant with another man's child. Though they divorced in 1920, Stephanie kept her title and, more important, her connections to more than half the royal houses of Europe. It didn't take long for her to realize the value of her high-society contacts. She'd always had a taste for luxury (this was the woman who had brought her servants *and* a bathtub to the front lines while serving as a nurse in World War I), so when the cash ran out, she took to selling the only assets she had left: introductions and connections.

And perhaps more. By 1928, Stephanie was under the watchful eye of British and French intelligence. Documents found in her Paris apartment in 1932, shortly after she made a quick getaway to London, revealed that she was being paid by the Germans to befriend Lord Rothermere, owner of the *Daily Mail*, Britain's most popular newspaper. She was tasked with convincing him to use his papers to campaign for the return of German territory lost in the Treaty of Versailles. She eventually got to Rothermere, and her relationship with him was quite lucrative for both her and her Nazi connections. The same year she left Paris under a cloud of suspicion, she inked a deal with the press baron to be his European "society columnist" for £5,000 a year (about $433,000 in today's money), with an additional £2,000 for every completed assignment. Rothermere asked Stephanie to introduce him to Hitler, the new chancellor of the Reich, which was exactly what the fledgling Führer wanted. (He knew the value of good propaganda.) With Stephanie's coaching, Rothermere became one of the Nazi Party's most outspoken supporters in Britain. In 1938, their relationship ended, after Rothermere complained that she was asking for money all the time.

But Rothermere wasn't Stephanie's only gig. Throughout the 1930s she'd become increasingly valuable to the Nazis, especially because her conquests reached to the very top of the British aristocracy: King Edward VIII and the woman for whom he abdicated, Wallis Simpson. In fact, the only thing that stopped Stephanie from succeeding in keeping the pro-Nazi king on the throne was Parliament's dislike for the twice-divorced American commoner with a man's name.

By the mid-1930s, Stephanie had "wormed her way into society circles in London," according to her official secret service file, gathering intel on the country's influential people, spreading pro-German propaganda, and seeding the elite with Nazi sympathizers. She was under near-constant surveillance, though the home office was reluctant to kick her out owing to the "milieu in which the princess moved" (read: powerful friends who'd pitch a fit).

Ins and Outs

Stephanie's star in the Nazi Party was rising. She was their favorite hostess, bringing together party officials and European leaders for cocktails and conversation. Hitler invited her to his mountain retreat and showered her with gifts: bouquets of roses, portraits of himself in expensive frames dedicated to his "Dear Princess," a sheepdog puppy she called Wolf, after his own German shepherd, even a castle. In 1937, she was awarded the Honorary Cross of the German Red Cross for her "tireless activities on behalf of the German Reich." In 1936–38 she received VIP invitations to attend Hitler's famous goose-stepping rallies, even sitting on the Reich's platform in 1938. That same year, she became an "honorary Aryan" when she was awarded the Nazis' highest honor, the Gold Medal of Honor.

Stephanie did her part, and more, for the party, but her efforts didn't make her popular with everyone in the Nazi hierarchy. Fickle, paranoid Hitler began to agree with what people were saying about the princess—that she was Jewish (which she was; her mother had converted to Catholicism), that she was a blackmailer (a known fact), and that she had fingers in too many pies (definitely true). In early 1939, when the Nazi Party cut her off financially, Stephanie was on her own.

She tried to get her old job back with Rothermere but he refused, so she decided to take a gamble. She sued him for breach of contract, claiming he'd agreed to pay her in perpetuity. It was a move that looked a lot like blackmail, particularly when Stephanie made it clear that if he didn't pony up, she'd publish her memoirs, revealing Rothermere as a treasonous Nazi sympathizer who liked to chase after much younger women.

Not one to be bullied, Rothermere let the case go forward, and in November 1939 it reached the British high court. Stephanie lost, and even worse, the trial had shown her to be close with Hitler, which was really bad because, by then, Britain was at war with Germany. Shortly after the trial ended, a group of society ladies at the Ritz shouted at her, "Get out, you filthy spy!"

So she did. With nowhere left to go, 48-year-old Stephanie headed to America. When she and her 106 pieces of luggage landed in New York in December, the press was waiting for Hitler's precious princess, as was the FBI. Both trailed her assiduously (although it was the paparazzi she once found in her hotel bathroom). Ever the survivalist, Stephanie once again started seeding Nazi sympathy among high society, probably in an attempt to regain favor with her old friends. The American government didn't take kindly to her efforts, and when her temporary visa expired in November 1940, an extension was denied by J. Edgar Hoover himself.

It was then that Stephanie got desperate—and dramatic. She appealed directly to President Franklin Roosevelt, but he showed her little sympathy. She threatened suicide and claimed to be "too ill" to testify at her deportation hearing, even going so far as to arrive on a stretcher delivered by an ambulance. All to no avail. On March 7, 1941, Roosevelt gave a direct order to get "that Hohenlohe woman" out of the country. The next day, she was arrested.

Stephanie's son later said that she had a "special talent for turning former enemies into devoted friends." Which is quite an understatement, given her next feat. In the space of a few hours, the prisoner princess met and seduced the head of the Immigration and Naturalization Service, a married father of four named Lemuel Scholfield. On May 19, he allowed Stephanie to be released on bail. Handily, one of the conditions was that she remain in contact with her INS regional director—Scholfield, with whom she was now having frequent sleepovers.

Stephanie may have gained a temporary reprieve, but on December 8, 1941, the day after the Japanese attack on Pearl Harbor and America's entrance into World War II, she was arrested yet again. This time, no one was taking any chances—she was placed in solitary confinement at an immigration center in New Jersey. The besotted Scholfield tried using his influence on Hoover but only succeeded in enraging him; he was forced to resign. Stephanie was transferred to an internment camp for enemy aliens in Seagoville, Texas, where she spent the rest of the war behind barbed wire by order of the president. She was the last detainee to leave the camp, in 1945, and Scholfield was waiting for her; they lived together until his death in 1954.

Amazingly, Stephanie was able yet again to claw her way back onto the society pages and into the good graces of powerful people. In 1965, 20 years after her release from the internment camp, she was invited to Lyndon B. Johnson's presidential inauguration. Stephanie died in 1972, at the age of 80, and though she was old and ill, her death still came as a shock to those who knew her. Given how deftly she'd managed the trick of survival, no one thought the resilient princess would ever let go of life.

Survivors

PRINCESSES WHO
MADE CONTROVERSIAL
AND QUESTIONABLE
CHOICES

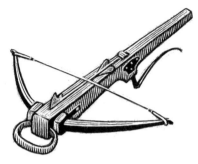

Lucrezia

The Renaissance Mafia Princess

April 18, 1480-June 24, 1519
Italy

*I*t was said that the beautiful Lucrezia Borgia wore a hollow ring filled with poison, convenient for slipping the stuff into unattended drinks. It was said that she murdered her lovers when she was done with them, and that she bathed in blood to maintain her flawless skin. It was said that she and her brother, the prodigiously homicidal Cesare, were lovers. It was unsurprising, really, that people whispered such terrible, tantalizing things about her—after all, her family's reputation as a proto-Mafia clan remains potent even today.

But the real Lucrezia Borgia wasn't a murderess, and she probably was never intimate with her brother. In fact, despite a rocky young adulthood that saw her married three times before the age of 22, she eventually blossomed into a woman you might actually like to have tea with. Just maybe pour your own cup.

MEET THE BORGIAS

By the time of Lucrezia's birth, in 1480, the Borgia family was one of the most powerful clans in Renaissance Italy and Spain. It was certainly one of the most corrupt: Borgias murdered, married, lied, and cheated their way into power, and once they had it, they went to great lengths to keep it. They were, effectively, a Renaissance mafia family, but with even fewer laws to curtail their crimes.

Lucrezia's father, Rodrigo, was a nephew of the late Pope Calixtus III. Though clearly not suited for the celibate life, at age 25 he was made a cardinal, a position that came with a lot of power and a massive income. At the time, the Roman Catholic church was the political, as well as the spiritual, center of Western Europe; it governed the Papal States, a region that encompassed a wide swath in the center of what is now Italy. The church and its head, the pope, wielded major influence over other Italian city-states, including the kingdom of Naples to the south and powerful Florence to the north, as well as the Catholic monarchies of Spain and France. It was also as corrupt as any ruling institution can be, which explains how Rodrigo could be considered a legitimate ecclesiastic leader while hosting wild parties replete with young ladies, wine, dancing, and lots of unpriestly sex. He reportedly fathered as many as nine children, at least four (including Lucrezia and Cesare) with his longtime mistress, the married noblewoman Vannozza Cattanei. But if the Borgia children were illegitimate, they were never made to feel that way. Beautiful Lucrezia was treated every bit like the princess she would later become.

When Lucrezia was 12, Cardinal Rodrigo was elected pope, taking the name Alexander VI, a triumph that cemented the Borgias' fortunes and made her father the most powerful man in Europe. It also meant that pretty Lucrezia, who according to contemporaries had long blonde hair,

hazel eyes that could appear gray or tawny, and an "admirably proportioned" bust, was the Borgias' new most-valuable asset.

Pope Alexander was exceptionally adept at marrying off Lucrezia
for maximum gain—each of her three marriages was to a more politically
important family. The first, when Lucrezia was just 13, made her the wife
of Count Giovanni Sforza, member of a rival clan and ruler of Pesaro, a
city-state on the Adriatic coast. But Sforza proved a disappointment:
though terrified of his new relations, he was equally afraid of his own
family. Lucrezia's father determined she would be worth more were she
married to someone else, and so when she was 17, he moved to have her
marriage annulled. He was the pope, after all, but he had to claim that
Sforza was impotent and the marriage was never consummated. That
Sforza's first wife had died in childbirth would seem to indicate that he
was able to perform his husbandly duties, but overlooking that fact wasn't
nearly as difficult as getting Sforza to agree to sign the divorce papers.
The count, as you can imagine, was not enthusiastic about telling the
world he was impotent, but ultimately he capitulated to pressure from
the Borgia family as well as his own.

Meanwhile, Lucrezia embarked on an ill-fated dalliance with independence. While her family wrestled over her divorce, she removed herself to a convent outside Rome. But if you think she couldn't get up to
much trouble there, think again—she soon found herself pregnant after
a passionate affair with Pedro Calderon, a Spaniard in service to her father. Within weeks of her family discovering the pregnancy, Calderon
was dead—Cesare supposedly stabbed him in the Vatican at the pope's
feet, although a papal scribe says that he "fell not of his own will into the
Tiber." The lady-in-waiting who'd tried to help Lucrezia cover up her
growing bump was pushed into the river after him. The fate of the child,
whom Lucrezia may have delivered in March 1498, is unknown.

Back to the Altar

Such conditions would have made any other woman unmarriable, and
gossips were calling Lucrezia the "greatest whore there ever was in
Rome." Yet suitors clamored for her hand, and by August 1498 she

was again at the altar. Her second marriage, to 17-year-old Alfonso of Aragon, the duke of Bisceglie and illegitimate son of the king of Naples, made Lucrezia a duchess and earned her the title of princess of Salerno. Lucrezia adapted well to her new husband, with whom, by all accounts, she was very much in love. Within six months, she was pregnant with their son, who was born on November 1, 1499. But people who became inconvenient to the Borgia family had a tendency to die, and the young duke was becoming very inconvenient, indeed.

Renaissance politics were as tangled as a bowl of pasta (sorry), but here's the long story less long: Cesare, who had recently married a French noblewoman, wanted help from France to conquer the city-states of southern Italy. Because France was warring against Naples, Lucrezia's marriage to a Neapolitan was an obstacle to family business. So one day in 1500, "unknown" assailants attacked Alfonso in St. Peter's Square, leaving him severely wounded but alive. Lucrezia nursed him back to health, only to have him later strangled by armed attackers. As a contemporary reported, "Since Don Alfonso refused to die of his wounds, he was strangled in his bed." There was no doubt who'd commissioned the murder—all signs pointed to Cesare. Aware that he was the prime suspect, Cesare claimed his brother-in-law had tried to kill him with a crossbow while he walked in the garden and therefore deserved to die. No one believed that story, and gossips claimed Alfonso was murdered not just for hindering the alliance with the French, but also because he'd replaced Cesare in his sister's affections.

Lucrezia was devastated by her husband's death. According to his former tutor, who was present at both attacks, Lucrezia filled the palace with "shrieking, lamenting, and wailing." Her constant weeping and raging against her father (who, incidentally, had no part in the murder) and her brother proved too much; they sent her and her infant son to Nepi, a small town 30 miles north of the Vatican, to recover her senses. And though she had loved her husband, Lucrezia loved her brother Cesare even more (how much more is open for debate); she soon forgave him. Next task on the family to-do list: find her another status-boosting husband.

Lucrezia's third and final walk down the aisle was with another Alfonso, this time Alfonso d'Este, duke of Ferrara. This match was the trickiest: at first Lucrezia seemed disinclined to remarry, complaining to her father that, to date, all of her husbands had been—*ahem*—"very unlucky." What's more, Ercole d'Este, Alfonso's father, didn't trust the Borgias as far as he could throw them, and so he spent years delaying the marriage. Courtiers continually tried to convince him of Lucrezia's personal modesty, her Christian devotion, and her good sense; Lucrezia, who was nothing if not ambitious, also started a frequent correspondence with Ercole in the hopes of impressing him. In the end, it was probably the sizable Borgia dowry and power, as much as her personal charms, that facilitated the match. Once again, Lucrezia bent herself to her family's will, leaving her 2-year-old son in Rome to wed the duke.

With marriage number three, Lucrezia's reputation was on the upswing. Even a spy in the employ of her new and distrustful sister-in-law declared that "every day she makes a better impression on me; she is a lady with a very good mind, astute, you have to keep your wits about you with her." And despite her husband's initial misgivings, he and Lucrezia got on like a house on fire. True, he spent his days prowling the streets for whores and hanging out in taverns, but he spent his nights with her. Lucrezia's relationships with her new in-laws were improving as well, which was probably a good thing, because the Borgias' roller coaster fortunes were about to take a nosedive.

THE REHABILITATION OF LUCREZIA BORGIA

In 1502, Cesare was the acknowledged military power in Italy, having attacked and taken control of several key city-states. He was a terror. Once, suspecting that one of his most trusted followers was plotting against him, he had the man decapitated, the head mounted on a lance and displayed in the town piazza. Anyone who stood in Cesare's way was likely to meet a similar fate.

By 1503, however, Cesare's fortunes were turning. In particular, his alliance with the French king was becoming a problem. Believing that Cesare was too powerful, Louis VII began blocking his acquisition of additional lands. Then the situation worsened—on August 18 of that year, Pope Alexander VI died. The man who had been the source of the Borgia authority was gone, and Cesare's mad scramble for power had made him more enemies than he could afford. The new pope supported him but wasn't around long enough to matter: the elderly man died only 26 days into his reign. The next pope to be elected was one of the Borgias' most hated rivals, and Cesare found himself a marked man. In 1504 he was arrested by papal forces and shipped off to prison in Spain. After a dramatic escape in 1507, Cesare was killed while fighting in the army of his brother-in-law the king of Navarre.

Lucrezia remained loyal to her brother until the end. By this time her own position was extremely perilous. Not only had her family's power and influence died with her father, but so far she had been unable to do the one thing she needed to do: produce an heir. Though pregnant in her first year of marriage, she had given birth to a stillborn daughter at seven months and nearly died from fever. Her husband had an easy out should he want one—everyone knew that the grounds for Lucrezia's divorce from Sforza were a sham, a claim that, if pressed, could mean that her current union had no legal basis.

But Lucrezia's new family didn't try to ditch her, for the simple reason that they liked her. That's as strong an indication as any that Lucrezia was not the evil incestuous murderess that contemporary and historical gossip claim she was. True, had her husband divorced her, he would have been obligated to return her exceptionally large dowry. But there is no evidence that any of the duke's family even raised the thought. On the contrary, her new family protected her, respected her, and even tried to help her wayward brother.

In some ways, the Borgia downfall proved to be Lucrezia's salvation—run-of-the-mill intrigue was far less deadly than Borgia-level intrigue. And though she had a few affairs—most notably with poet Pietro Bembo and her brother-in-law Francesco Gonzaga—for the most part she led a quiet life. She re-created herself as the quintessential Renaissance lady: a patron of the arts, charitable, pious, reserved, and nearly constantly pregnant. She eventually bore four sons and a daughter who survived infancy, though she was also plagued by multiple miscarriages and difficult births. Lucrezia's final pregnancy, at the age of almost 39, resulted in her death. She succumbed to postchildbirth puerperal fever five days after delivering another daughter, who also did not survive.

THE WICKEDEST WITCH OF THEM ALL?

By the end of her life, Lucrezia had become excessively penitential, whether for sins real or imagined, only she knows. How complicit she was in her family's crimes is unclear, but she certainly benefitted from them. The constant intrigues and murderous tendencies brought her power, wealth, and excellent marriages she couldn't possibly have made otherwise. But her brother murdered one of her lovers *and* one of her husbands *and* one of their own brothers, and her family's actions separated her from her firstborn son. Though her flirtations with independence didn't always go well, they did reveal a woman trying to break free from those who used her for their own ends.

Few women in history have been as demonized, even fetishized, as Lucrezia Borgia. Historians and novelists preferred to believe that her sins were real, and over the centuries many have added several she couldn't possibly have been guilty of. In 1833, for example, the French writer Victor Hugo wrote a stage play based on Lucrezia's life, depicting her as a lusty, amoral murderess who accidentally poisons her illegitimate son; the play later became Gaetano Donizetti's opera. In Hugo's preface, he makes his opinions unequivocally clear: "Take the most hideous, the most repulsive, the most complete moral deformity; place it where it fits best—in the heart of a woman whose physical beauty and royal grandeur will make the crime stand out all the more strikingly; then add to all that moral deformity the purest feeling a woman can have, that of a mother. . . . Inside our monster put a mother and the monster will interest us and make us weep. And this creature that filled us with fear will inspire pity; that deformed soul will be almost beautiful in our eyes."

It's this sexy, incestuous, philandering, murderous princess that people want to believe in, the one who makes the most scandalous story. But Lucrezia Borgia wasn't the slutty poisoner everyone wanted her to be. She was a woman who managed to survive not only the pit of vipers that was Renaissance Italy, but the pit of vipers that was her own family. And isn't that story more interesting?

Malinche

The Princess Who Served Her Country's Conquerers

CA. 1502-1529
AZTEC MEXICO AND SPANISH MEXICO

O nce upon a time, there was an Aztec princess. Her father was the *cacique* of a city-state near the Gulf of Mexico, but he died when the princess was very young. Her wicked mother soon remarried and gave birth to a little boy.

The little princess's mother and stepfather wanted their son to become the next chief, and the little princess was in the way. They couldn't let her marry because then her husband would have a claim to the throne. So the scheming parents hit upon an ingenious solution: they sold the girl to a group of Mayan slave traders and told everyone she'd died. The Mayans in turn sold her to traders from the city of Tabasco, where the princess came of age and was rescued by the brave knights of the Spanish Empire. She proved her worth by acting as their translator and guide, so fully embracing their religion that when once again confronted with her mother, she forgave the perfidious woman on the spot.

That's the fairy-tale version that later Spanish biographers would relate of the beautiful, noble, admirable princess known as Malinche. But that's not the story modern Mexicans tell. To them, La Malinche is one of the most reviled, controversial women in postcolonial history.

The real story, of course, is a lot more complicated.

LOST IN TRANSLATION

We don't know the circumstances of the young woman's birth or even her real name—Malinche was the Spanish garbling of Malintzin, the name she was called by the slavers who sold her. Though she probably was the daughter of a nobleman, the whole "princess" thing was added later by the Spanish who wanted to valorize her story. But it is true that at about 8 or 9 years old, little Malinche found herself sold into slavery. The institution was a deeply entrenched part of Mesoamerican culture at the time, and it was not uncommon for families to sell their children as slaves, who were typically used for manual labor or sex.

In 1519 the Spaniards arrived in Tabasco, and teenage Malinche's whole world changed. Led by the conquistador Hernan Cortés, the Spanish had come calling a few times before, and their interactions with the local Chontal people had not exactly been friendly. This time around, the Chontal tried to put up a fight, but the invaders had armor, guns, and horses. The Chontal lost 220 men in a matter of hours; surrender was the only option. Malinche, along with 19 other women as well as large quantities of gold and food, was offered up as tribute. She was baptized Marina—it was standard practice among the conquistadors to convert women and slaves to Christianity before having sex with them—and then passed off to one of Cortés's men.

This "most excellent woman," according to Bernal Díaz del Castillo, a foot soldier in Cortés's army writing in 1568, was "good-looking, intelligent, and self-assured." More important, she had a gift for languages that quickly made her indispensable. Malinche's native tongue was Nahuatl, but as a slave in Tabasco she'd learned two Mayan dialects and soon she set to learning Castilian Spanish from a friar in Cortés's company. Her facility was said to be so great that she was fluent in only four months. When Cortés realized her value, he made sure that she never left his side. She served so often as his mouthpiece, and the two were so closely identified with each other, that he was sometimes called "El Malinche" (kind of like Mr. Malinche) by the Mesoamericans.

But Malinche wasn't valuable only as a translator. She was familiar with native royal customs, owing to what Spanish biographers claimed was her childhood lived in a nobleman's home, and as a slave she'd spent time with several tribes. She understood how the indigenous peoples thought, what they believed, and how they worked. She could be exactly what Cortés needed: a guide in this strange new land.

It didn't take long for Malinche to prove her worth. She told Cortés that the Aztecs thought he might be the reincarnation of their god ruler Quetzalcóatl. She also explained that several of the tribes chafing under Aztec rule could easily be persuaded to help him take down their empire. Cortés depended on her to communicate with those who wished to join him and, after the Spanish defeated a tribe, to explain to the people that they'd in fact been conquered. Malinche even acted as a sort of spy. Once, playing the disloyal servant, she heard from a local woman about a plot to ambush the Spaniards as they were leaving the village of Cholula. She told Cortés, who then ordered the massacre of Cholulan leaders and warriors.

With Malinche's help, the Spaniards made their way to Tenochtitlan, Moctezuma's massive and glorious city. In late 1519, it was Malinche who translated the Aztec leader's first words with the foreign newcomers. Whatever Moctezuma actually said, and whatever Malinche may have translated, Cortés claimed to his king that the Aztec ruler had immediately agreed to cede his entire empire to Spain. That gave Cortés the pretext to subdue the Aztecs with force (technically, the Spanish king could not force a foreign people to serve him, but he could punish rebels who defied his rightful rule). In spring 1520, after several months of peaceful but tense coexistence, fighting broke out. Cortés blamed the Aztecs, claiming a plot was afoot to revolt against the Spaniards; on that pretext and a trumped-up treason charge, he arrested Moctezuma. What happened next depends on whose version you believe. Native records claim that it was the Spanish who struck first, slaughtering the Aztecs in one of the temples during a religious festival. Cortés's soldiers later said that the festival was just a cover for the warrior class and nobles to prepare to mount an attack on the Spaniards.

War was unavoidable. According to native accounts, Malinche tried to dissuade the Aztecs from revolting, pointing out that they were outgunned. But at first it was Cortés and his troops who were forced to retreat. Ultimately, though, the uprising was doomed to fail, not because of superior Spanish military might, but because of a much more insidious enemy: smallpox. The Spaniards had carried the deadly disease to the Americas, and native peoples had no natural defenses against it. Within weeks of their initial victory, thousands of Aztecs had died. At the end of April 1521, Cortés, with reinforcements from nearby Spanish-held Cuba, set out once again for Tenochtitlan, and this time he conquered it.

It's doubtful that without the aid of Malinche, the Spanish could have pulled off such an astounding conquest in the span of two years and with fewer than 1,000 soldiers. So why did she help the enemy? On the face of it, Malinche had little reason to want the precolonial system to endure; all it got her was a one-way ticket to forced bondage. And though she may have felt she had no choice, it's also possible that she was in love with Cortés. Whatever her feelings, in 1522 she bore him a son, whom they named Martín, after his grandfather.

Once the Spaniards had conquered the Aztecs, Malinche was much less useful, and Cortés was certainly not in love with her. His Spanish wife's suspicious death in 1522 (possibly at his hands) left him free to remarry, and he didn't waste the chance to forge a political union by marrying a native. Nevertheless, Cortés never entirely abandoned the woman who had been so helpful to him, and Malinche seems to have been made rich by her efforts; contemporary reports note deliveries of gold to her house. In autumn 1524, she was married off to Juan Jaramillo, one of Cortés's captains, and as a dowry was given the villages of Olutla and Tetiquipaque. As the wife of a wellborn, well-placed Spaniard, Malinche was able to avoid the fate that befell other indigenous women who bore mestizo (mixed native and European blood) children: being cast aside in poverty and shame.

Malinche and her husband remained in Cortés's service, and in April 1526 the couple welcomed a baby girl into the world. In 1529, just ten years after the Spanish arrived, Malinche was dead, probably the victim of one of the new European diseases still ravaging native populations.

THE MANY FACES OF MALINCHE

In Mexico today, a *malinchista* is a traitor to his or her people, just as Malinche supposedly was. She's been called the Mexican Eve, *La Traidora* ("the traitor"), and *La Vendida* ("the sell-out"), among other unflattering names.

It's impossible, however, to tease the true Malinche from the myth; she never recorded her feelings or thoughts or the reasons for her actions. We don't know if she was a nobleman's daughter, whether she loved her husband, or what she died of. The dearth of detail helps explain why it's so easy to turn a flesh-and-blood woman into a potent symbol—and why what she symbolizes has always been in flux. As the novelist Haniel Long wrote in 1939, "She represents more than any one moment of history can hold."

In Mexico's struggle for independence, Malinche became a representation of traitorous female sexuality, partly because she was so revered in the Spanish narrative of the conquest. Díaz del Castillo called her a "truly great princess" who, "although a native woman, possessed such manly valor . . . that she betrayed no weakness but a courage greater than that of a woman." In 1945, lashing out against the Spanish narrative, Mexican Nobel laureate Octavio Paz condemned Malinche as the root of Mexico's "anxiety and anguish." Calling her "*la Chingada*" (a naughty word, like "screwed" but more vulgar), Paz claimed that what Cortés did to this weak, passive woman was what the Spanish did to the Mesoamerican people. That Malinche "let" him seduce her is her betrayal; she is the traitor, and Cortés, though a villain, is blameless. That remained the prevailing perception for decades. In 1982, for example, a statue of Malinche and her son, representing the first mestizo of Mexico, was removed after local students protested; they didn't want a monument to a blood traitor in their neighborhood.

Dramatists, novelists, and filmmakers have also reinterpreted the story, with varying degrees of sympathy. In H. Rider Haggard's 1893 *Montezuma's Daughter*, she's a Pocahontas-like character, saving the conquistadors from being killed by her people; in Gary Jennings's 1980 historical novel *Aztec*, she's a schemer and a traitor. Sometimes Malinche is a mentally unbalanced she-devil who feels deep guilt for the atrocities the Spaniards inflicted with her help. She might be a woman so addled by her love for Cortés that she doesn't even care he's using her as a pawn; or she's a realist who sees that it's better to survive with the conquistadors than to die as a slave. She's a scapegoat, taking the blame for the fall of the Aztec nation, or she's the madwoman who gleefully engineered the bloody destruction of her way of life.

More recently, feminists have reclaimed Malinche, first as an icon of victimhood who was violated by the patriarchy of both the Aztecs and the Spanish, and later as a survivor who forged ahead when those around her died. Modern scholarship sees her as a kind of cultural and linguistic bridge between the Mesoamerican past and the postcolonial present. Her son Martín, the product of her relationship with Cortés, has come to represent the mestizo future.

No other Aztec princess made such an indelible mark on Mexican history, and certainly no other woman played such an integral role in the Spanish conquest of Mexico. But Malinche's legacy has endured, at least in part, because she is voiceless. She's been used as a mouthpiece by historians, novelists, feminists, and scholars, as much today as in her own lifetime.

History is full of bloody ends, inscrutable motivations, indecipherable decisions, and choices that we can never fully understand. That's what makes it so easy to manipulate, especially when facts are as thin as they are regarding this woman whose real name, let alone motivations, remains unknown. Ultimately, that's the true story of Malinche.

The War Booty Princess

For most royal women throughout history, having a title didn't mean having power. Their actions were mostly dictated by fathers, brothers, or husbands, and during wartime they often became an unwilling prize for the male victor. Such was the case of beautiful Nest of Wales.

In 1093, young Nest was taken hostage by invading Norman forces after her father, King Rhys ap Tewdwr, was killed. She ended up in her oppressors' court, where she caught the eye of Henry, William II's younger brother, later bearing one of his many illegitimate sons. After becoming king, Henry married Nest off to one of his mates, Gerald of Windsor. The couple returned to Gerald's stolen castle in Wales, where she bore him four children.

In 1109 a prince named Owain met Nest at a feast and fell in love with her. Like many local Welsh princes, Owain was trying to shake the yoke of Norman rule, and he and a group of his men decided to lay siege to Gerald's castle, supposedly to steal Nest away. Gerald escaped through the privy, but Nest was taken hostage along with her children, who were soon returned to their father.

Owain probably didn't love her, but rather abducted her to start a fight—he was taking a page out of a timeworn playbook that cast royal women as booty. His actions precipitated a war that inflamed the locals and earned Nest the nickname "Helen of Wales." Henry I, her former lover, leapt to her defense, offering Owain's rivals land in Wales if they fought to get Nest back. Within the year, Owain had ditched Nest and fled to Ireland. Nest rejoined her husband and children, but strife continued to plague the countryside—the rebellion that Owain started lasted until 1116.

Sophia Dorothea

The Prisoner Princess

SEPTEMBER 15, 1666–NOVEMBER 13, 1726
CASTLE ALDHEN, GERMANY

*I*t could have been a storybook romance, if the authors were the brothers Grimm, or maybe Stephen King. When Princess Sophia Dorothea was told she was to be married to Prince George Louis of Hanover, she fainted dead away. She collapsed again when she was expected to greet him as her fiancé. And when she was given a diamond-studded miniature portrait of her betrothed, she dashed it against the wall, screaming, "I will not marry the pig snout!" But on November 21, 1682, marry the pig snout she did. It was probably the worst mistake of her life.

Marriage on the Rocks

Sophia Dorothea of Celle was born in northwest Germany in 1666, the only child of George William, the duke of Brunswick-Lüneburg. She was a romantic and flighty child but was expected to fetch a fine husband, and at age 16, she did just that. Her fiancé, 22-year-old George Louis, was her first cousin and the son and heir of the elector of Hanover, ruler of the most important principality in Germany. He was also in line for the British crown and would be the future George I of England. The pair had known each other for much of their young adulthood, and they didn't like each other one bit. Though Sophia Dorothea was reckoned by most to be pretty, witty, and vivacious, George regarded her as his social inferior, a bastard child whose parents didn't marry until she was nearly 10 years old. Sophia Dorothea thought George was cold, rude, and overly formal. He was known in Hanover as "the pig snout," owing to both his appearance and his attitude.

The truth is that even George's own mother didn't like him very much. In a letter to a niece, she declared him "the most pigheaded, stubborn boy who ever lived, and who has round his brains such a thick crust that I defy any man or woman ever to discover what is in them." And for all he begrudged Sophia Dorothea her murky birth, George got an early start on making his own pack of illegitimate children, knocking up one of his sibling's governesses when he was just 16 years old. His mother warned him "not to have his name bawled from the housetops as the progenitor of bastards."

But as was often the case in royal matrimony, whether or not the couple liked each other was irrelevant. And at first George and Sophia Dorothea seemed resigned to their fate. Eleven months after the wedding, they welcomed their first child, a son and heir they named George Augustus. But the court at Hanover was smothering in its formality, and though her in-laws tried to be welcoming, they found Sophia Dorothea's etiquette lacking and declared her a "bad influence." Meanwhile, the young royals' relationship lurched from bad to worse. George ignored his high-spirited wife, and when he did notice her, he acted as if he were repulsed by what he saw. Even worse, when Sophia Dorothea was pregnant with their second child, her husband suddenly turned violent.

George had begun an affair with the youthful Melusine von der Schlulenberg, one of his mother's ladies-in-waiting. She was stick thin and a head taller than he was, so they made a pretty distinctive couple when they went out in public. Which they often did—George made no effort to hide the affair. One day his pregnant and tearful wife followed him into his study, demanding he tell her what she could do to win him back. George flew into a rage, shaking Sophia Dorothea violently and nearly strangling her to death. The attack left her bruised and desperately ill; she was confined to bed, and fears that she would miscarry gripped the Hanoverian court. George didn't visit his ailing wife until forced to by his mother; when he finally did, he sat sullenly by her bed, holding her hand like a bored child. Sophia Dorothea recovered, but the marriage never did.

In March 1687, Sophia Dorothea gave birth to a daughter, and George continued his affair with Melusine. Within two years, husband and wife were openly hostile to each other. George spent much of his time either away at war or in Melusine's arms—the first of their three daughters was born in January 1692. When Sophia Dorothea complained about her husband's infidelities to her parents, they advised her just to keep a stiff upper lip and ignore his behavior. When she complained to her in-laws—who were also her aunt and uncle—they also advised her to hold her tongue. As her mother-in-law reminded her, George might be king of England someday, and she could expect to be queen. (How a German prince could become king of England comes down to religion: George was Protestant, and British Parliament was about to declare a law that no Catholic could sit on the English throne, thus rendering illegal the succession of more than 50 other royals with stronger claims but the wrong faith.)

But it was only a matter of time before the pretty young princess sought a distraction of her own. She found it in Philip Christopher von Königsmarck, a dashing young Swedish count and colonel in the Hanoverian army. Königsmarck came from a distinguished military family and had a "poetic" nature that contrasted favorably with her husband's rather vile personality.

By 1689, Königsmarck and Sophia Dorothea were very much in love. He began writing her soppy love letters stuffed with romantic verses; at first she tried to resist such a dangerous flirtation, but by year's end she was writing back. She sewed his clandestine epistles into the linings of curtains or hid them in playing-card boxes in her room; he would find hers tucked into his hat or gloves by her trusted lady-in-waiting. It wasn't long before their letters shifted from the courtly pantomime of love to something more intimate. The depth of their affection is clear by April 1691, when Königsmarck signed off with "I embrace your knees." By March of the next year, their correspondence contained references to the act of *monter à cheval* ("horseback riding," wink-wink), the "transports of passion" they experienced together, Königsmarck's pleasure at "embracing the most beautiful body in the world," and his desire to "kiss that little place which has given me so much pleasure."

Who Knew? (Who Didn't?)

The affair was meant to be a secret, so of course everyone at court knew all about it. The lovers relied on too many people to help them pass their notes, which were written in an easily decipherable code. Though they used Sophia Dorothea's lady-in-waiting's room for trysts, or met in the garden at night, they gave themselves away in public with longing glances and prearranged signals. Still they believed they were getting away with it all: Königsmarck wrote to Sophia Dorothea, "What delight, *ma petite*, for us to communicate with impunity in the presence of thousands of people!"

Though everyone knew about the affair, no one quite knew what to do about it. Despite measures taken by Sophia Dorothea's in-laws and her parents to keep the lovebirds apart (including sending Königsmarck to the front—this being Europe in the 1690s, a war was always handy), the lovers still managed to sneak letters back and forth. Königsmarck even signed some in his own blood as a testament to his burning ardor. As the infatuation grew more intense, Sophia Dorothea's brittle, fragile marriage crumbled. An episode from 1693 highlights just how bad it was. While walking one night on the grounds of the Hanoverian palace, Sophia Dorothea came upon a small outlying building. She opened the door to find her husband holding hands with his mistress and gazing adoringly at his newborn daughter, his second child by Melusine. Affronted by this clandestine scene of domestic bliss, the princess began screaming at her wayward husband. George Louis responded by trying to strangle her once again and had to be pulled off by her ladies-in-waiting.

Unsurprisingly, Sophia Dorothea was now actively looking for a way to escape with Königsmarck. But upon reviewing her marriage contract, she was shocked to find that she had no money of her own—her father had signed over her entire dowry when she wed. She refused to live under the same roof as George, fleeing to her parents and demanding to live with them or be given her own household. But again her father failed her, refusing to allow her to stay longer than a few months.

Back at court in June 1694, a desperate Sophia Dorothea and her lover worked out a plan: they'd make for the German principality of Wolfenbüttel, where they could seek sanctuary with the sympathetic Duke Anthony Ulric. On July 1, Königsmarck found a letter in his rooms from Sophia Dorothea, asking him to come to her private apartment at 10 that night. A disguised Königsmarck snuck onto palace grounds and made his way to her room, where he gave their old signal (whispering "The Spanish Follies" at the door). She let him in, happy to see him, but was surprised—she hadn't sent any letter. Despite this ill omen, the couple agreed to skip town the next morning so that she could say goodbye to her children before leaving. They parted, elated and excited. Sophia Dorothea never saw Königsmarck again.

In fact, the meeting was a trap set by Countess Clara Elizabeth von Platen, the mistress of Sophia Dorothea's father-in-law and rumored to be an ex-lover of Königsmarck who was looking for an opportunity to remove Sophia Dorothea from court. When Königsmarck arrived at the princess's apartments, the countess ran to tell the elector, Sophia Dorothea's father-in-law, that the brazen couple was in the very act of making love. She could catch them, she said, and arrest them. The elector agreed.

When Königsmarck left Sophia Dorothea's apartments, the countess and her four accomplices were waiting for him. The men set upon him, swords drawn. Though Königsmarck managed to wound three of them before his sword broke in half, they soon overpowered him. As he lay bleeding to death, he gurgled his last words: "Spare the princess; save the innocent princess!" The countess reportedly then kicked him in the face with her diamond-buckled shoe.

Only then did she realize what she'd done. The elector had agreed to let her arrest Königsmarck, not to kill him. He was a nobleman, and a widely known one; people were bound to come looking for him. Panicked, the countess ran back to the elector and told him what had happened; he authorized her to do whatever was necessary to get rid of the problem. And so the countess had her courtiers stuff Königsmarck's body in a sack, weigh it down with stones, and dump it in the river. Those in court who knew about the murder now needed to cover it up.

LOCKED AWAY

The next morning, Sophia Dorothea, her bags packed, waited for her children to pay their usual morning call. Instead she was visited by a palace official, who came to inform her that she was confined to her rooms until further notice. Her belongings were searched; the incriminating letters were found. Three days later, her lady-in-waiting told her that Königsmarck was dead.

Sophia Dorothea was now in custody while her father and father-in-law argued over what to do. A divorce was clearly necessary, but they also knew that pressing the adultery angle would produce uncomfortable questions all around. Already people were wondering what happened to the dashing young count. The only viable solution was to claim desertion on her part. Thus on December 28, 1694, the marriage was dissolved; as the guilty party, Sophia Dorothea would not be permitted to remarry. But at least she'd be free.

Wrong. Yet again, her father betrayed her: Part of his agreement stipulated that Sophia Dorothea would remain a state prisoner at the castle of Ahlden, an estate protected by a river on one side and a moat on the other. The concern was that Sophia Dorothea might make a tempting hostage for George Louis's political rivals, notably France and those Britons who resisted the imposition of a German royal on the English throne. The

28-year-old princess simply could not be at liberty for the rest of her life.

It wasn't until she was locked away that Sophia Dorothea understood the full horror of what was happening: She was cut off completely from her two young children. Her father refused ever to see her again and would not allow her mother to visit. All her servants were forced to take an oath of loyalty to the elector and encouraged to report anything suspicious. Sophia Dorothea was allowed outside only after her doctors told her jailers that she needed fresh air. Even then, she was permitted nothing more than a short walk in the back garden, under guard. Entire areas of the castle were off-limits. Once, a fire started near her wing, but escape would have taken her through a gallery that was forbidden to her. Trapped, she waited at the threshold, clutching her jewelry box, for someone to escort her to safety.

The German public and nobility were shocked by Sophia Dorothea's unjust imprisonment, but the several attempts to rescue her failed. Now called the Duchess of Ahlden, she spent the last 33 years of her life at the castle. She died on November 13, 1726, at the age of 60.

The day he heard the news, George, now King of England, went to the theater to see a comedy with his two mistresses. He forbade his son, the future king George II, from making any public demonstration of grief. Only Sophia Dorothea's daughter, now the queen of Prussia, was able to mourn her mother publicly. George had Sophia Dorothea buried at the ducal vaults in Celle, at night and without ceremony, her grave marked only with her name and the dates of her birth and death.

In the end, however, Sophia Dorothea may have had her revenge, at least according to legend. Several years before her death, a French fortune-teller told superstitious George I that if he were at all responsible for Sophia Dorothea's demise, he'd die too within the year. (She'd been paid to say that by Sophia Dorothea's mother, *shh*.) The pronouncement spooked him, though not enough to free his poor ex-wife. But that wasn't all—on her deathbed, Sophia Dorothea supposedly cursed his name and wrote him a letter reproaching him for his cruelty. The letter reached him on June 21, 1727. Reading her last words calling him to appear before God and account for his crimes, George supposedly had a stroke and died.

Marriage or Insane Asylum?

Leopold II, King of the Belgians, was a cruel monarch and an even worse father. His wife, a woman who seemed to prefer her horses to her children, wasn't much better. Not surprisingly, then, the couple's eldest daughter, Princess Louise Marie Amélie, channeled her anger and frustration into making the many shopkeepers, dressmakers, and jewelry stores in Europe rich.

Born in 1858, Princess Louise was acutely aware that she was not the longed-for male heir her father wanted. She grew up in a household marked by coldness, indifferent cruelty, and austerity. At age 15, she married her second cousin, Prince Philip of Saxe-Coburg-Gotha, a heavily whiskered man 14 years her senior. She had absolutely no idea what to expect from their wedding night—no one had ever told her—and she ran away when she got an inkling of what was up. She was later found in her nightdress hiding in the greenhouses.

The newlyweds moved to Vienna, where the cosmopolitan lifestyle of the Austrian court soothed Louise's fears. She threw herself into flirtations, scandalous love affairs, pretty dresses, and buying lots and lots of stuff. Two children later, the princess still hadn't slowed down. Then, in 1895, after 20 years of marriage, she fell in love with Geza Mattachich, a Croatian count and dashing officer in the Austrian army who was 10 years her junior; the attraction, she'd later claim, was like an electric shock. Two years later, it was her turn to shock when she ran away with him. "You are taking big risks for a few passing successes of nice dresses, compliments or love declarations," her mother wrote in a pleading letter. "They won't last longer than bubbles of soap! Stop the stories that are circulating, dry the tears of your mother." Her father refused to allow her to divorce, but Louise was not to be dissuaded. She moved to France, settling in Nice, where she could live with her lover unimpeded by the court.

But Louise's profligate ways soon caught up with her. After spending everything on hotels, clothing, and jewelry, the broke royal was forced to sell it all off, right down to her underwear, in what sounds like a big, glittery yard sale. The proceeds still didn't cover the millions she owed. Both King Leopold and her estranged husband refused to cover her debts, leading creditors to break through her door and take everything that wasn't nailed down.

So Louise and Mattachich allegedly turned criminal, forging promissory notes in the name of her sister. (Some claimed that the charges were trumped up by her father and husband.) After a short time on the lam, Mattachich was arrested for fraud and thrown in jail. Louise, meanwhile, was given an ultimatum by her father: return to your husband or be committed to an insane asylum. She chose the latter and was interned at a hospital run by an Austrian court physician. In 1902 the *New York Times* reported that the princess, held "practically a prisoner" at a "retreat" for the past two years, had been declared "hopelessly insane."

Louise spent six years as an inmate until Mattachich broke her out. The couple escaped to Paris, where they lived in poverty. Even after Louise finally obtained a divorce in 1907, she and Mattachich were no better off. Louise's father disowned her, and she spent the rest of her life wandering Europe with Mattachich by her side, hounded by creditors. In 1921 Louise penned her memoirs, both in an effort to repair her tattered reputation and to earn some much-needed money. Though she dedicated the book to her father, "the great man" and "great king," she wrote, "I owe nothing but misfortune to my royal origin. Ever since I was born, I have suffered and been deceived."

Ever-faithful Mattachich died in Paris in October 1923; Louise would last less than a year, dying with his portrait clutched to her chest in March 1924.

Sarah Winnemucca

The Princess Accused of Collaborating

Ca. 1844–October 17, 1891
The northern Paiute nation and
the American frontier

The headline in the Washington, D.C., *National Tribune* read, "Princess Winnemucca: No Longer the Wild Indian Girl But a Lady of Culture From Boston." It was January 29, 1885, and Sarah Winnemucca Hopkins, popularly known as Princess Winnemucca or Princess Sally of the Northern Paiute people, was on a lecture tour in the Northeast.

Sarah, whose original name was Thocmetony (meaning "shell

flower"), was lecturing about the appalling conditions her people were subjected to while living on reservations, but you wouldn't know that from the article. In a mocking tone typical of writings about Native Americans during this era, the reporter noted that since Sarah had abandoned her heathen ways, her people regarded her with suspicion. "They know that she has adopted the garb of the white sisters and it is even suspected that she uses soap and comb occasionally. To the genuine Piute, these things are inconsistent with the traditions of the race." The conclusion: "She was regarded as a little queer by everybody."

The reporter got at least one thing right: Sarah *was* regarded as a little odd by just about everybody. Though they might champion her cause, most white Americans didn't think of the "Indian princess" as one of them, and the Paiutes sometimes saw her as a collaborator on the payroll of the U.S. government—a government that seemed to think the solution to the "Indian problem" was starvation and disease. Sarah just couldn't win.

In Like a Lion

Sarah is best known for her 1883 autobiography, *Life among the Piutes: Their Wrongs and Their Claims*, the first memoir written and published by a Native American woman. Her story begins: "I was born somewhere near 1844, but am not sure of the precise time. I was a very small child when the first white people came to our country. They came like a lion, yes, like a roaring lion, and have continued to do so ever since, and I have never forgotten their first coming."

When white settlers arrived in the American West in the 1840s, the Northern Paiutes were a small nomadic tribe of hunter-gatherers who crisscrossed what is now Nevada, California, and Oregon. The settlers, meanwhile, were hell-bent on westward expansion and digging for all the gold in them thar hills, and native tribes were in the way.

Sarah reported that when her grandfather, a chief, first met the settlers, he welcomed them and acted as their guide. Sarah's people kept the newcomers alive through a difficult winter and followed her grandfather's wishes to treat them as "brothers." Sarah's father, Chief Winnemucca, was more circumspect and tended to keep his distance from whites. Not surprising, given that the settlers tended to repay the natives by burning down their winter stores, indiscriminately shooting them, and polluting their drinking water. There were good white people, too, Sarah noted, those who gave the Indians clothing, who shared medicine with her when she was covered in poison oak, who recognized that the Indians should be treated with respect. But there weren't many of that sort, and more settlers arrived every month.

Early on, Sarah may have realized something that others did not: to survive the roaring lion, you had to know how to talk to it. Fortunately for her, she had always had a great facility with languages, having learned Spanish before the age of 10, after members of her family married Spanish colonials in California. She proved just as adept at English, which she learned from a white family while she was in domestic service in Nevada (this family was also probably first to call her Sarah). By 1859 Sarah was acting as a translator for her family when she realized that white settlers wanted to deal with someone they considered an authority. So she implied to several government agents that her father was the "Big Chief" of the Northern Paiute nation, not just the head of his band of 150 followers. This little white lie allowed Chief Winnemucca to speak on behalf of his people, and Sarah to call herself a princess.

Life could be extremely dangerous for an Indian trying to find a place on the border between the "civilized" and the "savage." One example of the danger Sarah faced appears in her book: she describes how a contingent of white soldiers, armed with a flimsy claim that her people had stolen some cattle, slaughtered an entire village, down to the last child. "It is always the whites that begin the wars, for their own selfish purposes," she wrote.

In 1872 the Northern Paiute were "given" the Malheur Reservation in Oregon, and Sarah's family moved there. At first, the site was overseen by Samuel Parrish, an agent who, Sarah said, treated the Indians fairly. After four years, he was replaced by the villainous William Rinehart, who stole their goods, refused to pay them for work, and cheated them at every pass. Under his feckless watch, many Indian families starved. Paiutes who were suspected of a crime were executed without a trial. Much of the land that was supposed to be set aside for them was illegally seized by white settlers, leaving the Indians less area for hunting and food gathering. He even closed the school. Sarah's efforts to secure sufficient food for her people and to alert the authorities about the conditions at Malheur were ignored, even though she signed her letters "Princess Winnemucca."

In 1878, those Indians who had remained on the reservation mounted a revolt, led by the Bannock tribe. Sarah and her family sided with the U.S. government. When her father and his band were captured and held captive by the Bannocks, Sarah rode 223 miles in 48 hours to free them, leading them to the relative safety of a U.S. Army fort. Later, she worked as a translator, guide, and scout for the American forces. After the Bannock War, however, the federal government didn't bother with distinctions of loyalty. All the Paiutes who may or may not have sided with the rebels were deemed enemies and became, overnight, prisoners of war. In January, they were forced to march 350 miles through waist-deep snow to Yakima Reservation in Washington. Nearly one in five died during the journey, many of them small children or the elderly. More would die when they reached the reservation, including Sarah's sister. There wasn't nearly enough food, warm clothing, or fuel for fires to keep the Indians alive.

THE PRINCESS AND THE PRESIDENT

Desperate to save her people from slow, certain death in Yakima, Sarah went east to agitate on their behalf and speak to officials in Washington, D.C. She went as a princess, a role with which she was more than familiar. In 1864 Sarah, her father, and her sister had toured as an Indian "royal family," acting out tableaux vivants of popular native myths and stories. Wearing feathered headdresses, the family would enter the theater in a sort of royal procession, surrounded by a phalanx of braves. They'd then perform stereotypical scenes, the "Noble Savage" ideal of the Pocahontas story, mingled with some "*Savage* Savage" takes on the "Grand Scalp Dance" and "War Dance."

That Sarah acted out roles ascribed by white culture is a complicated and uncomfortable fact of history. But one benefit of her days on the stage was that she learned how to get people's attention. For lectures and performances, she wore what she claimed—and what audiences assumed—was traditional native princess clothing: fantastic bedazzled and fringed ensembles, sometimes made of buckskin, other times of cloth, sporting the kind of ready-made decorations found on lampshades and curtains. To complete the look, her long black hair was loose and topped with a beaded or feathered tiara. She accessorized with beaded bangles and carried a velvet bag embroidered with a cupid. A picture of "Princess Sarah" in her "Native" costume serves as the frontispiece of her 1883 autobiography. Attendees at her lectures and public appearances could buy pictures of the princess in full regalia, with proceeds going to support her travel expenses and her tribe.

Sarah knew what she was doing. Her costume conjured a romantic image of the doomed, noble, white-friendly Indian princess, which struck a chord with those who felt a bit queasy about that whole Manifest Destiny thing. At the height of her popularity, stories of Sarah's family and life filled newspapers and magazines. As many as 1,500 people would file in to see her, and she gave more than 400 lectures in five years. She also grabbed the attention of social reformers like Mary Peabody Mann, widow of education reformer Horace Mann, and Mary's sister Elizabeth Peabody, who became Sarah's patrons.

But though Sarah used her "civilized Indian Princess" persona as a gimmick, once she had people's attention she didn't pull any punches. Between entertaining stories and tales of Native American history, she excoriated her public for the injustices being suffered by the Paiute and other tribes. In her autobiography, she writes, "Oh, my dear good Christian people, how long are you going to stand by and see us suffer at your hands?"

Sarah repeatedly used words like *savage*, *civilized*, and *Christian* throughout her autobiography, cleverly playing with the meanings of each. Writing about how her people helped the white settlers, she says, "They gave them as much as they had to eat. They did not hold out their hands and say: 'You can't have anything to eat unless you pay me.' No, no such word was used by us savages at that time." And though they may believe themselves to be civilized, white people are presented as hypocrites: "You dare cry out Liberty, when you hold us in places against our will, driving us from place to place as if we were beasts."

In late 1878, Sarah's repeated efforts to be heard by the federal government finally paid off: she was able to say her piece to President Rutherford Hayes and Carl Schurz, secretary of the interior. Not that it did a lot of good. Though she was given written promises that the Paiute would be escorted back to Malheur, such oaths were quickly broken.

Smear Campaign

The failure of the feds to make good on their commitments made Sarah's relationship with her people all the more problematic. Though she'd spent years working on their behalf, she was sometimes seen as acting in collusion with the U.S. government, a collaborator at best and a traitor at worst. Some of her most ardent efforts failed miserably. After the Bannock War, for example, she convinced her people to gather at Fort Harney so that they could be moved back to the Malheur Reservation. But the government had lied, and instead of Malheur they were forced on a death march to Yakima Reservation. When a group of five women tried to flee, Sarah and her sister were deployed to hunt them down and bring them back. That Sarah was on the federal payroll, reportedly given a yearly pension of $600 and a house in Orgeon for her services in the Bannock War, didn't help either.

The fact is, even though Sarah was working extremely hard for her people, she didn't necessarily want to live like them. In 1870 she told a newspaper reporter, "I like the Indian life tolerably well. . . . I would rather be with my people, but not to live with them as they live. I was not raised so. . . . My happiest life has been spent in Santa Clara while at school and living among the whites." Underscoring this point, she married a succession of three white men, including an agent of the very government agency that treated her people so badly. She was also a proponent of what sounds like assimilation, which angered people then just as it does now. But Sarah placed her people's physical survival over their cultural survival, meaning that, for her, assimilation was preferable to slow starvation on a reservation.

Sarah's image among whites was just as complicated. Her

outspokenness made her a convenient target for the American press, which described her as dirty, thieving, and prone to getting into fights. The Bureau of Indian Affairs, which had a vested interest in defaming her character, branded her a "common camp follower" (i.e., a prostitute) and a "harlot," as well as a drunkard and a gambler. When Sarah dared voice an opinion, she was thus easily dismissed. That willingness by the general public to believe the worst and laugh at the rest meant that her demands for her people were easily brushed aside. Still, Sarah didn't stop talking.

THE POWER OF THE P-WORD

The title "princess" can mean a lot of things—it's all in how you use it. The fact that the Northern Paiute didn't have a titled system of royalty didn't stop Sarah from using the word to make her voice heard by non-native Americans. But if the word *princess* made it easier for Sarah to be heard, it was also used to denigrate her.

Near the end of her life, Sarah said that she didn't believe she had accomplished much. This after years of bitter disappointment, of seeing her people die from starvation and cold, of being lied to by the president of the United States, of being personally attacked in the press. In 1884 she returned to Nevada to start a school for Indian children, but it closed after only four years. Some of the funds, provided by patrons and the sales of Sarah's book, were squandered by her gambler husband.

Sarah Winnemucca died on October 17, 1891. It is only with the clarity of hindsight that her legacy has come to be appreciated. In 2005 the state of Nevada gave a bronze statue of Sarah Winnemucca Hopkins to the National Statuary Hall Collection. It depicts her as she would have appeared to the crowds who came to hear her speak: about 35 years old, clad in a fringed and beaded dress of her own creation, and carrying the cupid bag. The plaque reads:

Defender of Human rights
Educator
Author of first book by a Native woman.

The description is accurate but doesn't really convey much about who she was: a complicated champion and controversial heroine who used the role she created to write a new story. She was one of the few Native Americans in her day whose voice could be heard in the conversation about what the United States owed the country's early inhabitants. Unfortunately, as Sarah herself wrote, "brave deeds don't always get rewarded in this world."

Sofka Dolgorouky

The Princess Who Turned Communist

OCTOBER 23, 1907–FEBRUARY 26, 1994
OLD RUSSIA; ENGLAND; A FRENCH
CONCENTRATION CAMP; THE U.S.S.R.

*I*n 1940, Sofka Skipwith, formerly Princess Sofka Dolgorouky, left the relative safety of England for Paris. Given the Nazis' imperial pretentions on the Continent, it was not the best timing. Her stated intention was to stay in France only six months or so, long enough to earn money for her mother and stepfather, a pair of displaced Russian émigrés living in France. She left behind her three sons; Patrick, the youngest, was placed in care of the "milkman's mother-in-law," and the two older boys were sent to live with their paternal grandparents; she also said goodbye to her husband, a Royal Air Force pilot. She could not have known that it would be four years before she would be reunited with her children. Or that she'd never see her husband again.

REGIME CHANGE

Sofka's story is related in a fascinating biography, written by her grand-daughter and namesake, as well as in her own 1968 autobiography. First, her princess pedigree is off the charts (although a bit illegitimate in parts); she was descended from the great royal houses of Russia, including that of Catherine the Great, and Kievan Rus, the proto-Russian state. Sofka grew up in St. Petersburg as many other noble children did then, with a grim British governess, tons of toys, playdates with the hemophiliac tsarevich, and no contact with common children. But her mother, Countess Sophy Bobrinsky, was different from other aristocratic wives. Though cold and inaccessible to her only child, Sophy was forceful and intense in ways that few other women of her day could be. She was an exceptional surgeon, one of the first female pilots in Russia, the only woman to drive in a 1912 motor car rally, and a writer of satirical poetry that was published under a pseudonym. And perhaps most shocking of all: she divorced Sofka's father, the charming if reprobate Prince Peter Dolgorouky, after only five years of unsatisfactory and unfaithful marriage.

Other events soon conspired to ensure that Sofka's youth was nothing like her parents'. The old regime, and Sofka's family along with it, was about to go barreling into revolution. World War I took her parents to the front lines—Sofka's father with the Horse Guards, and her mother as a surgeon with the Red Cross. The deprivations and deaths of Russian soldiers caused by World War I fueled revolutionary passions among the populace. As the conflict ground to its inexorable conclusion, Russia had another war to deal with, a civil one. Disturbed by the red Bolshevik banners blossoming in the marketplaces and shootings in the streets, Sofka's grandmother took the little princess to the Crimea, on the Black Sea. And that is where they were when the Bolsheviks executed the imperial family and when Sofka's father was declared an enemy of the people with a price on his head.

Life for Sofka continued precariously. She received a secret education in the revolutionary cause from the family groom, a Bolshevik of sorts, who explained to her the basic injustice of the aristocratic system. In April 1919, with danger increasing for the nobility, a nearly 12-year-old Sofka and her grandmother left Russia on a refugee ship bound for the British Isles. Once in England, Sofka's experience was similar to that of many White Russian émigrés, displaced nobility who—for the time being, at least—were considered romantic and pitiable. She was even featured in a magazine called *Eve*, posing with her dog; the article played up the glamour of her title and the Russian Revolution. Her teen years were spent bouncing between family in Hungary, Italy, and Paris. She was young, impetuous; she read Russian poetry and wandered the streets with her boyfriends. After failing her school exams, she found odd jobs until a Scottish duchess, a longtime family friend, hired her as a personal secretary.

But the seeds of revolution had been sown in Sofka's psyche back in Russia. And amid the wealth and privilege in which she lived, witness to the frivolous lives of people blind to the suffering and poverty of their own countrymen, those seeds would begin to germinate.

COMMUNIST IN THE MAKING

The innocence with which a teenage Sofka had pursued boys became something much less chaste by her twenties. Not to put too fine a point on it, she slept around. "When I say promiscuous, I mean the sleeping with the window-cleaner and postman sort of promiscuous," was how an ex-brother-in-law would describe her a decade after her death. Sofka herself boasted of having more than 100 liaisons in her lifetime. As she told her granddaughter, "It doesn't matter how many lovers you have, just don't have more than one at the same time."

Unfortunately, she didn't take her own advice. In 1931, Sofka married Leo Zinovieff, a fellow exiled aristocrat and an architect; the two were very different but seemed to be genuinely in love, at least for a while. Soon the cracks were starting to show: she'd had a brief affair that she described in her autobiography as one of the "worst things" she'd done. Leo didn't really like his wife's left-leaning friends and, as she discovered, had indulged in an affair of his own. Thus the scene was set when, in late 1934, Sofka met Grey Skipwith, the man she'd consider the love of her life. She was 27, and teaching him Russian; he was 23, the wealthy-ish son of a baronet. Within six months, their flirtation turned to real passion. Even though Sofka was pregnant with her second child (Leo's, in fact), she resolved to leave her husband. The couple separated in 1936 and divorced the next year. Two days after the divorce was finalized, Sofka became Mrs. Skipwith in a quickie ceremony at the Chelsea Registrar's Office; the couple spent a short honeymoon in Nice and then settled into a rural idyll in Maidenhead. Within six months, she was pregnant again.

Throughout her personal upheaval during these years, Sofka's political leanings matured into something that her aristocratic relatives would hate. She had known privilege as well as poverty (at one point Leo had lost his job, leaving the couple destitute), and she couldn't understand the gulf between the two. "Once one has experienced this," Sofka wrote, "one can never regard life in the same way as before." By the time she found regular work again (as a secretary to the actor Laurence Olivier), she was on her way to becoming a Communist, subsisting on a diet of Karl Marx, leftist ideology, and Soviet propaganda. She'd read the Communist Manifesto and "could see nothing to disagree with." But she still had doubts, later writing, "Our idea of Communism was that it was a world-wide conspiratorial organization to overthrow authority. Once you joined it, it ruled your life. Like the Mafia, there was no escape."

THE WAR YEARS

After war was declared in September 1939, Grey volunteered for the Royal Air Force; Sofka became so depressed, she started drinking wine in the mornings. She later claimed that her flight to France was at the request of her mother, who was running out of money (perhaps due to a morphine addiction). But the truth is that Sofka probably wanted a distraction from her life—she never was the type to wipe noses and change diapers anyway—and going to France as the Nazis beat down the door was as good as any. She arrived in Paris just in time for Germany to invade and France to surrender. The princess was trapped in a city on fire, amid millions of panicked people. Even worse, as a British citizen, she was an enemy in the eyes of the Germans. Her diary, which is written to Grey, records on December 5 that a fellow Russian hatched a plan for her to escape to an unoccupied country. Three days later, she wrote, "Darling. I do love you. It's agony cold today—a black frost. Bloody. G'night, beloved—please do not forget me." The diary ends there—the next day, she was arrested. She had just enough time to grab a fur coat, a copy of *The Brothers Karamazov*, and a loaf of bread from a bakery before she was taken to police lock-up and, from there, to the train station.

Sofka arrived at Besançon, in eastern France, after three days of traveling locked in a third-class train car with dozens of other women, all holders of British passports. The women were deposited in a drafty barracks turned makeshift prison camp. Despite the appalling conditions, Sofka adapted. She managed to advocate on behalf of the inmates to earn them hot showers and organized their daily rota; she was named her dormitory's *chef de chambre*, in charge of rations and fuel. Six months later, the women were moved to the Grand Hotel in Vittel, a popular spa resort requisitioned by the Nazis and turned into a model camp—a handy, picturesque refutation of the reports of horrifying conditions in the concentration camps.

At Vittel, survival was no longer as difficult. Sofka gave lectures in Russian poetry, started a dramatic society that performed Shakespearean plays, and taught Russian and English. She was effervescently active, engaging in at least one lesbian fling, staying up late playing cards, and, according to a good friend she made there, never allowing herself to mope. It was here that Sofka met real Communists, party members from way back, who convinced her that perhaps Communism wasn't quite the mafia she thought it was. "I felt that here was an ideology that could provide an equitable existence for humanity," she later wrote. Soon she became part of the Communist spy network, passing on information and helping other inmates escape.

In June 1942, Sofka's internment "idyll" came crashing down when she learned that her husband was missing in action; his death was confirmed that September. She refused to leave her bed or eat and was admitted to the camp's hospital. Grey's death shook Sofka to her core, but she found some comfort in the arms of a Jewish prisoner named Izio, who arrived at the camp in 1943 with his 4-year-old daughter and mother (his wife had been murdered by the Nazis). When the day came that the Nazis took the Jewish prisoners to the concentration camps, Izio could have escaped, but alone. Instead, he, too, went to his death. Sofka's grief turned to rage. She'd passed on information to the Resistance about the conditions the Jews were facing, about how 16 of them tried to commit suicide rather than leave Vittel, about how she smuggled out a newborn baby, sedated with pills from the camp hospital and swaddled in a blanket in a Red Cross box, after his mother was sent to her death. But it seemed like the Allies did nothing. Sofka continued to do what she could. In 1944, when she and some of her friends were allowed to leave Vittel, they carried the names of Polish inmates on pieces of paper sewn into the linings of their coats. After her death, Sofka's efforts on behalf of the Jews at Vittel were recognized by the Holocaust Remembrance Institute in Israel.

SEEING RED

As a war widow with children in Britain, Sofka was offered release by the Germans in 1943. She decided to stay at Vittel, saying later that the Communist Party thought she would be more helpful there. As the war neared its end, Sofka was invited by the German government to give propaganda broadcasts for Radio Berlin; she agreed, intending to escape German custody in Lisbon. That plan worked: Sofka and a fellow Vittel inmate were picked up by tipped-off officials from the British Embassy. By summer 1944 she was back in England, where she found a job through her old boss, Olivier. She drank heavily and had sex often and with many different men ("anyone who seemed pleasant and entertaining," she wrote), trying to fill the hole in her soul.

Sofka also threw herself into Communism. She joined the Communist Party, sold the *Daily Worker* on street corners, and visited the Soviet Embassy to watch Russian films on Sunday mornings. She was a true believer—party officials would show her off as "Comrade Sofka, our Communist Princess!" On Saturdays, she'd host "Sofka's Saturday Soups," inviting party members, journalists, writers, artists, and bohemians for potluck at her house. In 1946, she left her job to work as the secretary of the British Soviet Friendship Society, translating Russian propaganda.

Sofka's political views were extremely unpopular, especially with her fellow exiled nobles; she was not welcome at her former in-laws' home, where her two older sons were living. Given that the Bolsheviks destroyed Sofka's family's way of life, murdered their friends and relatives, and scattered the Russian nobility across Europe and beyond, their reaction is not surprising. As her former brother-in-law declared, "Becoming a Communist when you are a Russian refugee is like a Jew from Germany becoming a Nazi. There's no difference." Sofka's Communist activities also brought her under surveillance of the British secret service. According to files unearthed by her granddaughter, British intelligence at first thought Sofka "an invaluable recruit" for the Communist Party, furnished with contacts in many spheres. Later, they declared her "unreliable," adding that "she is oversexed and this has led to her having many affairs."

In 1949, Sofka finally found her calling: she started working with a Communist travel agency called Progressive Tours. Under the motto "Travel, Friendship, Peace," the company took people on tours of the Soviet Union and other eastern bloc countries. As tour leader, she excelled at bullying hotel managers into lowering prices, steamrolling bureaucrats, and shepherding her charges around monuments and apartment blocks of the Soviet Brutalist school of architecture. And she was being watched the whole time—MI5 had its own agent working for the company.

Sofka would remain a loyal party member and tour operator through the 1950s. Although she suffered doubts and a "lack of conviction," even revelations about the atrocities under Stalin couldn't shake her fundamental belief that Communism offered the only plausible way to an equitable society. She felt it was the duty of any party member to defend the Soviet Union, despite evidence that this particular experiment wasn't working out. And when she ushered tours through the palace that had once belonged to her grandparents and was now the University of Leningrad's geology department, she stressed that she quite agreed it all should have been taken for the good of the people.

ANOTHER WORLD

Sofka wrote in her 1968 autobiography, "The world into which I was born in 1907 seems as unimaginable today, sixty years later, as the way of life on some distant planet. In fact, it is far easier to envisage tourist traffic to outer space than a return to the conventions and prejudices, the strict rules of etiquette, the luxury and the misery, the culture and the ignorance of that age." That world was irrevocably destroyed by the time she was 12 years old. The world she knew as a young woman was itself swept away by war and class upheaval. And before her death in 1994, the Soviet Union—the world that this exiled Russian princess had grown to love—would fall, too.

In 1962, Sofka moved to Bodmin Moor with her last lover, Jack, whom she'd met on a Russian tour, and finally settled down. She became an eccentric, living in a filthy house (she was too busy thinking and reading to clean) and spending her days watching tennis on the television and mothering a pack of whippets. She penned a Russian cookbook in the 1970s, and although her relationship with her children had always been a complicated one, she found herself enjoying being a particularly nontraditional grandmother.

The once-princess Sofka died in February 1994, at age 86. Her granddaughter remembered one of Sofka's favorite sayings: "If you have enough for two loaves, buy one and buy some flowers." In other words, live life to the fullest—you never know when it'll all be taken away.

Partiers

PRINCESSES
WHO LOVED TO
LIVE IT UP

Christina

The Cross-Dressing Princess

DECEMBER 18, 1626–APRIL 19, 1689
SWEDEN

*C*hristina of Sweden's gender confusion started early—when she was born, she was immediately declared a boy. The mistake was understandable: court astrologers had predicted that the child would be the male heir that her father, King Gustav Adolph, so desperately needed. The newborn was dark and hirsute and gave a lusty cry when she popped out; she also had a caul covering the crucial bits. Plus the room was dim, lit only by a candle.

Christina would later claim that after everyone realized the *he* was a *she*, the terrified nurse carried her wordlessly to her father. Instead of being angry, the king held the infant in his arms, kissed her, and said, "Let us thank God. This girl will be worth as much to me as a boy. I pray God to keep her, since he has given her to me. I wish for nothing else. I am content." It's a sweet thought, but it's probably not at all true.

Girl Prince

The fact was, Christina's birth complicated matters. King Gustav's only other child was a boy, but he was illegitimate, so the threat of a dynastic crisis was acute. Making another baby was confounded by the fact that her mother, Maria Eleonora, was on her way to going crazy, and her father was usually on his way to war.

King Gustav tried to make the best of a bad situation. He gave explicit instructions that his little girl should be educated as a prince and get plenty of exercise. Then he went and died in battle when Christina was only 6 years old. Christina was proclaimed queen of the Swedes, Goths, and Vandals, great princess of Finland, duchess of Estonia and Karelia, and lady of Ingria, a hefty slew of titles for a little girl who, in a portrait painted at the time, resembled an elderly dwarf.

Christina later claimed that everyone confronted with this grown-up child-queen was impressed with her, the same sort of retrospective myth-making she'd applied to the story of her father's reaction to her birth. In a letter written to God (because she was like that), Christina declared, "They noticed that You had made me so grave and so serious that I wasn't at all impatient, as is the usual way with children." But until age 18, she was queen in name only—Sweden was ruled by five regents handpicked by her late father. The regents hoped that Christina would marry before reaching maturity, so that her husband could rule if not through her, then at least alongside her.

But another wrench was thrown into the works: her mother's mental state was disintegrating rapidly. When the king died, Maria Eleonora pitched herself headlong into a cult of mourning, becoming a black-draped hysteric who wept constantly. The girl she'd rejected for being female, hairy, and "swarthy as a Moor" was now her most treasured link to her dead husband, and she rarely allowed Christina out of her sight. After suffering through nearly three years of this suffocating mothering,

Christina was removed from her mother's care, and Maria Eleonora was packed off to a castle some 50 miles away.

Christina was then educated according to her father's wishes and, it seems, took well to the curriculum. One of her tutors found her sufficiently diligent to warrant a report to Parliament that she was "not like other members of her sex" and was "stout-hearted and of good understanding." As a child, her toys were lead soldiers, which she used to enact military maneuvers. She was a crack shot with a pistol, a keen horsewoman, and versed in sword fighting. She learned statecraft from biographies of Alexander the Great and Elizabeth I; she studied Latin, German, and French to converse with ambassadors; and she received sufficiently large doses of Lutheranism, the state religion.

In November 1644 Christina turned 18, ending the regency. She seized the throne with vigor but was young and inexperienced; she had so often told herself the fairy tale of her own greatness that it blinded her to her faults. Despite her education, she was no master of governance or politics. She was indecisive when she ought to have been resolute; acted out of spite rather than reason; wanted power without earning it; and opened her court to all kinds of intrigues she mistakenly thought she controlled. She also spent the crown's money as if it were her own, and when coffers dwindled, she started selling titles, flooding the country with earls and barons and reducing the tax base drastically. Before long, the Swedish piggybank had a tinny ring to it. To her credit, Christina spent Sweden's money mostly trying to buy culture and elevate the provincial tone of the Stockholm court. She amassed a valuable collection of books, paintings, sculpture, and objets d'art and imported legions of scholars from across Europe. The star of her collection was the great French philosopher René Descartes (of "I think, therefore I am" fame), whom she convinced to grace her court. Christina decided he would tutor her three times a week—at five in the morning in an unheated library in January 1650, "the coldest month of the coldest year in an exceptionally cold century." Descartes soon caught influenza and died. But Christina's plans for a big memorial to the great man were soon forgotten, and Catholic Descartes was left to molder under a rotting wooden plank in the unbaptized section of a Lutheran graveyard.

Though exceptionally clever, Christina was just a dilettante. She knew a little about a lot, learning only enough about each topic to impress her courtiers, and rarely stuck with anything for long. She was as prideful about her learning as the prince she was raised to be: "I never could stand being corrected," she once told the French ambassador.

ABDICATION AVENUE

Everyone knew that Christina disliked being a girl. As she wrote in her autobiography, "I despised everything belonging to my sex, hardly excluding modesty and propriety." Though she was petite—barely five feet tall—and delicate, Christina walked and talked like a man. She strode around in flat shoes, swore like a sailor in a deep gruff voice, and tended to smack her servants around. She slouched, preferred short skirts and trousers to overstuffed female fashions, and had no time or patience for things like embroidery and etiquette. She was often too busy to comb her hair and none too keen on bathing (in her defense, no one really was back then).

Christina was so determinedly boyish that in her own lifetime, she was dogged by a persistent rumor that she was a hermaphrodite. Her mannish ways gave rise to other, more titillating rumors, which she did nothing to quell. She often slept in the same bed as her favorite lady-in-waiting, whom she called Belle on account of the woman's beauty. This was normal enough for two unmarried women at the time, but Christina liked to insinuate more than just sleeping was going on. She once embarrassed the English ambassador to the court by whispering in his ear that Belle's inside was as beautiful as her outside.

When Christina was 22, she declared her intention never to marry and even named the man everyone thought she would wed, her cousin Karl Gustav, as her successor. Perhaps she was inspired by Elizabeth I, Britain's so-called virgin queen with the "heart and stomach of a king," whose biographies she'd devoured as a teenager. Of course, these actions only made whispers of her lesbianism/bisexuality grow ever louder. But though she talked a good game, there's not much evidence that she had a sexual relationship with anyone. Her decision not to marry seems more connected to her distaste for sex in general than an aversion to men. She once wrote, "Marriage is the best cure for love, and the marriage bed is its tomb."

While everyone was talking about Christina's odd habits and ambiguous sexuality, they completely ignored the most dangerous of her interests: a budding Catholicism. Like her compatriots, Christina was raised Lutheran, and, as queen, she was also nominally the head of the Church of Sweden. At this time in Sweden, Catholicism was punishable by banishment, torture, and death—even for the queen. But Christina was undeterred (or perhaps encouraged). Her attraction to Catholicism was multifold—many of the scholars she'd brought to court practiced that faith, she liked the church's strict hierarchy, and she appreciated its tradition of learning.

At the same time, Christina was growing bored of being queen. But in 1650, the year she declared she would never marry, she was officially crowned at her coronation ceremony, which had been put off for lack of funds. Yet even as she was being feted, she was contemplating abdication. She hated the restraints that her duties placed on her freedom. The crown was bankrupt, owing in part to her poor management, and the country was suffering from widespread famine, the result of a brutally cold winter. Discontent with the new monarch pervaded the royal court, but Christina would brook no criticisms.

It's no surprise that Christina wanted to abdicate, but given her unwavering belief in her own greatness, it's surprising that she did. In 1653, she declared her intention to give up the throne but retain the title of queen. (She kept her plans to convert to herself.) Amazingly, the Swedish parliament agreed to her demands, which also included land and income. And so on June 6, 1654, with a ceremony at a castle in Uppsala, Christina gave up her crown.

Postabdication Vacation

Christina's impatience to leave was obvious. She cleared out of Uppsala the same day she abdicated, even before the banquet celebrating her cousin's coronation had ended. Making for Denmark, she put on the men's clothes she would prefer to wear for the rest of her life, shaved her head, slapped on a men's wig, and strapped on a sword. "Free at last!" she supposedly exclaimed. "Out of Sweden, and I hope I never come back!"

She could have traveled in state by ship wherever she wanted to go, but Christina relished the hard-riding dusty overland approach, especially because such behavior was mildly shocking for a woman at the time (which seems to have become her MO from then on). She eventually made her way to Brussels, where she converted to Catholicism; from there, she went to Rome for her first audience with the pope. Just as she'd wasted no time casting off Lutheranism, Christina quickly engaged in some un-Catholic behavior. The night of her conversion, she was overheard making fun of transubstantiation, which she'd just sworn an oath to respect. She had a habit of talking in church, and her taste for nude paintings and sculptures had little to do with the contemplation of divinity.

Christina was also hemorrhaging money. Ensconced in a borrowed villa in Rome, she was so broke she couldn't afford to pay her servants, who took to stealing the silver. Even more scandalously, she had fallen in love with Cardinal Decio Azzolino, the pope's young, clever, not-hard-to-look-at representative. For a short time, she even stopped wearing men's clothes in favor of dresses, which were cut so low as to earn her a reprimand from the pontiff. Azzolino was seemingly in love with Christina as well, and rumors abounded that she'd borne him a child. In reality, the two probably never slept together, despite all her naughty talk and the claim by her former employee that she was "the greatest whore in the world."

By now Christina had turned to other worldly matters, including political intrigue. She set her sights on becoming a real queen again by taking the throne of Naples, the southern Italian kingdom, which France and Spain were perpetually squabbling over. In early 1656, Christina secretly agreed with French spymaster Cardinal Jules Mazarin to take the Naples throne, with the help of 4,000 French soldiers, and keep it warm for young Philip of Anjou. Excited, she bustled up to the top of Castel Sant'Angelo and fired off a cannon . . . only she'd forgotten to aim, and the cannonball lodged itself in the side of a building. Oops.

But political winds shift, and within a year and a half, the plan to make Christina the queen of Naples was shelved. She took out her anger and frustration on one of her own: Gian-Rinaldo Monaldeschi, her master of the horse (an accurate appellation because she really did have just the one horse). While in France awaiting word from Mazarin about the Naples plan, Christina discovered that Monaldeschi was writing letters containing all kinds of evil gossip about her. On November 10, 1657, she pronounced him guilty of treason and ordered her men to execute him that same day. She may have been a queen without a country, but she was still a monarch and therefore had the right of judgment over her "subjects," including Monaldeschi. Though his murder was legal, it was cruel and horrifying. The pope, once so pleased with his queenly convert, denounced her as a barbarian and refused to receive her in Rome.

At only 32 years old, Christina had worn out the goodwill of most of Europe's political powers. Her occasional forays into world politics were met with smirks, and she ended up spending much of her time in a garden at her villa in Rome. By the end of her life, she cut a small, portly figure in her men's clothing, short hair, and wispy lady whiskers. For a woman who desperately wanted to be taken seriously as an intellectual, a leader, and a political force, it must have been galling to know that she was viewed as faintly ridiculous.

That is, if she ever realized it. The somewhat admirable thing about Christina was that, throughout her life, she steadfastly believed the myth of her own importance. In her unfinished autobiography she wrote, "My talents and my virtues raise me above the rest of mankind." When she died in April 1689, her will revealed just how inflated her ego truly was: she left legacies, jewels, and property to various servants, retainers, and ladies-in-waiting. In reality, little of it was hers to give.

In 1933, Greta Garbo starred in a black-and-white film about Christina's life called *Queen Christina*. Though also Swedish, the lovely Garbo bears less than a passing resemblance to the hirsute Christina, and the plot bears less a than passing resemblance to the unvarnished truth. But Garbo's representation of a defiant queen is, in its way, an accurate picture of a woman who never lost conviction in her own legend. It's pure fiction, but it's what Christina would have wanted to believe.

Caraboo
(a.k.a. Mary Baker)

The Phony Princess Who Hoodwinked England

NOVEMBER 23, 1791-DECEMBER 24, 1864
THE (FICTITIOUS) MALAYSIAN COUNTRY OF JAVASU

O n the night of April 3, 1817, the overseer of the poor in the English village of Almondsbury, a tiny cluster of houses near Bristol, encountered what must have been one of the weirdest things he'd seen in his entire provincial life. The local cobbler's wife had come to him with a problem. Apparently, a "young Female" had walked uninvited into her cottage and indicated—by lying down on the sofa—"that it was her wish to sleep under its roof." She could have been just a vagrant, but she didn't speak English or any language they'd ever heard. Stymied, the overseer and the cobbler's wife thought it best to put the matter before their social betters. So the neighborhood gentry, Samuel Worrall, Esq., and his American wife, Elizabeth, trekked the mile into town to figure out what the heck was going on.

Mystery Woman

What they found was a girl wearing a black gown accessorized with a black and red shawl "loosely and tastefully put on in imitation of the Asiatic costume," according to a contemporary account. She was petite, standing only about five-foot-two, "attractive and prepossessing," with dark hair and eyes, and appeared to be around 25 years old. She had little in her possession to offer any clue to her identity, and she communicated largely by making signs. Her behavior was particularly strange. When shown into the parlor of the inn, she seemed affected by an engraving of a pineapple on the wall and communicated to her hosts that it was a "fruit of her own country." She prayed before drinking her tea and didn't seem to know what a bed was.

The Worralls decided to put her up for the night at the inn, after which she was taken to St. Peter's Hospital for the poor and vagrant in Bristol. Local residents, having heard about the strange visitor, brought around other foreigners to try to talk to her. But no one spoke her language, and the woman's spirits seemed to deteriorate; she refused to eat or drink and barely slept. Mrs. Worrall, moved by pity, rescued the woman and installed her in the family's townhouse. Through a bit of pantomime, Mrs. Worrall managed to learn the unfortunate creature's name: Caraboo.

Despite this breakthrough, the Worralls were still no closer to figuring out where Caraboo came from or what had happened to her. Finally, after two weeks, a piece of luck arrived: a Portuguese man, who just happened to be in the area and had been to Malaysia, heard about the lost young woman and stopped by to meet her. Miraculously, he could understand what she was trying to tell them.

Caraboo's story unfolded in one long dramatic narrative, punctuated by wild hand gestures and weeping. Her Chinese father was a man of rank; her Malaysian mother was murdered by cannibals. While walking in her gardens on her island home, Javasu in the East Indies, she was kidnapped by the crew of the horrible pirate captain Chee-min. Gagged and bound hand and foot, she was dragged aboard their filthy vessel; her father attempted to swim after it, and Caraboo herself fought like a tiger, killing one of Chee-min's men and injuring another. But all to no avail. After eleven days aboard the pirate ship, she was sold to the captain of a brig making for Europe. Months later, the brig entered Bristol Channel, and she decided to make a swim for it. On dry land, she traded clothes with an Englishwoman and spent the next six weeks wandering the countryside before she was taken in by the kindly Worralls.

In the two months that followed this revelation, Princess Caraboo of Javasu was treated as a visiting royal, ensconced at the Worralls' comfortable country home near Almondsbury. Her hosts continued to make every effort to learn more about her, and she obliged, divulging as many details as their limited shared language could allow. She recounted that her mother, before her untimely death at the hands (and teeth) of cannibals, wore a gold chain that extended from her pierced nose to her right temple; her father had three other wives, was carried on a sedan chair, and wore peacock feathers in his hat and a gold chain signifying his rank. The greeting customs of her land involved prostrating oneself; her father's servants played a kind of clarinet with a built-in harp; the black cannibals, whom she called "Boogoos," cut off the arms and heads of white people to roast and eat.

Every day, the pretty princess became more theatrical. She carried a bow and arrow slung across her back, which she could fire off with great accuracy while at a full run, and a wooden stick at her right side in imitation of a sword. She prayed to "Allah Tallah" and worshipped the rising sun from the rooftops once a week, as well as the lake every time she passed it. She drank only water and ate only food that she'd prepared herself (she was "partial to curry"). She was extremely cautious around men, refusing to allow them to take her hand; if they brushed against her, she would change her clothes.

Caraboo taught the Worralls words in her language and wrote in a script that seemed to resemble Chinese. She even showed her hosts how to dress in the Javasu style: a dress with a calf-length skirt, belted around the ribcage, and long wide sleeves. She topped it with a turban accessorized with a few peacock feathers stuck in at a jaunty angle and a pair of open sandals.

And all of it was, of course, a load of crap.

Liar, Liar

Caraboo didn't hail from as far away as the East Indies—Javasu isn't even a real place. In fact, she was from barely as far away as the next county. It seems that the more her rescuers and their friends tried to uncover her history, they more they helped create it. Thinking she neither spoke nor read English, they showed her books and images of her supposed homeland and talked openly about all the exotic "Oriental" customs they knew. Caraboo used those details to furnish her fiction, and she wasn't picky about which ones—she was equally excited about a Chinese puzzle as she was for an Eskimo soapstone carving.

After that initial boost supplied by the Portuguese traveler, whose motivations remain unclear even today, she was off and running. It all must have been fascinating to hear, and she was very good at keeping up the pretense: "They never found her tripping or off her guard, either in her conversation or her general manners, always observing the custom of washing her tea cup, etc.," a contemporary account claims. Even attempts at surprising her into giving herself away didn't work. When two suspicious servants burst into her room shouting "Fire!" the princess just stared at them.

But by early June, keeping up appearances was increasingly difficult, especially after her story became known as far away as Scotland. Caraboo fled the Worralls and made for nearby Bath, a fashionable spa town. But if she meant to lie low and wait out the sensation her story had caused, she failed. When Mrs. Worrall found her runaway charge, she was "at the very pinnacle of her glory and ambition," ensconced in the drawing room of some notable personage, surrounded by "fashionable visitants" all trying to make her acquaintance.

Caraboo managed to convince Mrs. Worrall that she'd only run away to try to get back to Javasu. Within days, however, her fiction began to unravel, undone by the public sensation she'd caused in Bath. At the same time her former landlady was telling Mrs. Worrall that the unfortunate princess bore a more than passing resemblance to an erstwhile and very English lodger, a young man surfaced who remembered Caraboo and added that "when in his company spirits and water were not quite so repugnant to her taste as they had been."

Caraboo was caught. With no alternative, she told Mrs. Worrall the truth. Or something like it . . .

Caraboo of Javasu was in fact Mary Baker, née Willcocks, of Witheridge, Devonshire (now just Devon). At age 16, Mary was made a servant in a farmer's household but left when they refused to give her a raise. After bouncing around a series of menial jobs, she found herself destitute and begging door to door. She didn't want to return to her family in Devonshire and the tiny village where she was related to pretty much everyone. Eventually, she made her way to London, where she fell ill and spent months in the hospital before being taken in as a maid by a local family.

After a misunderstanding caused her to leave her post, a despondent Mary entered what she thought was a nunnery in Blackfriars. Turns out that Magdalen Hospital was a home for "penitent prostitutes," and she was kicked out when it was discovered she hadn't ever been a lady of the night. From there, she tried to get back home to Devonshire; along the way, she cut her hair short and dressed as a man to find work. She fell in with some highwaymen who hired her as a groom and an apprentice robber. That ruse fell apart after she was unable to fire a pistol, and the brigands forced her to promise on pain of death not to betray them.

Mary finally found her way back to her parents, who demanded that she find real work. But she lasted only a few months at everything she tried—she left the tanner's because she was made to haul the hides out of the cart; she left her next job because she was forced to venture into a deep snow and nearly died of exposure; she left her post as a cook because "the fire did not agree with her."

Back in London in 1814, Mary supposedly met and married a Frenchman, who left her shortly after she became pregnant. Unable to support a baby and with no idea if her husband would ever return, she gave the boy up for adoption after his birth in 1816. When she found out the baby had died in the orphanage's care, she left her servant position in London, wandered the countryside, and traveled with gypsies for a time. After leaving the gypsies, who'd begged her to become part of their clan, Mary began roaming the countryside trying to earn money for passage to America. Begging under the guise of a foreigner seemed a fast, easy, and exciting way to do it. And that, she said, was about when she made her way to Almondsbury and the kind ministrations of the Worralls.

It was as close to the truth as anyone was going to get. Some of her story was corroborated by her father, a perplexed Devonshire cobbler. He was of the opinion that his daughter, though clever, "was not right in her mind" and hadn't been since she was struck by rheumatic fever at age 15.

THE WHY BEHIND THE LIE

Mary was not a con artist, not exactly. All accounts of her hoax note that she never stole or took anything that didn't belong to her. So why did she do it? Initially, at least, her reason may have been to stay out of prison—English law at the time dealt harshly with beggars and vagrants. If she was discovered to be just a broke English girl, rather than a friendless foreign princess, she could have spent more than a year in jail.

Contemporary investigators had other theories. One craniologist (a person who examines the shape of the skull for clues about a person's character) declared her "cold," noting that she possessed "boundless ambition." Surprisingly, he found that she had little "secretiveness" but exceptional "wariness" and "vanity," indicating to him that her object in this little game was, "I, I, I, it is I, who can nose-lead you, and make fools of ye all!" Investigations into her character conducted by the indefatigable John Matthews Gutch of a local Bristol newspaper reveal a woman who had an incredible imagination and loved attention. Gutch found that everyone who knew Mary remembered her as an eccentric or a teller of tall tales "which never did harm to any body, but seemed to arise from the love of telling something extraordinary." Gutch was clearly impressed with Mary, writing, "That the talents of such a girl should have been hitherto directed to no better purpose, every one must lament."

But Mary's fantasies bordered on pathological. Even her "real" story was riddled with lies, many of them bizarre. Unlike the story she told Mrs. Worrall, she was clearly aware of the nature of Madgalen Hospital, the home for former prostitutes. She'd told the admitting officials she'd been led to a dissolute life by a gentleman who seduced her, and rather than be kicked out, she'd left of her own accord. She hadn't been prostituting herself, so why she went to Madgalen Hospital is unclear. Whether she was ever married is another instance where her narrative detours from provable truth, though contemporary sources all agree that she did have a child and that the boy died around four months old. If anything, her stories and lies became more fanciful after her child's death.

Such behavior is consistent with the idea that stress can bring on a mental breakdown, especially if the person was predisposed to a manic state. Which Mary may have been—people who survive rheumatic fever also suffer a higher incidence of neuropsychiatric disorders, including manic depression. So maybe her father's claim that she'd been a bit strange since suffering a fever wasn't too far off the mark.

As to why people believed her, that's clear: she was a good actress, and they wanted to. The Romantic ideal of the "Orient" was incredibly fashionable at the time, permeating popular culture through art, poetry, picture books, even interior design. Having a Javasu princess pitch up in one's quiet village must have seemed incredibly exotic. Who wouldn't have wanted to believe she was the real deal?

After Mary's deception was uncovered and published in local newspapers, interest in the erstwhile princess of Javasu only increased. Curiosity seekers from all walks of life—earls, doctors, and an unceasing parade of Christian ministers hoping to save her soul—came to town to meet her.

But in 1817, only a few months after she was found out, Mary left Bristol on a ship bound for America, her passage paid by the estimable Mrs. Worrall, whose kindness evidently knew no bounds. Tales of Mary's hoax preceded her arrival in Philadelphia. The city's wharves were crowded with curiosity seekers, and plans were already afoot to get her onto the stage, playing herself as the character she'd made up. "Carraboo," as she was called in America, was a phenomenon, fueling a passion for turbans among fashionable ladies. But Mary soon became the subject of ridicule. Certainly, an element of teasing the gullible British characterized local newspaper reports of Miss Carraboo's American exploits, including swimming *up* a waterfall. But there was also a good deal of moral outrage that this girl, who'd "made her self notorious" in her native country, as one editorial boomed, would show herself in America.

By 1824, Mary was back in London, exhibiting herself at a New Bond Street public room as Princess Caraboo. Paying customers were few, and income didn't cover the cost of renting the rooms. Fame, it seems, lasts only so long. But all did not end badly for the wannabe royalty. Mary returned to Bristol, where she started a business supplying medicinal leeches to the local hospital and pharmacies. She married Richard Baker and had a daughter, also named Mary, who kept up the business after her mother's death. Mary the younger may have also inherited her mother's colorful nature—she became the town's crazy cat lady.

Mary Baker, a.k.a. Princess Caraboo, died in Bristol on Christmas Eve 1864, at the age of 75. Her story has continued to fascinate, resurfacing periodically in popular culture in the years since her grand adventure. In the 1990s, it was made into a film starring Phoebe Cates, a play in Bristol, and a BBC television program. Mary would have been proud. After all, she sure loved a good story.

Six Ways to Fake Princesshood

Princess Caraboo was by no means the only woman who ever tried to pass herself off as a princess. History is littered with royal imposters who, for reasons of love, greed, or insanity, pretended to be someone they most certainly were not.

Most rely on a "Princess and the Pea" strategy: talk like a princess, act like a princess, make a fuss about vegetables under your mattress like a princess, and maybe everyone will believe you *are* a princess. Other imposters have bet on their audience's ignorance and willingness to believe; like Caraboo, these were usually exceptional actresses gifted with an incredible imagination (and gall). And in some cases, the fiction worked because the would-be princess came to believe her own crazy story.

So if you're thinking of giving it a go as a royal fake, here are six notable attempts to learn from.

1. MAKE A NAME FOR YOURSELF: PRINCESS TARAKANOVA

In 1774 a young woman surfaced in Paris claiming to be the legitimate daughter of Russian tsar Peter III's aunt, Empress Elizabeth, and her secret husband, Count Aleksy Razumovsky. Had that been true, her claim to the throne would have been greater than that of the reigning empress, Catherine the Great, who'd achieved her power through marriage rather than by blood.

The woman bizarrely called herself Princess Tarakanova, or Princess Cockroach (*tarakan* means "cockroach" in Russian). She claimed it was a pet name given by her illustrious mother before she sent her to be raised in Persia. Beautiful and well educated, Tarakanova had attracted a few European aristocrats to be part of her entourage. (Note: When pretending to be a princess, it's helpful to have some real royalty on hand to bolster your claims.)

Her timing was bad. Catherine the Great had just had her boozy husband murdered in a bloody coup and was in no mood to entertain claimants to her throne. The self-proclaimed princess, now living on borrowed splendor in Italy, graciously offered to split the Russian empire with Catherine, noting that she didn't want to have to resort to calling on the Turks for military support. But Catherine was not one to hesitate about squashing little bugs. Especially when evidence turned up that Princess Cockroach had been put up to the plot by Polish rebels looking to sow the seeds of revolution in Russia.

Still, Catherine worried that the notoriety and support the girl was attracting could lead to rebellion. So she sent a former lover, Count Alexei Orlov, to Italy. The plan was to gain the princess's trust, pretend to support her claim, seduce her, and then kidnap her.

It worked. Orlov lured Tarakanova onto his ship with the promise of marriage, and when she was safely on board he sprang his trap. The princess was arrested and returned to Russia. She died in prison in 1776, barely a year after her capture, still awaiting trial. At the time of her death, rumors circulated that she drowned in her cell during a flood. In reality, she died of an illness no doubt exacerbated by life behind bars.

2. DRESS THE PART:
PRINCESS SUSANNA CAROLINE MATILDA

In the early 1770s, the sister of Queen Charlotte—wife of England's George III and namesake of plenty of cities, counties, roads, and pubs in the British colonies—visited the New World. Colonial gossips, starved for news of the old country, were all atwitter. Never heard of Princess Susanna

Caroline Matilda? She was evicted from court after a scandal. But isn't Queen Charlotte from Germany? Why doesn't Princess Susanna speak German? Why, that's because she is refusing to speak her native tongue until she's reconciled to her most beloved sister. Royal scandal! everyone squeaked.

For a year and a half, Princess Susanna was *the* social accessory in Virginia and the Carolinas, passed from house to house and put up in lavish comfort. So imagine everyone's shock when the princess was revealed to be not a disgraced royal but an escaped convict.

Princess Susanna was in fact Sarah Wilson, born in Staffordshire and hired in London as a maidservant to Caroline Vernon, one of the queen's ladies-in-waiting. After a short time in Vernon's employ, it was discovered that Wilson had managed to steal a fine dress, a miniature portrait of the queen, and some jewels, among other things. She was tried and sentenced to death; thanks to Vernon's kind intervention, her sentence was commuted to transportation to the colonies.

Wilson arrived in Baltimore in 1771 and was sold as an indentured servant to William Devall, a plantation owner in Maryland. Somehow she escaped and ran away to Virginia, taking with her the ill-gotten dress, jewels, and portrait (which, incredibly and inexplicably, she'd managed to hang on to throughout her trial, sentencing, and transatlantic voyage). These items would serve her well in her new identity, as would the court gossip she'd picked up as a servant.

So furnished, Wilson became Princess Susanna for the excited locals, who put her up in their guest rooms and allowed her to hold court in their living rooms. She was, it appears, an exceptional actress: meticulous in her details, she had even embroidered little crowns with her monogram onto her linens. She adopted the attitude of an exiled aristocrat, letting it be known that she still had some influence in the royal houses of Europe and implying that kindness toward her might bring financial rewards. How long she intended to keep up the fiction is unclear, but in the meantime she was doing a brisk business in favors.

Word in the colonies didn't travel fast, and it wasn't until months after Wilson's escape that Devall heard about the exiled princess. He sent one of his men down to South Carolina, where she was then residing, to bring her back into custody. The man found Wilson happily holding court at a local worthy's house. After unmasking her true identity, he ushered her out the door at gunpoint.

Back in Devall's service, Wilson spent two years as a humble servant until fate once again gave her an opportunity to escape. When another Sarah Wilson arrived in the colony, she managed to switch places with the woman. The erstwhile princess later married a British officer, and the couple set themselves up in business using the money she'd amassed during her time as an exiled aristocrat. They lived happily ever after, growing a big family and enjoying life in postrevolutionary America.

3. Publish your story: Princess Olive of Cumberland

Olivia Serres, née Wilmot, was a woman who sometimes found herself in debt. And when she did, well, the most expedient thing to do was to claim that she was not just Olivia Serres, semi-successful landscape painter and novelist, but Princess Olive of Cumberland, the sometimes-legitimate, sometimes-illegitimate daughter of the king's brother.

Olivia first made her claim in 1817, putting forth a petition to King George III (who was by then irretrievably mad) that she was the illegitimate daughter of the late Henry Frederick, duke of Cumberland. This, however, wasn't enough to keep Serres out of debtors' prison, so in 1820 she revised her claim: she was his *legitimate* daughter, born April 3, 1772, of his secret marriage to Olive Wilmot, which had taken place on March 4, 1767.

Olivia wasn't content to appeal just to the British royal family; she took her case to the court of public opinion. Repeatedly. A prolific writer, she published pamphlet after pamphlet explaining her contradictory claims; she once had London papered in posters that read "The Princess of Cumberland in Captivity!" In 1822, Olivia published her pièce de résistance, the aptly titled "Princess of Cumberland's Statement to the English Nation." Ridiculously long and meandering, it includes descriptions of an episode in which the young princess is rescued from drowning by a dog and another in which she is beset by robbers in her own home.

More to the point, Olivia claimed that her uncle, Dr. Wilmot, was in fact her grandfather, and that he'd secretly married a Polish princess. The product of that union was Olivia's mother, who'd caught the fancy of the duke of Cumberland and married him in 1767. But their domestic bliss was tragically torn asunder. The duke abandoned his wife, who died soon after, and bizarrely abandoned his daughter into the care of a Warwick house painter with a tendency to embezzle.

Happily for Olivia, everyone who could have attested to the truth of her claims was dead: the duke died in 1790; King George checked out in 1820; and Olive Wilmot, her mother, "died of a broken heart" sometime at the beginning of the princess's narrative. Olivia backed up her claim with a lucky resemblance to the deceased duke and a bit of theatricality. She had the royal arms painted on her coach and hired footmen dressed in royal livery. The rest of her "proof" consisted of copies of letters between herself and members of the royal family and various ministers, as well as signed affidavits purporting to support her claims—all of which were forgeries.

Olivia upheld the fiction, often in print, until her death in debtors' prison in 1835. One of her last pamphlets, titled "Wrongs of Her Royal Highness the Princess Olive of Cumberland," was published in 1833 and declares that "every law, both human and Divine, has been violated in the person of this lady." It ends, "This Subject to be Continued . . ." And it was. After Olivia's death, her daughter took up the cause and demanded to be recognized as Princess Lavinia of Cumberland. Unsurprisingly, she was denied.

4. CLAIM TO BE ONE OF MANY: PRINCESS SUMAIRE

In July 1940, Princess Sumaire, an elegant 22-year-old sometime fashion model, arrived in Shanghai to enliven the international expatriate community. She was, she claimed, the daughter of Maharajah Bhupinder Singh of Patiala, and she duly took up residence at the swanky Park Hotel. Shanghai at that time was a film noir come to life: glamorously violent, a dark demimonde of European refugees, gangsters, and conmen. Sumaire fit right in. She was rumored to have been disowned by her family for her "loose morals," to be a "follower of the Lesbian cult," and to be a nymphomaniac from whose amorous clutches even hotel bellboys weren't safe.

But the "princess" didn't confine her below-board activities to scandalizing the good people of Shanghai with her sexual appetite. She was also an intriguer of the highest order who was at the center of a web of pro-Japanese criminal and political movers; among those who visited her lavish hotel apartment were known Axis agents. So British intelligence and police did a little digging. Turns out Sumaire's real name was Rajkumari Sumair Apjit Singh, lately the wife of an official of the Indian state railways. It was easy for her to get away with calling herself the maharajah's daughter, because he had 23 of them and couldn't be bothered to keep track. Sumaire did have some relationship to the maharajah's family, but it's unclear exactly what; British police in Shanghai claimed that she was the maharajah's niece and his lover.

By December 1941, Sumaire was in a bad way financially, forced to give up her suite at the Park Hotel. But her fortunes were reversed yet again when her allies the Japanese invaded. Soon she was back at the Park, throwing cocktail parties for socially and politically connected Germans, Italians, and Japanese as well as people known to be working for Axis intelligence services. In 1943 Sumaire married a Japanese American, one of Japan's Shanghai-based criminal contacts.

The liberation of Shanghai in September 1945 meant that Sumaire was on the wrong side of the power divide. She penned distraught letters to the maharajah claiming to have been a victim of Japanese depredations while under occupation and begging for money to pay her "debts of honor." The last sighting of the princess, as she was still calling herself, was when she tried to marry an American ex-Army officer in 1946 and earn a ticket to the United States.

Or was it? In 1951, a Princess Sumair, also claiming to be the daughter of the maharajah of Patiala, surfaced in Paris as a haute couture fashion designer, creating Indian-inspired dresses for the filthy rich. Roughly 30 years after that, she pops up in America, married to a fur dealer named John Boughton and preparing to launch her Fifth Avenue store. In 1979, the *Palm Beach Daily* interviewed the "princess" about her collection and her fabulous upbringing in the maharajah's palace. In May 1980, *People* magazine profiled the designer, now dividing her time between Palm Beach and Manhattan, whose clothes were in the "if you have to ask, you can't afford it" price bracket. Mentions of this Princess Sumair drop off precipitously after about 1983. The last trace of her online is a record indicating that a Sumair Boughton died in Milwaukee on May 15, 2003, at the age of 74, giving her date of birth as June 17, 1928.

Were they the same woman? Possibly. Photos show a physical resemblance between the nymphomaniac Axis sympathizer of Shanghai and the Palm Beach fashion designer. In addition, both princesses had no problem using their name and supposed maharajah connections to get what they wanted, whether social recognition or dinner reservations. If they are one and the same, then it looks like Princess Sumaire may have gotten away with it in the end.

5. Cultivate a psychological disorder: Princess Antoinette Millard

In the early 2000s, one face—sometimes topped with a diamond tiara—made frequent appearances in New York's society pages. She was petite and pretty, with blonde hair, exquisite bone structure, and great taste. She seemed to know all the right people. She wore extravagant jewelry from all the best jewelers in Manhattan, went to all the best parties and fashion shows, and seemed to be on all the important charitable boards. She was Princess Antoinette Millard, a Saudi Arabian royal who'd recently converted to Judaism. And she was not a real person.

The princess persona was the creation of Antoinette Lisa Millard, also known as Lisa Walker, a 40-something divorcée from Buffalo with an unchecked mental illness. This princess wasn't even her only identity: she was also an investment banker; a lawyer with a degree from Boston University; a model for Bergdorf Goodman's catalogue; a divorcée waiting for her husband's $7 million settlement; a Jewish convert; one of a set of triplets (that one is actually true); and the sufferer of a tumor near her heart that needed urgent surgery.

Millard perpetrated the various ruses for more than two years, until the whole charade came crashing down in 2004. Between November 2003 and January 2004, she'd charged more than $1 million on her American Express card, buying more than $492,000 worth of jewelry from various Manhattan jewelers, all of which she then insured. But she told the insurance company that the jewelry had belonged to her mother and aunt, supposedly Saudi royalty, and she had documents to prove it. And then, the coup de grâce: the day after Millard insured the jewelry, she said it was stolen when she was mugged, and then she made a $262,000 claim.

That's when investigators discovered that 12 of the 23 pieces she reported stolen had in fact been sold to a pawnshop the month before Millard insured them, and that the document she'd used to prove their existence was a forgery. On May 6, 2004, she was arrested at her apartment, an ordinary one-bedroom flat at 89th Street and Third Avenue. Unable to post the $100,000 bail, Millard was packed off to Rikers Island. Newspaper reports gleefully noted that she was not, and never had been, a princess.

In 2005, Millard pleaded guilty to grand larceny and insurance fraud and might have spent up to 15 years in prison, but the district attorney recommended that she be admitted to a psychiatric facility. A psychiatrist testified that she suffered from depression, bipolar disorder, and anorexia. Her lawyers claimed that her condition was due to the trauma of witnessing the terrorist attacks on the World Trade Center in 2001. They also assured the judge that Millard would be admitted to the psychiatric unit at New York-Presbyterian/Columbia hospital for a year, with the doors securely locked. Millard was asked to pay $540 in legal fees; she couldn't come up with the money.

A year later, Millard was arrested in Jacksonville, Florida, on charges of evading justice. What happened after that is unclear, but in 2010 she made headlines once again. It seems that the brazen pseudo-princess filed a lawsuit against one of the companies whose jewelry she'd tried to hock during her insurance fraud days, claiming they'd overcharged her. To the delight of the New York tabloids, the judge literally ripped up her complaint, forcing her to drop the $1.1 million suit.

6. Get wrapped up in the role: The Persian Princess

When authorities busted an illegal antiques-dealing ring in Pakistan in October 2000, they found what appeared to be the only Persian mummy in history. Dubbed the "Persian

Princess" and estimated to be about 2,600 years dead, the discovery could have rewritten the history books, but it was all a hoax. Authorities eventually figured out that the ancient royal was likely a modern murder victim.

The story began when Karachi police, acting on a tip, found video evidence of a man named Ali Akbar attempting to sell a mummy. This was a violation of Pakistan's Antiquity Act, but Akbar was just the middleman. He led investigators to the home of a powerful tribal leader near the Afghanistan–Iraq border, where the mummy was found in a crawl space hidden under a carpet in a locked room.

The mummy, in a wooden sarcophagus with a stone cover, was lying on top of a reed mat coated with honey and resin. She wore a golden crown and a hammered gold mask. On her chest, an inscribed gold breastplate proclaimed, according to a cursory reading, "I am the daughter of the great King Xerxes . . . I am Rhodugune." The owner told police that he got the mummy from an Iranian man who claimed it had surfaced during an earthquake.

If real, the body would have been an indication that the Egyptians imparted their mummification techniques to trading partners in the region. Not only did the discovery whet archeological appetites worldwide, but it also threatened to spark an international incident. Pakistan found the mummy, but because the cuneiform writing on the breastplate indicated a Persian origin, Iran claimed the artifact as part of that country's royal heritage. Even the Taliban got involved, saying that the mummy was smuggled into Pakistan from nearby Afghanistan and that they'd caught and executed the smugglers.

The mummy remained in the custody of Pakistan's National Museum, and the more experts examined it, the more things started to look suspicious. Investigators noticed that the breastplate inscription contained grammatical errors, and the gold jewelry was of poor quality, especially for a princess. The royal symbols carved on the wooden sarcophagus had clearly been drawn in pencil first. And the reed mat was, according to radiocarbon dating, only 50 years old at most. It seemed that everything associated with the mummy was fake. But people have tried to pawn off real mummies as fake royalty to inflate their worth. Was the mummy itself genuine?

Here's where things got disturbing. Whoever had removed the woman's internal organs had taken them all—including the heart, which in Egyptian practice would have been left in the body—and had done so through a slit in the abdomen that looked worryingly like a stab wound. The brain had been pulled out through her mouth, not her nose, also contrary to Egyptian practice. She was also missing all of her teeth.

And then, the clincher: CT scans revealed the presence of tiny bones in the inner ear that could not possibly have survived two millennia. In fact, the woman could not have been dead more than a few years. Further investigation revealed that the woman's lower back had been broken by a violent blow. Peeling back the bandages for an autopsy, investigators found a middle-aged woman who had died in 1996. Cause of death: broken neck. The fake mummy princess was starting to look like a very real victim of foul play.

It's impossible to know from the autopsy if the woman had been murdered or suffered an accident, with a team of forgers simply recovering the body after death. Nevertheless, the whole thing pointed to a sinister ring of antiquities fakers, especially since this wasn't a one-man job. Once they had their body, the forgers had yanked out her internal organs and packed her body with baking soda and table salt before taking great care to dress it up in mummy wrappings. A stonemason made the slab she was lying on, a woodcarver made the sarcophagus, a goldsmith beat out the mask and breastplate, and someone with a working knowledge of Egyptian mummification practices as well as Persian history and cuneiform writing took care of the rest. All that effort was not without potential reward; the tribal leader who was trying to sell the mummy claimed he had a buyer on the hook for $1.1 million (the asking price was $11 million).

The anonymous woman's broken neck and back were enough to prompt the Pakistani police to launch a murder investigation. But eventually interest in the victim dissipated. As of 2008, the last mention of her in the press, Pakistani police no longer seemed to be actively investigating the crime. Even worse, the unknown woman's body remained unburied, left in cold storage at the morgue; according to officials, they were still awaiting permission to bury her.

Charlotte of Prussia

The Princess Who Threw a Sex Party

JULY 24, 1860-OCTOBER 1, 1919
PRUSSIA

*I*t was a cold, snowy night in 1891 when sleighs arrived at the Jagdschloss Grunewald, a hunting lodge in the woods. Dozens of the Prussian court's noblest aristocrats and most important officials, clad in furs against the winter chill, had come to the oldest Prussian palace in Berlin for a night of drinking, dancing, gambling, and sex. The furs were soon discarded, and it wasn't long before the inhibitions were, too. Partners were exchanged, new positions tried out—all under the glassy eyes of countless stuffed deer heads, as well as the watchful eye of at least one enterprising noble.

The next morning, after the cavorting aristocrats had departed with fond memories, a bit of a hangover, and possibly some exciting new venereal diseases, they began receiving anonymous letters threatening to reveal exactly what they'd gotten up to at the secluded schloss. And just in case the swingers couldn't remember everything clearly, the letters helpfully included explicit details, which were accompanied by pornographic drawings and collages. Even worse, the descriptions went well beyond what happened at the castle. According to a 1904 biography of the Prussian emperor, the letter writer "was in the habit of trotting out old and long-forgotten skeletons, mauling over half-healed sores, and telling of nasty or dishonourable actions, some of them true, others invented." That meant that the author of the missives was not only an attendee at the party, but also someone with real access to the Berlin court. Before it was all over, the scandal would reach all the way to the German Reichstag, money would be paid to keep the blackmailer silent, and at least one career would be ruined and one life would be lost.

So who wrote the letters? The person at the top of the list was the one who'd thrown the sexy shindig: a chain-smoking princess named Viktoria Elisabeth Auguste Charlotte, granddaughter of Queen Victoria, daughter of the Prussian rulers, and younger sister of Kaiser Wilhelm II, the last German emperor.

Empty on the Inside

Princess Charlotte, as she was called, was the oldest and least promising daughter of the Prussian crown prince and princess. Growing up, she'd had no head for learning, was inclined to be snobbish and rude, and frequently butted heads with her mother. By the time she reached her teen years, Charlotte had earned herself a reputation as the "most arrogant and heartless coquette at court." As her mother lamented, "that pretty exterior and the empty inside, those dangerous character traits! Everyone is initially enthralled, and yet those who know her better know how she really is—and can have neither love nor trust nor respect!" Ouch. (As for Charlotte's "pretty exterior," well, she was short, with a long body and stubby limbs, an immense bust, and one shoulder higher than the other. She also suffered from thinning hair. Maybe you had to see her in the right light?)

In February 1878, 17-year-old Charlotte married Bernhard III, duke of Saxe-Meiningein. He was nine years older than she and had a "finicky and old-maidish" air, but Charlotte felt herself to be in love with him. In May of the next year, she had a daughter named Feodora, her only child. Not much into mothering, Charlotte soon left the child in the care of a nurse and returned to Berlin to inflict herself on the social scene.

Charlotte was a typical mean girl—she pretended to be friends with people only to gain their confidence, learn compromising things about them, and then tell everyone. Her own brother called her "Charley the Pretender," for her two-faced nature. She had a wicked tongue and aimed to rule Berlin's court as its gossipy queen bee. At the same time, Charlotte was admired for her sense of style, her French dresses, her cleverness, and her taste in horses, music, and flowers. She also threw great parties. And when her brother became Emperor Wilhelm II, Charlotte was suddenly highly sought after in Berlin society.

Sex, Lies, and Porno Letters

Soon after Wilhelm II's ascension came the sex party and blackmail scandal. Charlotte, with her love of malicious chatter and trouble-making tendencies, was the first to be suspected of writing the letters even though she received several, too. Her enemies, of which she had a few, claimed she wrote the letters to herself and that she'd thrown the party to entrap the guests.

In all, some 246 letters passed between blackmailer and victims. Despite censorship laws, a lot of the dirt came out in the press, prompting much moaning about moral decline. And because politicians also love gossip, heated debates broke out in the Reichstag, triggering a police investigation and a round of incriminations. But although she loved passing on tittle-tattle, it turns out that Charlotte was *not* the letter writer. After the spotlight left her it then landed on the unfortunate Count Leberecht von Kotze, one of her former friends; in June 1894, he was arrested.

Although eventually cleared of all charges, he never felt fully vindicated and challenged everyone involved to duels. In 1896 he fought and killed Baron von Schrader, the man who had ordered his arrest.

A police investigation lasting several years ultimately revealed that the real culprits were none other than the kaiser's brother-in-law, Duke Ernest Gunther of Schleswig-Holstein, and his French mistress. The duke had long been the black sheep of the empress's family, and he'd been at the sexy swingers' ball. After his role was revealed, he was essentially banished from court. His mistress, meanwhile, was escorted to the German border under armed guard and kicked out with a warning never to return.

But Charlotte was not entirely innocent. Much of the material for the letters had come from her diary, which she lost while on holiday with the Kotzes (the dueler and his wife). In it, she'd recorded scandalous secrets about her own family and members of the court; the diary somehow landed in the hands of the duke's naughty mistress (possibly via the Kotzes, with whom Charlotte had quarreled), who passed it on to her lover. The police found the diary during the investigation and handed it over to Wilhelm. The kaiser was incensed—relations were already tense between him and his sister, owing to Charlotte's hatred of his wife (and his wife's for her). Charlotte's husband was transferred to a regiment stationed in some dull German backwater and she went with him, suffering a de facto banishment from the society she so loved. The kaiser and his sister never reconciled. (Remarkably, the sex party scandal was almost immediately forgotten. It wasn't until 2010, when a German historian cracked the Prussian State Archives, that the story came to light.)

Like Mother, Like Daughter

For all her cattiness, Charlotte does deserve some sympathy. After all, she had grown up an unloved child, afflicted with a nervous tendency to bite her nails and suck on her clothing, tics that were only exacerbated by her mother's constant criticism. Victoria (Queen Victoria's daughter) genuinely seemed to dislike her daughter, calling her "stupid," "backward," "naughty," "very troublesome," and "ungraceful"; Charlotte's natural quick wit was taken as rudeness. Years later, when her mother was dying of cancer, Charlotte was the last of the children to learn the news.

Given such a fraught relationship with her mother, perhaps it's not surprising that Charlotte turned out to be a pretty crappy mother herself. She hated being pregnant, not to mention the restrictions that it and motherhood imposed on her. After Feodora's birth, Charlotte decided to have no more children. Feodora grew up as unloved as her mother had been, abandoned to nurses and governesses and with few other children to play with. By the time Feodora was a teenager, her grandmother complained that the girl would be "her Mama over again," that all she cared about were dresses and what people wore and that she had a tendency to tell lies. Relations did not improve after Feodora married (at age 17, to Prince Henry XXX Reuss, a relatively poor aristocrat 15 years her senior). When Feodora, who desperately wanted children, was unable to conceive, Charlotte was less than sympathetic. To the idea of grandkids, she snapped, "No thanks, I can live without the damned brood!"

Charlotte found Feodora increasingly "incomprehensible," saying, "It's of no use, so I must keep aloof & let her go her own way." She alienated her daughter and son-in-law to such a degree that public insults were the accepted form of communication between them. Feodora's father, Bernhard, complained with a startling lack of awareness about his daughter's "passion for gossip and calumny which she has certainly not inherited from us." Not even Feodora's failing health could elicit maternal feelings from Charlotte, who bitched about how "pale, thin, [and] ugly" her daughter was, declaring, "I could hardly believe this curious, loud personage had been my Child! . . . I cannot love her!" By the turn of the century, Charlotte had even begun telling people that her son-in-law had given her daughter a venereal disease, and she demanded that Feodora submit to a doctor's examination to prove that he hadn't. The vitriol was so shocking that gossipmongers in Berlin began to question the mental health of both women. And with good reason.

Charlotte's behavior had long been put down to a willful, malicious nature and her insatiable appetite for drinking, smoking, and gossip. In reality, Charlotte may have been suffering from porphyria, the same painful and rare blood condition that was behind the "madness" of her maternal great-great-grandfather, King George III (though recent evidence suggests that George may have been mentally ill, after all). Later in her life, Charlotte was plagued by ill health—rheumatism, aches, kidney pains, colds, bowel issues, swollen joints, and weird blood conditions that doctors thought were severe anemia. She was also depressed, unable to sleep, and plagued by itchiness. And it probably didn't help that she smoked, known to exacerbate porphyria. Her mother once described her complexion as "yellow" and claimed that "she smells like a cigar shop, which for ladies is not the thing."

Feodora suffered from the same condition, which manifested in her around age 11. By the time she was in her thirties, her medical complaints, which were frequent and very real, were dismissed by her family as hypochondria and "mental apathy." Her husband claimed that she was too lazy to take care of herself: "She grossly exaggerates her illnesses and causes me and others quite unnecessary anxiety." In addition, Feodora was likely manic depressive or bipolar, swinging daily from ecstatic joy to "depressed unto death."

On October 1, 1919, Charlotte died of a heart attack at the age of 59. She and her daughter never reconciled. Feodora spent the next 25 years in and out of sanatoriums, a victim of horrible health, infertility, and her husband's insensitivity. She committed suicide on August 26, 1945, by sticking her head in a gas oven at the clinic where she was a full-time inmate. Fifty years after she was buried, her body was exhumed, and researchers confirmed that she had indeed suffered from porphyria.

Where her mother's death had occasioned a short sentence in the *Times'* News in Brief column, Feodora's went completely unremarked. Both women lived through a tumultuous period of upheaval in what had been for centuries the "natural order"; neither managed it with particular grace, but neither had it easy, either. We could write off Charlotte and her daughter as vain, self-centered women who cared only about themselves. But that's sort of all they could be—princesses like Charlotte and Feodora were expected to be meek, docile creatures who did what they were told. The problem with that life is that it's boring and limited, and doesn't allow for untreated mental illness or swinging sexual experimentation. Being born in a palace may be great, but it isn't terribly free.

Clara Ward

The Princess Who Ran Off
with a Gypsy . . . and a Waiter . . .
and a Station Manager

JUNE 17, 1873-DECEMBER 9, 1916
GOSSIP PAGES ON TWO CONTINENTS

*P*aris, 1896. A young, beautiful, vivacious princess and her much older husband are seated at a smoky café, a notorious nightclub patronized by the wealthy and fashionable. Despite the November chill, it's almost too warm inside, and the princess's round white shoulders are nearly bare, her ample bosom only just contained by her corseted dress. Bored, she toys idly with her glass of champagne. As the band strikes up a haunting gypsy melody, the keening wail of a violin pierces the air.

The violinist, a small man with black hair and dark flashing eyes, sizes up the audience as he moves through it. The princess catches his attention. He walks toward her, playing more intensely. She smiles.

Ten days later, the gypsy violinist and the princess flee Paris, leaving behind her indifferent husband and two young children and the pressures of high society. It wasn't the first time this princess made headlines across the globe, and it certainly wouldn't be the last.

An American in Paris

The Princesse de Caraman-Chimay, also known as Clara Ward, wasn't born a princess, but she was as close as most Americans got. Her father, Captain Eber Ward, known as the "King of the Lakes," was a wealthy shipping tycoon and lumber industry magnate. Michigan's first millionaire, he'd scandalously married Clara's mother after his first wife (and mother of his seven children) divorced him on the grounds of serial infidelity.

Clara was born in Detroit in 1873. Her father died when she was barely 18 months old, leaving most of his $6 million fortune to her mother and their children together. (Pointedly, he left much less to the children from his first marriage.) Clara's mother moved the little girl and her brother to New York and then, after marrying a Canadian, to Toronto. When Clara was 15 years old, she was sent to a London finishing school.

Actually, *several* finishing schools. According to a contemporary newspaper, Clara's reputation in London soon "became anything but what a mother could desire," and she was obliged to find a new school. One story claimed that she disappeared from her school in Paris and was found 18 days later in the garret of a starving student; another claimed she escaped school by hitching a ride on the roof of her mother's carriage. Yet another account describes how Clara was sent to an Italian convent school, where she "shocked the good nuns" and had to be removed. Take these stories with a big block of salt—turn-of-the-century newspapers were not exactly devoted to accuracy. But though she had earned herself a reputation before being launched on the polite society of Europe, Clara's wildness would by no means get in the way of the good old-fashioned husband-hunting her mother had in store.

Clara's sizable fortune—at least $50,000 a year from her father's estate—and voluptuously Victorian figure made her an instant sensation. "Lips like a pomegranate and the heart of a saint," one enthralled contemporary declaimed, though neither of those things rings true. "As beautiful as she is wealthy," as another paper reported, sounds about right.

When Clara met Prince Joseph de Caraman-Chimay, son of a Belgian foreign affairs minister, he was about $100,000 in debt and owned a crumbling chateau in desperate need of repair. He was not, it appears, a handsome man. He was 15 years older than Clara, and his personality barely merited a mention in even the most gossipy newspaper reports about the couple. But he had a title, and that's what mattered. He proposed, and the two were married in Paris on May 20, 1890. Clara, wearing a $10,000 dress, was only 17 years old; she had just become the Princesse de Caraman-Chimay, one of only a handful of American women to gain a royal title (see "The Dollar Princesses," page 196).

The newly minted princess and her husband spent their time traveling among his estates, the Belgian court, the Riviera, Paris, and every other fashionable European hotspot. Though she had a daughter, the countess Marie, in 1891, followed by a son in 1894, rumors persisted that Clara was involved with other men and that the prince didn't care enough to stop her.

Life as a princess wasn't all it was cracked up to be. Speaking to the press after her divorce (it's probably not a spoiler to reveal that the couple separated), Clara claimed that she had no choice but to leave the Belgian court after King Leopold II "showered" her with attention, neglected his other guests in favor of her beauty, and made her a social pariah. Sure, she said, she encouraged him. But in so doing, she earned herself the wrath of the court, especially the queen. Clara's humiliation was complete when she "stood alone on one of the steps of the great staircase leading into the palace conservatories. As I entered the great hall, every woman there turned her back, or gazed at me contemptuously." She warned other American women not to be dazzled by the promise of a title: "Few American-bred women could feel themselves really happy in the high European, especially Continental, society," she declared.

No longer welcome at court, Clara and the prince spent time in

Paris, which was then in the grips of a fin-de-siècle passion fueled by scandalous dancing, Champagne, and art nouveau. Clara seized upon life with reckless abandon, making a name for herself as the wildest American that side of the Atlantic.

All this raucous living put her on a collision course with a scandal involving the affections of a Hungarian gypsy fiddler named Rigo Janczy on that November night in 1896. A diminutive man with a massive handlebar mustache and much-pomaded hair, Rigo was not classically handsome. The *Chicago Tribune* sneered that he was a "monkey-faced brute," and a Scottish newspaper wrote that "he is said to be pock-pitted, of small stature, and everyone wondered what she saw in him." He was also already married.

None of that mattered to Clara. The first night she saw her Rigo, she turned from her husband to smile at him and never looked back. Ten days later, according to Rigo, the pair ran off together "like gypsies" in the dead of night. The press went crazy—papers across Europe, Britain, and America carried news of the princess's flight.

Postcard Pinup

Armed with his wife's notoriety, Prince Joseph won a divorce by January 1897, less than two months after Clara abandoned him and their children. At the hearing—which saw all of fashionable Brussels fighting to get into the courtroom, but no Clara—even her lawyer declared her a "fiery untamed steed" with a "wild, savage, eccentric nature." The prince retained custody, and Clara was forced to pay him child support; she was never allowed to see her children again.

Clara had fallen so far so fast that there would never be any going back. Not that she cared. As she declared in a statement made at the divorce hearing, "I am done with it all. I wanted to be free. I am at least out of the rotten atmosphere in which modern society lives. It does not want me and I do not want it—so we are quits." The loss of her children may have been collateral damage in Clara's quest for freedom, though in the absence of any letters or comment, we cannot know for sure how she felt. Whatever her true feelings, she certainly threw herself into her new peripatetic lifestyle with gusto.

The first place the illicit couple went was the mountainside cottage of Rigo's mother, a far cry from the royal court and Parisian nightclubs the princess had known. Supposedly Clara was so grateful to the Hungarian woman that she bought the mountain and gave Rigo's mother a pearl necklace, which she hung on a nail by the fireplace.

Once back in Paris, Clara's scandalous behavior had gotten her ostracized from respectable society. But the former royal had money, and money fixes everything. When the local worthies succeeded in pressuring hotels and innkeepers into refusing to rent her rooms, she simply got herself a house. She took to riding a bicycle down the boulevards, clad in bloomers and "low socks like a man." She smoked cigarettes in public and was featured frequently in articles in the foreign press lamenting the city's moral decline.

Emboldened by this most bohemian of lifestyles, in April 1897 Clara began earning money posing in skin-tight flesh-colored costumes on the stages of the Moulin Rouge and Folies Bergère. She called her art *"poses plastiques"*; she was accompanied by Rigo, playing the violin and dancing around her like an organ-grinder's monkey. Somehow Clara managed to scandalize even the worldly Parisians. Her first show was canceled after police learned that friends of the prince were planning to show up to pelt her with "live rabbits, rotten eggs, and other equally objectionable missiles," according to one newspaper report. Paris might have been outraged, but locals still ponied up to see Clara Ward sort-of naked, as did art lovers in other European capitals. When the couple played in Berlin, they reportedly brought in $6,800 in one month (about $181,000 today).

Clara also posed for postcard pictures wearing her *poses plastiques* body suit, with her wavy brown hair tumbling past her rather sturdy bottom, and topped by a crown seemingly fashioned out of light bulbs and coat hangers. More scandal ensued: in August 1897, her ex-husband demanded that police raid several photographic shops and seize pictures of Clara in, according to the newspapers, "all sorts of costume." Clara's naughty photos were reportedly banned in the German Empire because Kaiser Wilhelm II found her "beauty" so disturbing. That's probably an exaggeration, but it is true that people were arrested for peddling and mailing the taboo images of the ex-princess.

Unlucky in Love

This was about the time that Henri de Toulouse-Lautrec, the famous Belle Époque painter of prostitutes, created a lithograph of Clara and Rigo. The two are sitting in an orchestra pit in a Paris nightclub, Clara's hair an impossible yellow, Rigo mustachioed and swarthy. Called "Idylle Princière," it captured them at their most fashionable, amorous, and interesting. Things pretty much went downhill from there.

The couple lived in sin until 1898, when Rigo was finally granted a divorce, setting him free to marry Clara, which he then did. Their passion was intense; supposedly, during a trip to Japan they had each other's portraits tattooed on their biceps. Clara showed her devotion by spending ridiculous amounts of money on her new husband. A grinning Rigo told reporters that she bought him a menagerie of baby elephants, lions, and tigers, just to amuse him, as well as a new violin and a casket full of jewels. They traveled across Europe and spent two years in Egypt, literally building palaces wherever they wished.

Eventually, all this prodigious spending came to the attention of Clara's mother. Scandalized by her daughter's behavior, she was even more worried about the state of the family finances. So she moved to have Clara cut off, asking that the wayward ex-princess's uncle be appointed conservator of her estate. In 1898 the court agreed, and Clara was given a yearly income of £12,000 (nearly $2 million in today's money), out of which £3,000 went to her ex-husband to pay for the children's living expenses. But Clara's spending continued unabated. In 1901 she was officially declared a spendthrift after her uncle was forced to dip into her capital to pay off her debts. He revealed that over the course of seven years Clara had spent $750,000 (about $20 million today), the bulk of it "frittered away in company with the sparkling-eyed Rigo," according to the *Detroit Free Press*.

Meanwhile, life with Rigo wasn't all zoo animals and palaces—the two fought often, loudly and publicly. In January 1897, right about the time her husband was divorcing her in Brussels, Clara and the gypsy violinist had a violent quarrel at a Milan hotel, stunning guests with their shouting and screaming and door-slamming. Clara left Rigo in the lurch, paying only her share of the bill and putting him, as the *New York Times* noted, "in an awkward position." Little else is recorded about their life together, but it couldn't have been easy. Even "loose" society rejected them: in 1902, the couple was viciously booed at the Folies Bergère when Rigo was performing with his orchestra. The strain may have been too much for their marriage; they were divorced by 1904, and Rigo moved to America. He claimed that Clara left him because she'd taken up with a grubby railway worker.

At least part of Rigo's statement appears to be true, because in the same year of her divorce, Clara married her third husband. Guiseppe "Peppino" Ricciardi was a waiter on a train, or a baggage clerk, or a canvasser for an Italian tourist agency, or a manager of a railway station of the Mount Vesuvius Funicular—his professional situation remains unclear. What is certain is that he was very good-looking, known as the "handsomest man in Naples."

Throughout her new marriage, Clara remained a mainstay of society and gossip column reports, with varying degrees of accuracy. The press reported that she was performing on the vaudeville stages in America (she wasn't), had been declared insane by her family (nope), was completely cut off from her family's fortune (not exactly), and had been marrying and divorcing (yep). In 1910 her unerring bad luck in men made headlines once again. Ricciardi left her, claiming she was having an affair with the butler. Clara declared herself innocent, saying, "These Neapolitans are so jealous!" The pair was officially divorced by July 1911.

DEFIANT TO THE END

Clara wasn't lonely for long. Upon her divorce from Ricciardi, she supposedly said, "I cannot be alone. I am unhappy like that. I shall marry yet once again." She did, although even less is known about her fourth husband; it seems he was one Signore Abano Caselato (or Cassalota, Casselletto, or Casaloto) and was possibly a butler, or a chauffeur, or a station manager, or an artist. The first her family heard of the man she'd been married to for at least five years was when he telegrammed to say that Clara had died of pneumonia on December 9, 1916, in Padua, Italy; she was only 43.

Reports claimed that Clara was penniless, but in fact the money that had buoyed her through her scandalous life never deserted her, even when nearly all of her husbands, family, and friends did. Her $1.2 million estate was split among her children, Ricciardi, and a cousin in America. Her last husband was not included in the will, which had been drawn up in 1904.

Clara's life was a study in rebellion. One paper declared, "From her earliest youth, Clara Ward seems to have had a loadstone desire to scandalize the world; to break down all the baririers [*sic*] of convention and be at least [as] bizarre and unusual for one woman to be." Another wrote that some would say the "devil stood sponsor when Clara Ward was born and that she had always been more or less proud of her godfather." Her fabulously embroidered obituary in the *Detroit News* lamented, "She died a woman without illusions. She had gone the pace. She lived intensely, a slave of her desires; she died an outcast, an old woman of 43 years, just when she should have been in her prime."

Clara did burn bright and fast—but she did it on her own terms. Talking about her flight from the Belgian court, she once said, "I defied them, as I have all my life defied everyone." She certainly did, for better or for worse.

The Dollar Princesses

Clara Ward was just one of many American heiresses who married European royalty in a mutually beneficial partnership that saw the Americans gain social standing while the Europeans refilled their empty coffers. Called Dollar Princesses, these young beauties kept Old World aristocrats afloat for decades. Sometimes the union of old nobility and new money worked, and sometimes it didn't. But without the wealth of these women, the noble houses of Europe surely would have been crushed under the weight of their own history.

Wanted: American Money

The first American woman to become a princess by marriage was Catherine Willis Gray, great-grandniece of George Washington. In 1826 she wed Prince Achille Murat, son of the former king of Naples and Napoleon's sister Caroline. Her entrée into European royalty didn't exactly open the floodgates, but by the time the nineteenth century came to a close, the number of American princesses had risen exponentially.

That was for two reasons. First, the old order in Europe was crumbling in slow motion, shaken by revolutions, abdications, assassinations, and social unrest. Second, businessmen in America were getting rich, and fast. The era saw the rise of American men of industry, many of them barely a generation removed from poor immigrants who'd left Europe in search of fortune abroad. They wanted their daughters to have access to the place in society they hadn't enjoyed, and so they purchased status along with everything else. The practice was so acknowledged that American newspapers published articles instructing hopeful millionairesses where to set their sights: "Dukes are the loftiest kind of noblemen in England," one printed in 1886, going on to detail which of the 27 such men in the United Kingdom would be available for marital conquest. On the other side of the Atlantic, the British sense of decorum didn't stretch so far as to keep one "English Peer of a very old title" from advertising in the *Daily Telegraph* in 1901 that he was looking for a "very wealthy lady" to marry: widows and spinsters okay, no divorcées need apply.

By 1904, more than 20 American women, most of them heiresses, could call themselves Princess Something or other. By 1915, that number had more than doubled, to 42. And it wasn't just princesses—American women were duchesses, countesses, marchionesses, and more. In 1914, 60 peers and 40 sons of peers of Britain were married to American heiresses, so many that Britain's prime minister, Lord Palmerston, commented, "Before the century is out, those clever and pretty women from New York will pull all the strings in half the chancelleries in Europe."

But a fancy title doesn't always bring happiness, as Clara Ward cautioned. Members of entrenched European nobility were apt to regard newcomers with suspicion, no matter how desperately they craved their cash. Jennie Jerome, Winston Churchill's allegedly tattooed American mother, wrote in her diary about the welcome such princesses received: "Anything of an outlandish nature might be expected of her. If she talked, dressed and conducted herself as any well-bred woman would . . . she was usually saluted with the tactful remark; 'I should never have thought you were an American'—which was intended as a compliment. . . . Her dollars were her only recommendation."

GOOD MONEY, BAD MARRIAGE

A lot of these unions didn't work out. Gladys Deacon, for example, the beautiful daughter of a millionaire Boston banker, had huge blue eyes, a classic profile, and a forceful personality that would have been much less enchanting in someone less attractive. In the late 1890s, she met the duke of Marlborough, whose palatial estate, Blenheim Palace, was immensely appealing. He, however, was already married to another Dollar Princess, though both were itching for a divorce. That didn't happen until 1921, when Gladys was 40 and had already ruined her good looks. (At the age of 22, she'd injected paraffin wax into her nose in a bid to maintain its shape, which was just as bad an idea as it sounds.) The duke married her anyway, but life with this millionairess didn't prove any better than with the last one. Gladys once brought a revolver to dinner and, when asked why, remarked, "Oh, I don't know, I might just shoot Marlborough." Hubby had her committed, and she spent the last 15 years of her life confined to a hospital. She died in 1977, at the age of 96.

Happily ever after

Others did find happiness, of a sort, and Winnaretta Singer was one of them. She was the twentieth of sewing-machine tycoon Isaac Singer's 24 children (fathered through two legal and three common-law marriages). Born in America, she grew up in Britain and France; when her father died in 1875, 11-year-old Winnaretta was left with a $900,000 fortune (more than $18 million today). Her first marriage was to Prince Louis-Vilfred de Scey-Montbéliard, in 1887. Family lore claims that the groom entered the bridal suite to find his new wife armed with an umbrella and perched atop the wardrobe, threatening, "If you touch me, I'll kill you!" No surprise that they separated after only 21 months and were divorced in 1891. It becomes even less surprising when one knows that Winnaretta was a lesbian.

The one good thing that came from this failed marriage was that, once wed, Winnaretta was free to conduct avant-garde *salons*, those meetings of artists, novelists, philosophers, composers, and musicians. These would spark her fruitful life-long career as a patron of the arts, most especially of modern music. She encouraged Igor Stravinsky, Claude Debussy, and Jean-Baptiste Faure and hosted soirées with Marcel Proust, Virginia Woolf, and Oscar Wilde. The musical and artistic landscape of Paris—and, indeed, of all Europe—was infinitely enriched by her presence.

Her next marriage was also to a prince, but this time it was a much better match: Prince Edmond de Polignac was 31 years her senior, a musician and composer, and gay. His friends and family knew that Winnaretta was looking for a *mariage blanc*, that is, a union that would never be consummated. They also realized that Edmond was broke, and, to persist in hosting *salons*, Winnaretta needed a certain aristocratic rank. The deal was done.

The two were married on December 15, 1893, and in many ways it was a true love match: their mutual love of *salons*, of music and art, meant that they never lacked for things to talk about, were always each other's best friend, and could still enjoy romantic relationships on the side. Winnaretta's Sapphic conquests were numerous and simultaneous: she was widely assumed to be a part of a lesbian artistic and aristocratic sub-culture, called "Paris-Lesbos," that included women like the writer Collette, the poet Renée Vivien, and the marquise de Morny. Edmond died in 1901, after nearly eight years of domestic harmony. Winnaretta remained a patroness and bene-factor until her own death on November 25, 1943.

Gloria von Thurn und Taxis

The Punk Princess
Who Went Corporate

Born February 23, 1960
Germany and the Überrich devastatingly
decadent landscape of the 1980s

The year was 1986, and Prince Johannes von Thurn und Taxis's million-dollar sixtieth birthday party had been going on for days. His health had been toasted at a white-tie lobster and caviar dinner, at a lobster and pheasant luncheon, and at a lobster and roasted-pig dinner. But the final evening's entertainment was by far the most sumptuous: an outlandish, preposterous eighteenth-century costume ball that began at 9:30 that night and ended at 9:30 the next morning. Conspicuous consumption doesn't even begin to describe it.

The 500-room castle, Schloss St. Emmeram, was teeming with celebrities such as Mick Jagger and Jerry Hall as well as greed-is-good-decade richies like Saudi arms dealer Adnan Khashoggi. All were dressed, without a whiff of irony, as the doomed, diamond-bedecked aristocracy of prerevolutionary France. Guests arrived at the castle's courtyard to find servants in peasant getups plucking chickens and building bonfires (of the vanities?); they wandered through a disco maze of lights and mirrors, to be deposited in the Hall of Muskets, whose beams were festooned with strings of sausages. There were mountains of lobster, fountains of champagne, and a cake decorated with 60 marzipan penises serving as candles.

At last, Princess Gloria von Thurn und Taxis made her entrance. She was dressed, of course, as Marie Antoinette, wearing a powder-pink $10,000 bespoke gown and a two-foot-tall powdered wig topped with the French queen's own pearl tiara. Later that night, she sang "Happy Birthday" to her beloved husband from atop a gilded cloud while accompanied by the Munich Opera. But the high times weren't to last, and Princess Gloria was destined to come crashing down to earth.

FROM BARMAID TO SCHLOSSWIFE

Gloria had become Princess von Thurn und Taxis—or, to give her official title, Mariae Gloria Ferdinanda Gerda Charlotte Teutonia Franziska Magarethe Frederike Simone Johanna Joachima Josefine Wilhelmine Huberta Princess von Thurn und Taxis—in 1980, when she married Prince Johannes. He was 53 when he met the 19-year-old barmaid in Munich; they hit it off and were hitched within a year. He was a big personality who made no secret of his romantic interest in both sexes, and he enjoyed pulling pranks on unsuspecting friends, such as lacing banquet dinners with laxatives and dropping herrings down women's dresses.

The bisexual jokester was also the wealthiest noble and biggest landowner in Germany. (Though the German nobility was dismantled in 1919, at the birth of the Weimar Republic, nobles got to keep their titles and their money.) His family could trace its fortune back to thirteenth-century Lombardy, when they got in on the (very) ground floor of the Holy Roman Empire postal service. The Tassis family (from the Italian word for badger), as they were called back then, earned their wealth and status operating a local courier service; by 1489 Franz von Taxis became the empire's official postmaster and held a virtual monopoly. In 1512 the family von Taxis was given their patents of nobility from Holy Roman Emperor Maximilian I, and by the seventeenth century they got to add Thurn, a derivative of Torre, to their name, on the claim that a way-back ancestor was a Torriani duke. (Really, it was just a great opportunity to add a tower next to the badger on the coat of arms.) In any case, 700 years and several banks, timber mills, breweries, and private forests later, Johannes was worth a reported $3 billion.

Though Gloria was also an aristocrat—a countess by birth—her family wasn't wealthy. But growing up without money didn't seem to impair her ability to spend it. She and her husband bought huge amounts of art, traveled the globe, and became fixtures of tabloids and glossy mags the world over. They threw wild parties that lasted days; his birthday fete was just one of many held at their massive castle in Bavaria, a stately pile that Gloria once said "makes Buckingham Palace look like a hut."

In 1985 an interviewer for *Vanity Fair* magazine dubbed Gloria "Princess TNT, the dynamite socialite"—the name stuck and Gloria more than lived up to it. She barked like a dog on *Late Night with David Letterman* and got busted for possession of hashish at the Munich airport. She wore sweaters made out of teddy bears and received Holy Communion wearing a witch's hat. She dyed her hair every hue of the rainbow, wore it in a Mohawk, or teased it up like the plumes of a peacock, earning her the additional sobriquet "Punk Princess." She rode Harleys and horses, partied with Prince and princes, danced on tables in a Paco Rabanne chainmail minidress, and dressed as a cowgirl for fancy balls.

The High Cost of High Living

But after the boozy excess of the '80s came the swift and devastating hangover of the '90s. In December 1990, Gloria's wild partying ended abruptly with the death of her husband—and the discovery that their estate was a stunning $576 million in debt. At least $80 million was in owed death and estate taxes; a recessionary climate and bad investments made up the rest. Gloria also had three children under the age of 10, including 8-year-old Prince Albert, who would inherit the property and the debt when he turned 18.

The punk princess needed to make some big changes if she hoped to preserve the family fortune. As she told London's *Daily Telegraph*, "My fairy story is over. You can't be a fairy and meet a payroll." And so the pink hair went, as did a number of family treasures. Almost immediately, Gloria settled with the state of Bavaria, which took $30 million in art and artifacts in lieu of the unpaid taxes. She sold 24 of their 27 cars, laid off the liveried staff at the family's six castles, and sold a few unused properties. Then she enlisted the aid of Sotheby's to get rid of even more family possessions, earning $13.7 million. The following year she held a second auction, which included 75,000 bottles of wine, netting another $19 million.

Her economy, however, did not endear her to her late husband's family, who balked at auctioning off her son's inheritance and questioned her right to do so. Father Emmeram, an uncle on her husband's side and a 91-year-old Benedictine hermit, denounced the princess as a "ruthless minx." But Gloria was a realist—some things in the family vaults were more valuable than others. "Albert can buy a new tureen anytime he needs one," she said, "but he can hardly go out and buy a forest." She soon realized, however, that pawning all the silver wouldn't be enough to put the family fortune in the black. So she dug in further: she reviewed the family portfolio, cut bad investments, sold a few banks that weren't performing. And she got creative. The castle, which had been a private residence for hundreds of years, was opened to the public for tours. She also wasn't above trading on her own colorful image to reel in the tourists. "At the end of the day, my green and blue and yellow hair made me interesting and made this place interesting," she said in 2006. "If I have 150,000 visitors a year, it's not only because they want to see the history of the Thurn und Taxises, but also where Gloria lives." Parts of the castle were also rented out for office space.

The punk princess spent the decade teaching herself corporate law and economics; the chainmail minidress was replaced with Chanel suits. She largely disappeared from the pages of the tabloids that had once thrilled to her every hair-color change and bizarre ensemble. "I didn't see anybody socially, because I was so tired in the evening," she told *Vanity Fair* in 2006. "But I got to know all the companies, and I got to know the problems, and I could make decisions." The 1990s weren't easy, but by 2002 Gloria's efforts had paid off. According to *Bloomberg BusinessWeek*, the family conglomerate was enjoying a 10 percent return.

By the turn of the twenty-first century, Gloria's transformation from TNT into an upstanding businesswoman and representative of German nobility was complete. In 2001, she even wrote a best-selling guide to good manners, *Our Etiquette: The World of Good Manners from A to Z*, coauthored with her good friend and fellow aristocrat Alessandra Borghese. Even more important, she managed to avoid becoming another parable of the price of 1980s greed culture.

THE PRINCESS AND THE POPE

But there was more to the new image than just keen business acumen. Gloria had found God. She'd always had her faith: "Even when I was partying and going to Studio 54, I was still attending church," she told the *New York Times* in 2008. "Maybe just not the early Mass." But for a while, religion took a backseat to meeting rock stars and spending money. As she explained to *Vanity Fair* in 2006: "Once I met them, the myth collapsed. With the Church, it was exactly the contrary. When I met Pope John Paul, he was even more than I thought he would be."

When Gloria's fortunes hit rock bottom, she turned to religion: "That crisis was when I really went back to praying regularly," she said. In 1991, she volunteered for the first time at Lourdes, the town in southern France where the Virgin Mary was said to have appeared in 1858 to a 14-year-old peasant girl. She helped the sick and dying who were seeking a miracle cure there. Fourteen years later, an auction house sold off 100 of her old couture dresses, with the proceeds going to the relief organization of the Order of Malta, a Catholic charity that organizes pilgrimages to Lourdes. Throughout the 1990s, she had cultivated relationships with powerful Catholic leaders, with the express wish to revive the relationships between old aristocratic families and the Roman Catholic church. And when Pope John Paul II died in April 2005, she was one of the first laypeople to be received by the new pope, Benedict XVI. Reconciling the hard partier and the hard prayer was easy for her. "Catholicism is a very sensual religion, which means that flesh and soul are compatible," she told the *New York Times*.

It's fitting that Gloria wore Marie Antoinette's pearl tiara at her husband's birthday. Like the famous French queen, the fashionable Princess TNT has a flair for excess and loves a good party. But unlike her guillotined counterpart, Gloria faced devastation and kept her head. Does she miss the '80s? Probably a little. But she doesn't regret what she called her "spoiled brat" years: "I think it's the privilege of youth to be curious, fun-loving, even wild. I also think that every age has its own behavior," she told *W* magazine in 2012. "You don't want to behave like you're 70 when you're in your 20s. And vice versa."

Princess Excess

Does being a princess automatically come with an insatiable need for worldly goods? Yes, at least according to the examples of these regal shopaholics.

Marie Auguste von Thurn und Taxis

Wife of the ruler of a powerful German principality, Princess Marie Auguste von Thurn und Taxis was in many ways not your typical eighteenth-century royal lady. She was a skilled political operator who used intrigues, covert diplomacy, and her feminine wiles to influence the court. She could be forthright and passionate, loudly speaking her mind on matters of the state. Her husband became so irritated at her influence that he made her promise, in writing, not to meddle.

But Marie Auguste was stereotypical in one sense: she liked pretty clothes. Her closet contained some 228 dresses, including seven state gowns, those massive confections of sumptuous fabrics, frilly lace, and all kinds of frothy trimmings. The most expensive cost 500 florins, more than 30 times the annual income of a servant in her court. Her jewelry collection was valued at 89,000 florins, an astronomical sum equal to a year's wages for more than 5,000 people.

Marie Auguste used her wardrobe and her jewelry to impress upon the court her importance and her rank; it was as much a part of her efforts to influence policy and policymakers as any of the intrigues she may have conducted. But it didn't make her terribly popular with her subjects, especially because, at least in part, it was the country's money she was spending. Moreover, she couldn't afford all that stuff. When she died in 1756, she owed 50,402 florins to various shopkeepers, dressmakers, and craftsmen, as well as to her own put-upon servants.

Elizabeth I of Russia

Marie Auguste's wardrobe was positively empty compared to that of her contemporary, Empress Elizabeth I of Russia. And speaking of empty, so was Russia's treasury.

That's because Elizabeth was rumored to have spent it all. When she died, she was survived by 15,000 dresses, not to mention the countless sets of men's clothing she liked to wear, two trunks full of stockings, and several thousand pairs of shoes. Unsurprisingly, Elizabeth changed clothes multiple times a day and never wore the same outfit twice. She also took pains to ensure that of all the ladies at court, she was the most fashionable. She passed laws requiring foreign fabric salesmen to offer her first dibs, on pain of arrest. Wearing the same hairstyle or even a similar accessory or ensemble as the empress would spark her anger, so much so that she sometimes turned violent.

Elizabeth hosted two balls every week, and her dinners were perhaps the best place to witness her conspicuous consumption. She had more silver and gold tableware made during her reign than any other Russian ruler. And gracing those settings were fresh fruits, a rarity in those days, and wine and Champagne by the bucketload.

That taste for the finer things set the tone for Elizabeth's court. Her courtiers fancied diamond-studded buttons, buckles, and epaulettes; they ordered their suits by the dozen and dressed their own servants in gold cloth. Elizabeth did have her good points—she was an intelligent woman, a keen diplomat, and a pacifist who maintained that she would never sign a death warrant (and she didn't). Moreover, her demand for exotic and luxury goods stimulated the growth of infrastructure, such as the postal service. Still, she spent money as if it didn't come from the blood, sweat, and tears of her subjects, and when she died in 1762, she was up to her eyeballs in debt.

Maha Al-Sudairi

Modern-day princess Maha Al-Sudairi has a taste for the finer things—she just doesn't like paying for them. In June 2012, she was nearly arrested in Paris after she and her retinue of 60 servants were caught trying to sneak out of the exclusive five-star Shangri-la Hotel at 3:30 in the morning without paying their $8 million tab. It may have been the fleet of limousines parked at the curb that tipped off management that she was doing a runner.

The ex-wife of Saudi Arabian crown prince Nayef bin Abdulaziz had been staying in the hotel since December, when she'd taken over the entire forty-first floor. But the hotel had to eat the cost of her stay. When nabbed trying to skip out, the princess claimed diplomatic immunity, leaving Parisian police with their hands tied. She decamped to another five-star hotel, the Royal Monceau, this one owned by a friend of the family.

It wasn't the only time the princess racked up a huge bill and refused to pony up. In June 2009 she also claimed diplomatic immunity after amassing a stunning $24.2 million in unpaid shopping receipts, including $94,000 on lingerie alone. That time, too, the French were left holding the bag.

Srirasmi of Thailand

Princess Srirasmi has lovely breasts, and her ex-husband really likes their dog. These two facts collided when Prince Vajiralongkorn, Thailand's crown prince, threw a lavish birthday party for Foo Foo, their fluffy white poodle, and Princess Srirasmi was seen celebrating in nothing but a G-string and a hat (with strains of George Michael's "Careless Whisper" audible in the background). Notably, everyone else—including the dog—was fully clothed. Also notably, Foo Foo holds the rank of air chief marshal in Thailand.

The topless pooch-party incident would have remained a private affair had the whole thing not been caught on video, with the footage somehow finding its way to an Australian TV station in 2009. Criticism of the royal family is outlawed in Thailand, but the video drew the ire of the nation.

As you might expect from a woman who hangs out at her dog's birthday party in her own birthday suit, this wasn't the only time Princess Srirasmi made international headlines. In October 2012, she upheld her reputation for excess when she descended on an English antiques center and spent $40,000 during an eight-hour shopping spree that saw her literally stripping the shelves. Most items only cost between $15 and $60—that's a lot of china dogs and silver tea services.

Floozies

PRINCESSES
NOTORIOUS FOR
THEIR SEXY
EXPLOITS

Caroline of Brunswick-Wolfenbüttel

The Princess Who Didn't Wash

MAY 17, 1768-AUGUST 7, 1821
BRITAIN AND VARIOUS
CONTINENTAL TOURIST SPOTS

G eorge, Prince of Wales, met his intended bride, Princess Caroline of Brunswick-Wolfenbüttel, for the first time two days before their marriage. Etiquette demanded that he embrace her, which he did—then recoiled and fled the room, crying to his servant, "I am not well; pray get me a glass of brandy." He stayed drunk for the next three

213

days. The relationship went downhill from there.

Nobody knows what it was about Caroline that turned off the prince so violently at that introduction. She wasn't storybook beautiful, but she certainly wasn't run-away-and-get-drunk ugly. And though she was known for being less than dedicated to her personal hygiene, contemporary accounts claim that she'd been groomed particularly well for the meeting. Nevertheless, the two had barely exchanged conversation before George decided she was his intellectual and social inferior, a woman to be endured, not enjoyed. And the prince's good opinion, once lost, was lost forever.

Not that he was any catch, either. "Prinney," as the 32-year-old prince was widely (and absurdly) known, was vain and snobbish but could be extremely charming when he wanted to be. He was also a corset-wearing drunk who would later tip the scales at more than 240 pounds. A terrible gambler and talented spender, he was always in debt. And then there was the little detail that he was already married, and had been for 10 years, to the very patient Maria Fitzherbert.

None of that mattered a bit in the royal marriage market. Mrs. Fitzherbert was a commoner and, even worse for the Protestant crown, a Catholic; the pair had wed without the king's consent, so technically the marriage didn't count. And what did a few extra pounds and an awful personality matter next to the fact that he'd be king? By royal logic, the prince was the most eligible bachelor in Europe.

Kissing Cousins

Prinney needed to get hitched—and fast. By 1794, he was an incredible £650,000 in debt (more than $40 million today), having spent wildly on art, building projects, fancy clothing, wine, and racehorses. Crisis hit when several angry tradesmen to whom he owed money filed a petition demanding payment. Parliament would agree to pay the debts only if the prince married. No one, least of all Prinney, cared who the bride was, as long as she was a princess, a Protestant, and in possession of a pulse.

Princess Caroline, the extremely available daughter of a powerful German duke, was the prince's first cousin. It's likely that hers was the first name mentioned and that Prinney, anxious to get out from under his weighty debt, seized on it. Had he done even the slightest bit of homework on his would-be wife, perhaps the whole farcical tragedy that followed would have been avoided. Because, unfortunately, his 26-year-old cousin was the rotund embodiment of everything he loathed.

Though good-natured, Caroline was untidy, graceless, and chubby. She was also loud, vulgar, and devoid of tact or discretion. She liked to flirt, earning her a reputation as "very loose" and guilty of "indecent conduct." She wasn't stupid, exactly, but she was shallow. She loved gossip, asked impertinent questions, had a crude sense of humor, and was often childish and disrespectful. Adding to this pretty picture, Caroline didn't wash, or at least not enough; her undergarments, too, went overly long between launderings. Were there ever two people more ill-suited for each other?

Worst. Marriage. Ever.

Things only got worse after their first meeting. Once the prince beat his hasty retreat, Caroline declared that he was fatter than in his portrait. At dinner that night, she was her worst possible self (trying to be clever but coming off as unhinged), as was Prinney (cold, rude, and drunk). But the show had to go on, and the couple was married two days later, on April 8, 1795. According to contemporary reports, the bridegroom looked "like death" and was obviously wasted; weepy and loud, he had to be held up by his groomsmen. According to Caroline, he spent their wedding night passed out in the fireplace. They went on their honeymoon with all of his "constantly drunk and dirty" mates, plus his mistress to boot.

Surprisingly, the pair did manage to get on well enough for Caroline to become pregnant almost immediately, though the birth of their daughter Charlotte, on January 7, 1796, did little to foster a rapprochement. Three days after she was born, George made out a new will leaving everything to his "wife" (dear Mrs. Fitzherbert) and "one shilling" to Caroline.

By June 1796, Prinney's hatred of Caroline was intractable. "My abhorrence of her is such . . . that I shudder at the very thoughts of sitting at the same table as her, or even being under the same roof," he wrote. The feeling was mutual. Just a year later, they officially separated. But what God and country had joined, no man could put asunder; neither the king nor Parliament would grant permission to divorce. Protestants (ironically, see Anne Boleyn) took divorce very seriously, and the marriage was important diplomatically. They were stuck with each other.

Of the two of them, Prinney was undoubtedly better off. As a male royal, it was expected that he would have mistresses. But for Caroline, adultery would mean a wealth-stripping split. That left her in a delicate position, which was particularly difficult for a woman with no sense of delicacy whatsoever.

European courts practically ran on rumor, and Caroline's behavior did little to stop the chatter. She was a big fan of the plunging neckline—as in, nipples out—and appeared to apply her makeup with a trowel. She could be a charming hostess but was also an incorrigible flirt who sometimes disappeared for hours with a gentleman friend, leaving her other guests to try to politely ignore her absence. Even worse, Caroline allegedly boasted that she took a "bedfellow" whenever she wanted and "the Prince paid for all." Sprinkled liberally with this kind of manure, rumors quickly sprouted that the princess was conducting several affairs. For a while it was just talk, but then Caroline gave the prince *almost* the scandal he needed to divorce her.

Caroline had a weird habit of collecting babies. To her credit, she seemed chiefly concerned with finding good homes for the foundlings. But in 1802, she adopted a baby boy named William Austin, known thereafter as Willikin, and bizarrely pretended that he was her own. Why she thought it would be funny to say so is unclear, but it's likely she just wanted to cause a fuss. Her allies, including her father-in-law, King George III, dismissed the stories of a bastard child as idle talk, and her foes could prove nothing because there was nothing to prove.

But by 1806, Caroline had committed a critical error: she made enemies of the Douglases, her former friends and neighbors. It was to Lady Douglas that Caroline first pretended that Willikin was her child. After a few months of close friendship, however, Caroline grew bored with the couple and was rude when Lady Douglas came to call. When

Lady Douglas wrote to Caroline implying that she had secrets about the princess she was willing to spill, Caroline reacted in a spectacularly ill-considered fashion. She sent her former friend obscene and harassing "anonymous" letters featuring poorly drawn pictures of Lady D performing a sex act. The Douglases were quite sure the letters were from Caroline—at least one bore her royal seal.

The offended Douglases (who, it should be noted, were also perpetually broke) marched straight to the prince and made it clear they would swear that Willikin was Caroline's bastard child. For good measure, Lady Douglas even accused the princess of trying to touch and kiss her inappropriately. Armed with such evidence, the prince demanded an investigation into his estranged wife's supposed infidelity. The ensuing "Delicate Investigation," as it was called, was conducted by a secret government committee. Witnesses included everyone from Caroline's footman to her portrait painter, Thomas Lawrence. Ultimately, Willikin's real mother testified that she'd indeed given him up to the princess when he was four months old, and the commission had no choice but to clear Caroline of all accusations. Prinney wouldn't get his divorce so easily.

Caroline had also won another decision, this one in the court of public opinion. Because the investigation was meant to be secret, it was, of course, common knowledge among the gossips at court. Details filtered down through the newspapers in a series of leaked documents. Caroline won the sympathy of the British public by portraying herself as a maligned wife and mother who was denied access to her child. But most of her support came because everyone hated Prinney. The British people and press had no use for fools, especially fat drunken ones who wasted taxpayer money on mistresses and wine. Novelist Jane Austen, writing in 1813 about Caroline, summed it up best: "Poor woman, I shall support her as long as I can because she is a woman and because I hate her husband."

Life on the Lam

However much the public loved Caroline, her aristocratic peers did not. Her social isolation was nearly complete after King George III was declared insane in 1811; the prince officially then became regent, which meant that friendship with Caroline was a political liability for anyone who wanted to be received at court. Moreover, she had committed the one sin that fashionable English society could not forgive: she'd become a bore. Caroline's exasperated ladies-in-waiting were fed up hearing about how she'd been monstrously treated by the royal family, how she hated them, and the various creative ways she'd like to see them die. (Sometimes after dinner, Caroline would spend the evening sticking pins into a wax doll made to look like the prince, before melting it over the fire. This same behavior would have gotten her beheaded had she lived in Anne Boleyn's day; see "The Sorceress Princesses," page 85.) In August 1814, Caroline left England, spending the next six years traveling. In Geneva that October, the now blowsy woman of 46 embarrassed herself and everyone around her by attending a ball in her honor "dressed *en Vénus*, or rather not dressed further than the waist." The next year, an English aristocrat who met Caroline in Genoa described her as a "fat woman of fifty years of age, short, plump and high colored," wearing a "pink bodice cut very low and a short white skirt which hardly came below her knees." Another recalled her black wig and "girl's white frock" cut "disgustingly low" to her stomach.

Caroline bounced around Europe and the Mediterranean, sometimes received by aristocratic houses but more often snubbed, especially as stories of her strange behavior spread. Having lost the last of her respectable entourage by the end of 1815, she was attended by a ragtag group of hangers-on and adventurers, itinerant show players and musicians, and scandalous persons of low birth. She engaged in affairs wildly and publicly, canoodling with everyone from the king of Naples (brother-in-law of Napoleon and therefore an enemy to England) to her Italian valet, or so the gossips said. So complete was her break with the court that no official word was sent of her daughter Charlotte's marriage on May 2, 1816. When Charlotte died in childbirth on November 6, 1817, Caroline, then living in an Italian villa on Lake Como, found out by reading about the tragedy in the newspaper.

In January 1820, poor mad George III died, and Prinney became His Majesty George IV. But he flat-out refused to allow Caroline to be queen. In June of that year, his ministers offered her an astounding £50,000 a year (about $6 million) to renounce her title and never return. Instead, she came bustling back to England, aglow with righteous indignation and bleating about her rights.

Pains and Penalties

Caroline did have supporters back home. Despite her long absence, the British public loved her even more when they saw her thumbing her nose at the much-hated royal family. Her return was attended by pro–Queen Caroline rallies, most of which turned into window-breaking riots, while mobs stood under the king's window and called him "Nero." Even the military seemed on the verge of mutiny. Meanwhile, the country's two main political parties girded their loins: Caroline's side was taken up by the opposition party, the Whigs; they were opposed to the Tories, who were the king's favorites and the party in power. The king declared he'd rather abdicate than recognize Caroline as queen.

With rebellion staring them in the face, the British government was forced to act. In August 1820, the Pains and Penalties Bill was brought before Parliament, an effort to legally dissolve Caroline and George's marriage by declaring her guilty of adultery. But if the government was trying to *avoid* a scandal, they failed spectacularly—the resulting trial aired all sorts of shocking and ridiculous details. First to take the stand was an Italian servant of Caroline's who testified that her supposed lover, the Italian valet Bergami, did not often sleep in his own bed. Further, he claimed he once heard sounds "like the creaking of a bench" coming from a tent in which Bergami and Caroline were together. Another witness claimed that the chamber pots in Caroline's rooms contained a "good deal" more than a single person could produce. And still another claimed that he'd come upon Bergami and Caroline asleep in a carriage, her hand upon his "private part" and his upon hers.

Caroline, meanwhile, acted like a parody of herself, wearing a startling black wig over a face caked in rouge, sometimes nodding off during the duller parts of the proceedings. But however she conducted herself, and however damning the evidence was against her, public support for

Caroline only increased. So, too, did libel against the king and his supporters. Realizing there was virtually no chance of getting the bill through both the House of Lords and the House of Commons, the measure was withdrawn.

Victory was hollow. Caroline was savvy enough to realize that although she had political supporters, she had virtually no friends. She was shunned by most of society, and the king's allies made sure that anyone who tried to befriend her saw their reputation shredded in the press. Moreover, the public was fickle and lacked patience for bad behavior. One bit of doggerel popular at the time went:

> *Most gracious Queen, we thee implore,*
> *To go away and sin no more;*
> *Or if that effort be too great,*
> *Go away at any rate.*

But she didn't, and her humiliation wasn't over yet. On July 20, 1821, the date of the king's coronation, Caroline was denied entry at Westminster Abbey. As she had for most of her life, she doggedly refused to concede defeat, despite having the door literally closed in her face. She wrote to His Majesty that afternoon: "The Queen must trust that after the Public insult her Majesty received the morning, the King will grant her just Right to be crowned on next Monday." The king did no such thing. Less than a month later, a sad and deluded Caroline died. Just 53 years old, she'd been suffering from an obstruction of her bowels, probably cancer, and had been in near-constant pain for most of the summer.

In death, Caroline won a final battle, this one for posterity. The British public mourned their queen's passing with nationwide weeping. Even those aristocrats whose friendship she'd worn out were inclined to think of this unhappy woman kindly and with pity. Conversely, when George IV died nine years later, no one shed a tear. The *Times* declared, "There was never an individual less regretted by his fellow creatures than this deceased King."

Death and the Victorian Age

The daughter of a marriage as unhappy as that of Princess Caroline of Brunswick and the Prince of Wales was unlikely to have an easy life. And Charlotte, a spoiled tomboy with a mercurial temperament, certainly did not. Wedged between her mother and father, the little girl spent the first part of her life as a pawn in their game of one-upmanship. The prince won, and Charlotte was given over almost solely to his care.

Some care. Virtually a prisoner, she was shepherded from one gloomy palatial estate to the next. Nearly every aspect of her life was controlled by her father or the women he appointed to mind her. She was too like her mother to inspire any real affection in dear old Dad, and he usually spoke to her only when he found fault. Nothing was done with Charlotte's comfort or happiness in mind.

Not that her mother would have filled the void any better. By the time Charlotte was 10 years old, Caroline's interaction with her daughter was restricted to a weekly visit. Just 18 years old when her mother left for the Continent, in 1814, Charlotte was devastated, writing, "I am so hurt about it that I am very low." Meanwhile, her father was attempting to arrange her marriage to William, the hereditary prince of Orange, a skinny kid whom Charlotte once said was so ugly, it was all she could do not to turn away when he spoke to her.

The marriage was eventually called off and Charlotte found another suitor whom she came to love immensely. Prince Leopold of Saxe-Coburg-Saalfeld, seven years her senior, smoothed out her rough edges, and she blossomed into the kind of prudent, feminine, and sweet princess everyone had wanted her to be. And here's where the story turns even sadder: the couple had only 18 months of marital bliss before

Charlotte died in childbirth; their son was stillborn.

The nation's outpouring of grief was intense. Charlotte had come to represent the British people's hope for the monarchy; their immense love for her matched their great hatred for her father. Had Charlotte lived, she would have become queen; her death left George III with no legitimate grandchildren. Ultimately, George's fourth son, Edward, wed a suitable princess, who gave birth to Alexandrina Victoria, fifth in line to the throne. Twenty years after Charlotte's death (and the deaths of her uncles), young Princess Alexandrina became Queen Victoria, Britain's longest reigning monarch (so far). Without her, the country might have missed out on all the good stuff associated with the 63-year Victorian era, from Christmas trees to sexual repression.

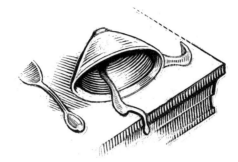

Pauline Bonaparte

The Exhibitionist Princess

OCTOBER 20, 1780-JUNE 9, 1825
NAPOLEON'S EMPIRE

I n 1804, the master sculptor Antonio Canova was commissioned to create a portrait of Pauline Bonaparte, the younger sister of the great Napoleon Bonaparte and an Italian princess by marriage. Pauline wanted to be depicted as Venus Victorious, the triumphant goddess of love. After all, she was in the prime of her beauty—lithe and long limbed, small breasted, milky skinned, wonderfully proportioned. These were her "advantages of nature," as she called them, and she wanted to show them off.

Canova, however, thought that a nearly naked goddess of love might be a bit too sexy for polite society; he suggested Diana, the *clothed* virgin goddess of the hunt and the moon. Pauline scoffed. "Nobody would believe my chastity," she said.

She was right. This was a woman who had her strapping young male servant carry her naked to the bath; who'd been rumored to have slept with half the Caribbean colony of Saint-Domingue; who was painted wearing a sheer dress that showed off her nipples and often wore that same diaphanous negligee to court; who'd had a golden cup fashioned in the shape of her breast; and who liked to entertain male guests while lounging in her bath. Not for nothing did Napoleon's enemies claim that Pauline had been a prostitute at age 14 in a Marseille brothel, or that she and her brother were lovers.

When it came to the sculpture, Pauline got her way (as she usually did). She posed reclining luxuriously on a chaise longue, nude from the waist up, one bare leg peeking out, her feet unshod, with only a draped cloth to protect her modesty (not that she had any use for modesty). When it was unveiled that summer, the plaster model of the statue caused a gossipy sensation in Paris and beyond.

Pauline loved it.

THE ROAD TO ROYALTY

Pauline, called Paoletta as a child, grew up during restless times on the island of Corsica. When she was 13, her family was forced to flee to mainland France after their house was burned to the ground by partisans. She could clearly remember when the Bonaparte clan was just a pack of refugees living in a tiny house in southern France, subsisting off the town's charity and taking in washing to make ends meet.

Pauline grew into an undereducated, oversexed vixen. But she was beautiful, and with her brother's star very much on the rise as a general of the French Revolution, she set her own sights on total social domination, especially if it meant she got to wear pretty dresses.

Pauline married General Victor Emmanuel Leclerc in June 1797, when she was just 17 years old and he was a brilliant young commander in the new army (a "blonde Napoleon," as some called him). Marriage did little to mature her. A contemporary recalled that at dinner one night, she chattered endlessly, laughed at nothing, imitated her elders, and stuck her tongue out at her sister-in-law Josephine behind her back. "She was devoid of principles, and if she did good she did so from caprice."

Pauline's behavior only worsened when she arrived in Paris. She was determined to be the most beautiful woman in the room, a feat that would be a whole lot easier if she was the one making up the guest list, so she started throwing parties. Along with entertaining and buying lots of pretty dresses, Pauline spent her time conducting love affairs. Though content with her "little Leclerc," she was equally happy to spread her affections far and wide. With her husband away on a military campaign, Pauline launched her own offensive on the menfolk of Paris. One story claims that she had simultaneous affairs with three generals, playing them off one another. When they figured it out, they dropped her.

The only thing keeping Pauline's amorousness in check was fear of her brother. He was the sun around which she orbited. When she and Leclerc had a son in 1798, the boy remained nameless until Napoleon, his uncle and godfather, bestowed one upon him (he chose Dermide). Napoleon was her father figure, the family's protector, and the only person who could control her or make her feel ashamed. Though they often fought, Pauline loved her brother truly and deeply.

ISLAND LIFE

And that love was rewarded. In late 1799 Napoleon named himself first consul of the government after a coup toppled the republican regime. He was now the only star in the sky as far as France was concerned, and Pauline cashed in. Sort of. After years of angling for a post that would lead to some glory or remuneration, her husband was made governor general of the island colony of Saint-Domingue (now Haiti). It was a post that could prove quite lucrative, if it didn't kill him first.

Saint-Domingue had shrugged off French rule in 1791 after a slave revolt led by Toussaint Louverture. But the French were hard-pressed to let it go—after all, it was home to some very profitable coffee, sugar, indigo, and cotton plantations. And so in 1801 Napoleon decided to take it back, sending Leclerc, Pauline, and 30,000 troops to do it. When they arrived in February 1802, they were confronted with a terrifying scene. Le Cap, the capital, was an inferno, the commanding rebel having set it alight rather than surrender it to the French. It took only 40 days for Leclerc to regain the colony; Louverture was taken prisoner, and Leclerc promised not to re-enslave the population. But a far deadlier enemy was about to strike: the mosquito. Yellow-fever season hit, killing men at a rate of 50 to 100 a day; within weeks, 25,000 soldiers had died.

Meanwhile, Pauline ruled the island as a queen, throwing balls and hosting musical events and earning a reputation for promiscuous behavior. Napoleon's enemies would later claim that she'd experimented with island men and women, that she slept her way through the officers' ranks, that those nightly musical events were really just orgies. The rumors were mostly untrue; people were too busy dying to worry about having sex.

But the situation in Saint-Domingue was becoming untenable, and local rebels revolted once more. Despite the danger and her husband's insistence, Pauline vowed to stay put. She very much enjoyed being first lady, even if her "paradise" was crawling with angry insurgents and deadly insects. On September 16, the rebels launched an assault on the recently rebuilt capital. Pauline refused to leave the palace, even though she knew that if the rebels reached her, they would rape her and murder her child. Other women pleaded to be allowed to flee. Pauline, either stupid or brave, scoffed at them: "I am the sister of Bonaparte and I am afraid of nothing." As the sound of fire neared, she turned to her husband's secretary and demanded that he kill her and her son should the rebels reach them. He refused and dragged her from the palace. Little Dermide was carried out by a soldier which playing with the plume on the man's helmet.

At the last moment, as the French guard contemplated dumping a struggling Pauline into a galley to row her to a waiting ship, Leclerc appeared—the French had won; the rebels were scattered. "I have sworn to return to France only by your side," Pauline declared, with tears in her eyes. And that's exactly what happened, though not in the sense she intended. Leclerc caught yellow fever and died on November 1, 1802. Seven days later, a weeping Pauline, their son, and her husband's coffin sailed for France. Before leaving, she sheared off her long dark hair, placing the locks next to Leclerc's skin. As for Saint-Domingue, France would lose the colony for good the next year.

Pauline truly mourned her husband, but such a woman was unable to keep it up for long. She was only 22, still beautiful, and, most important, politically valuable. Napoleon had other plans for his sister than a life in widow's weeds, like marrying her off to a prince, thereby tightening his grip on the empire.

Princess Pick-Me-Up

The prince in question was handsome, rich, and well connected. He was also as dumb as mittens on a cat. Prince Camillo Borghese came from one of the oldest families in Rome. Coincidentally, Napoleon needed to endear himself to the Italian principalities and city-states chafing under French rule, and gaining a Borghese brother-in-law would certainly prove beneficial. Pauline was happy to help, especially since Camillo came with money, a palace, and a heavy box full of family jewels.

Pauline remarried in August 1803, less than a year after the death of Leclerc, and moved to the prince's villa in Italy. But within a few months, she realized that everyone was right about this guy—he *was* dumb. And even the second time around, matrimony didn't keep her from pursuing her favorite pastime: sex with lots of different men. On the heels of one love affair that became too public, her brother forbade her to leave her husband and return to Paris, no matter how much she complained about Camillo's "difficult and disputatious character." But however much she disliked her vapid mate now, she would absolutely *loathe* him very soon. Because the same summer that sculpture of Pauline's nearly naked body caused titillation in Italy and France, her dear son Dermide died, and it wasn't until 10 days later that she knew anything about it.

Camillo, who'd never warmed to little Dermide, had convinced Pauline to leave the boy with his brother while the couple took a cure at a popular spa town. While they were away, Dermide caught a fever and died. Fearing Pauline's anger, Camillo hid the child's death from his wife. Turns out he was right to be afraid—when Pauline learned the truth, she flew into a rage. "Leave, Monsieur, I cannot bear the sight of you!" she cried. "You, the butcher of my son!" Pauline was utterly broken. Once again she cut off her hair and instructed that it be put in Dermide's coffin. She also threatened to retire from public life forever. It was only her brother's demand that she be present when he crowned himself emperor that kept her from making good on her promise.

But that was the end of cordial relations between the Borgheses. By 1806, Pauline was referring to Camillo as "His Serene Idiot." When he was heading off to war with Prussia, Pauline publicly asked her brother to secure for her husband, "after a useless life, a glorious death." When Camillo sent her notes addressed to the "Princess Borghese," she sent them back; she opened only those addressed to "Her Imperial Highness the Princess Pauline," the title her brother had bestowed on her in 1806.

If Pauline had been promiscuous before, she now pursued infidelity with truly reckless abandon. Her seductions were legendary: her lovers included Thomas Dumas, the famous mixed-race general and father of Alexandre, the future *Monte Cristo* writer; various generals under her brother's command; her chamberlain; a famous actor or two; some musicians; various princes and minor royalty; her first husband's secretary (when no one else was there to fill in); and pretty much anyone else who came knocking. Her affections flared wildly and were extinguished quickly. She tried to keep her affairs hidden from her brother, but he heard the whispers nevertheless. Those who were involved with her often found themselves conscripted into the army and sent to the front.

Popular rumor claimed that Pauline's frequent sexual liaisons had rendered her too weak to walk, which explained why she insisted on being carried everywhere and was so often confined to her bed. For once, gossip might have been correct. Dermide's birth had left Pauline with chronic pelvic pain, which some biographers believe could have been caused by salpingitis, an inflammation of the fallopian tubes; this condition would have made walking very painful. But salpingitis can also be caused by, well, too many sexual partners and the venereal diseases they can bring. The one thing that probably would have helped was the one thing that Pauline wouldn't do: give up her lovers.

And among those lovers may have been her brother. Empress Josephine claimed that she'd caught the two siblings in the act, and another courtier asserted that Pauline admitted the incestuous transgression to him. One modern biographer maintains that, given the reputed sexual appetites of both brother and sister, as well as their natural affinity for each other, it is probable the pair did experiment sexually together.

Whatever the truth behind their relationship, one fact remains: Napoleon watched over his sister devotedly. More than once he stepped in to save her from creditors, often paying, with minimal grumbling, the many hefty bills she racked up in her travels. Pauline certainly loved to spend money: she bought a yacht she never set foot on, traveled constantly between spa towns and water-cure resorts, and threw sumptuous balls. Along with her excessive consumption was a streak of diva behavior, which asserted itself in the sorts of outrageous requests that only royals can make. For example, she bathed in milk to preserve her white skin, which was as inconvenient as it sounds. Once, Pauline dropped in on a hapless relative and demanded that he procure milk for her bath, adding too that she would require a shower after. The poor man explained that he didn't have the equipment for such an undertaking. "Nothing so easy," Pauline responded. "Just make a hole in the ceiling above my bath, and have your servants pour the milk through when I am ready." She left his home after just one night, leaving behind a hole in the ceiling and a miasma of soured milk.

Traveling with this royal pain was also no picnic. Pauline had a habit of stopping her entourage so that she could switch from carriage to sedan chair, rearrange her clothing, or nap in a meadow. To ensure a comfortable snooze, she liked to use people as furniture. She would order one guard to sit upright so she could lean against him and another to lie down so that his stomach could serve as a footrest. Putting her feet on people seems to have been one of Pauline's favorite pastimes. One duchess recalled entering her boudoir to find a lady-in-waiting stretched flat on the floor, Pauline's feet resting on her throat. The poor woman cheerfully declared, "I am well used to it."

PARTY IN EXILE

But however much of a handful she could be, Pauline still had one virtue: loyalty. When Napoleon was down on his luck, she was the only sibling to support him. When he divorced the wife he loved, a move born of the necessity to produce an heir, Pauline threw no less than ten grand balls to cheer him up (true, she'd never liked Josephine anyway). And though she may not have agreed with his imperial pretensions, she sold her jewels to pay for his armies (extravagance is sometimes a good investment).

Even as forces within the French empire conspired against her brother, Pauline could be counted on. In April 1814, after a decade as emperor, Napoleon was ousted and exiled to the island of Elba, a rocky but beautiful outcropping off the Mediterranean coast of Italy. Pauline went with him. "If he will permit me to follow him, I will never leave him. . . . I have not loved him because he was a Sovereign, but because he is my brother," she said. To scare up cash, she sold properties and more jewelry. Just as she had been on Saint-Domingue, she became first lady of Elba, organizing balls, theatrical presentations, and receptions for the exiled emperor, holding court with local leading families and a growing retinue of hangers-on and exiled French officials. Napoleon even bestowed on her the awesome title "Organizer of Entertainments on the Island of Elba," which sounds like the nineteenth-century equivalent of "Cruise Director of the *Love Boat*."

This little island kingdom didn't last, however. By February 1815, Napoleon was ready to try his luck at reclaiming his empire. His plans failed. After only 100 days in power, he was defeated at the battle of Waterloo. Sewn into the lining of the carriage he abandoned there was a diamond necklace Pauline had given to fund his cause.

It was all over for the emperor, Pauline, and the Bonapartes. Joining Napoleon in exile in St. Helena was out of the question, though Pauline repeatedly asked for permission from the British authorities who sent him there. Meanwhile, she needed to figure out how she was going to live, especially after her long-suffering husband, Prince Borghese, sued for divorce. In June 1816, the couple was granted a decree of separation, and Pauline came out the victor: she got a 20,000-franc annual income and use of the Borghese palace.

With her existence somewhat secure, Pauline spent the next few years entertaining, visiting spas, and trying to help her brother, to no avail—

Napoleon died on May 5, 1821, still in exile. Pauline found out months later, and it was as though the light inside her went out. She'd grown thin worrying about her brother, and her beauty had faded. She demanded that the Canova statue, the one she'd so loved to show off, be put in storage. Though she still took lovers and sometimes entertained gentlemen guests while in her bath, Pauline largely retreated from the partying life she had once led. Her health, never robust, declined precipitously.

By all accounts, Pauline was an indolent and vain woman chiefly concerned with money and sex. But she was also fiercely devoted to her family and could exhibit some of the most daring qualities of bravery when her loved ones were in danger. When she died at the age of 44, her famed beauty was gone and she was in constant pain. Her will, however, made it clear what she'd valued most; she left everything to her family, including a villa for her estranged husband, with whom she'd reconciled. It made no mention of any of the men who'd been her lovers.

Margaret

The Princess Who Caused a Bank Robbery

August 21, 1930–February 9, 2002
Great Britain

The heist made headlines, and rightfully so: on the night of Saturday, September 11, 1971, a gang of thieves tunneled into the safety-deposit box vault at a Lloyd's Bank and made off with an untold fortune. The perpetrators had rented a storefront two doors down, at the corner of Baker Street and Marylebone Road. Under the cover of renovations, they dug a tunnel about 40 feet long, passing under a Chicken Inn restaurant and emerging inside the vault. At the crime scene were the scrawled words "Let Sherlock Holmes try to solve this."

Estimates at the time put the haul at around £500,000, but in fact it was much more—it's impossible to know the full value of the contents of the safety-deposit boxes. In the end, it didn't take the legendary detective to figure out who did it. In 1973 four men were arrested and jailed for the crime, although the mastermind was never apprehended.

But just four days after this incredible story broke, the newspapers stopped talking about it. In the world of British tabloids, that was extraordinary. Rumors spread that the authorities had put out a "D-notice," effectively a gag order preventing media from discussing details that might compromise national security. A few reports in the London *Times* followed, but the story was basically swept under the rug. Why?

The producers of the 2008 crime film *The Bank Job* claim to have the answer: the heist was, in fact, set up by British Security Service, better known as MI5, to steal compromising photographs of Princess Margaret, Queen Elizabeth II's wayward sister. The film suggests that Margaret, whose marriage was in steep decline and who was enjoying a lot of time on the Caribbean island of Mustique, had been captured in blurry images participating in a threesome with a nameless man and woman. More recent chatter suggests that if the robbery was set up by MI5, then the pictures were of Margaret and small-time gangster John Bindon, who'd also spent time on the island. Bindon claimed in 1972 that he'd engaged in an intimate relationship with the princess and had photos to prove it.

Was the bank robbery done in service to the crown? Possibly. The producers of the film claim they got the inside scoop from those in the know, but of course they would say that. Even if it's not true, there's no denying that Princess Margaret was a frequent fixture in the British gossip pages. Long before Prince Harry learned the hard way that what happens in Vegas doesn't always stay in Vegas, his great-aunt was giving the palace serious palpitations.

CLOUDY SKIES

Margaret was born in Scotland in 1930 during a late-summer thunderstorm. If you're inclined to see these sorts of things as omens, then you could say she lived the rest of her life directly under that dark cloud.

When Margaret was six years old, her uncle David, known officially as King Edward VIII, abdicated the throne over his refusal to give up Wallis Simpson, the twice-divorced American temptress with Nazi sympathies. Margaret's father, Bertie, became King George VI, and her older sister, Princess Elizabeth, became heir apparent. And Margaret? She was heard wailing, "Now that Papa is king, I am nothing."

Royal or not, the sisters fell into a pattern familiar to many parents. Elizabeth, four years older, was the serious and dutiful one. Margaret was the fun-loving spoiled prankster of whom little was expected. The sisters fought (Margaret was a biter); Elizabeth complained, "Margaret always wants what I want." Their childhood was as normal as could be expected. Margaret excelled at music, loved blood-soaked pirate comic books, and was a natural comedian. In 1939, as the outbreak of war forced the royal family to decamp to Windsor Castle, Margaret whined, "Who is this Hitler, spoiling everything?"

While Elizabeth was groomed to be the next queen, Margaret was left to founder. By the time she was 20 years old, her older sister was already married and had two children. Margaret's greatest talents seemed to be mastering the latest dance steps and being bright and funny; her only purpose was to marry a rich aristocrat. While waiting for that eventuality, she threw herself into partying and clubbing, staying out until four in the morning, smoking in public, and generally having a jolly good time.

DUTY CALLS

But the first man Margaret fell in love with was not a rich aristocrat. He was a dashing middle-class fighter pilot named Peter Townsend, who had shot down the first German bomber on British soil. At age 29, he was considerably older than 13-year-old Margaret when he came into her father's service as equerry (i.e., the guy who announces visitors to the king). And he was a married man. Margaret developed a "terrific crush" on him, one that would blossom into full-blown infatuation a few years later. He accompanied her on her official duties, and she could often be found hanging around his office, a perk of his promotion to deputy master of the household.

When she was 22, their affair began in earnest; Townsend's marriage was by then breaking up, and Margaret wasn't a child anymore. At first, it seems, both the Queen Mother and Queen Elizabeth—who had ascended the throne on February 6, 1952, after the death of their father—were prepared to accept Townsend. But Margaret was not a private citizen, and marriage was not hers to decide, a fact that highlights one of the most bizarre aspects of modern royal life.

According to the Royal Marriages Act of 1772, until she reached the age of 25, Margaret could not marry without the queen's consent. After that, her nuptials would have to be agreed on by British Parliament as well as the Parliaments of Commonwealth countries. The queen couldn't help a sister out either, because the monarch is also the head of the Church of England, and Townsend, as a divorcé, was not acceptable to the church. The queen would have to win agreement from the prime minister, Winston Churchill, who thought it would be a bad idea for Elizabeth to give her consent before her coronation (set for June 2, 1953).

It's strange to think that, having just survived World War II, the country would be so concerned over the marriage plans of a 22-year-old woman, regardless of her royal rank. But Britain had only just moved beyond the 1936 abdication crisis triggered by Wallis Simpson's divorce record. Now, despite efforts to keep the story under wraps, British tabloids had gotten wind of Margaret's romantic travails. According to the BBC, rumors began circulating after Margaret was seen brushing a piece of fluff from Townsend's jacket at Elizabeth's coronation. Bad press began to accumulate. As one newspaper sniffed, "It is quite unthinkable that a royal princess, third in line of succession to the throne, should even contemplate a marriage with a man who has been through a divorce." The state moved to part the lovers, and in July 1953, Townsend was assigned to a position abroad. The couple wouldn't see each other again for a year.

And so Margaret waited. When she finally reached her twenty-fifth birthday, she was cautiously confident that Parliament would at last give its seal of approval. But the politicians had other ideas—the princess was told that a sizable faction threatened to resign in protest if she married a divorced man. Marriage to Townsend was still possible, but only in a civil court. And that would mean giving up her rights of succession, her duties and privileges as a princess, and, crucially, her income. She would, like her uncle before her, be forced to move abroad for an indeterminate time. That was too much to ask. On October 31, 1955, the BBC interrupted its normal broadcast to read a statement from the princess, in which she told the nation she had decided not to marry Townsend. "I have been aware that, subject to my renouncing my rights of succession, it might have been possible for me to contract a civil marriage. But, mindful of the Church's teaching that Christian marriage is indissoluble, and conscious of my duty to the Commonwealth, I have resolved to put these considerations before any others."

Margaret had always been given everything she ever wanted, but she couldn't have love. "If I had been allowed to marry Peter, I am sure we would have been happy," she later lamented. "And who knows? It might have lasted." Sadly, her real marriage did not.

SWINGING SIXTIES

The official royal family biography of Margaret is a bare-bones affair: married to Antony Armstrong-Jones on May 6, 1960, at Westminster Abbey, two children, divorced in 1978. Just the facts, none of the juicy reality.

Here's what really happened: After the Townsend affair, Margaret found herself with few matrimonial prospects; all the nice young men who'd once been a part of her "set" had been taken by other women while she was waiting for permission to marry. So once again she threw herself into wild living, visiting nightclubs and dancing the cha-cha, jitterbug, jive, and charleston. (After meeting the princess following one of his shows, Louis Armstrong pronounced her "one hip chick.") Margaret could sing well, if a bit huskily after a decade of heavy smoking, and she liked a good drink. None of that made it difficult for her to perform her daytime duties, which included opening schools and cracking bottles of Champagne on various things. If Margaret resented her sister, she showed it by not arriving to the queen's tenth wedding anniversary celebration until after midnight (and staying for less than an hour).

Margaret met her future husband, Antony Armstrong-Jones, when he was working as a photographer at a party she attended, though she probably didn't remember the encounter afterward. When they crossed paths again, this time at a party he was invited to, Armstrong-Jones was then an up-and-coming society photographer taking pictures for glossy mags like *Tatler*. The two soon became friends, with Margaret frequenting his Pimlico studio/apartment.

Armstrong-Jones—Tony—was not at all the sort of man Margaret usually hung out with. After he moved out of his studio, for example, he rented a room in a friend's house in London's Docklands, where he shared a toilet with the landlord. This was a far cry from the Scottish castles and grand country estates Margaret grew up with. Tony was the son of a successful lawyer, which was a plus, but his parents were divorced, which was not. He was so not Margaret's "sort" that one of her friends made him use the servants' entrance when he visited. He was also rumored to be gay. But he was fun and exciting and, well, she'd just found out that Peter Townsend was marrying again, so . . . just like that, she agreed to marry Tony. This time, her family didn't put up a fight.

The couple wed with great pomp and extra circumstance at Westminster Abbey on May 6, 1960. Margaret's first child arrived a year later, just a few weeks after her husband was made earl of Snowdon and viscount Linley (couldn't have the boy be born without a hereditary title). Tony, meanwhile, continued to earn a living as a photographer and later a documentary film producer, convinced of the need to pay his own way.

The marriage worked, for a while. Tony and Margaret made friends with all kinds of swinging sixties types: comedian Peter Sellers, writer Gore Vidal, designer Mary Quant, the Aga Khan. They partied with booze (her) and pills (him), and they had a lot of sex. Just not always with each other.

THE PRINCESS AND THE PUNK

The cracks in the marriage that had started to form in the mid-1960s were veritable chasms by decade's end. The couple was staying together for the children and for the country—divorce was still scandalous, after all—but both were having affairs, Tony with a 23-year-old and Margaret with men closer to her own age and social status. She also began spending more time on Mustique, the hedonistic Caribbean island where a friend had given her a plot of land as a wedding gift.

By 1973, Margaret's friends felt that she needed a lover, so they set her up with Roddy Llewellyn, a vaguely aristocratic and sexually confused sometime–punk rocker 17 years her junior. The two met during a holiday at a friend's estate in Scotland; before the week was over, they were in love. (Their meeting was, apparently, fated: Roddy had visited a fortune teller five years earlier, who said he'd meet someone whose name began with "M" and with whom he'd spend a lot of time in the West Indies.)

At the beginning of the relationship, Roddy had help from Margaret's friends, who groomed him to be her lover. After a year, however, he chafed at the strictures of being involved with a married princess—Tony wasn't above being jealous—and so he took off, first to Guernsey (too close) and then to Turkey, without telling anyone. Margaret was reportedly so distressed that she swallowed a handful of sleeping pills. Upon his return, the lovers decided to take a breather. Roddy's behavior grew increasingly unhinged—after a bender in Barbados and a breakdown on the plane ride back home, he was checked into a mental facility to rest.

Meanwhile, Tony had fallen in love with his assistant, a woman whom Margaret called "that thing." He was also drinking heavily and barely disguising his hostility for his wayward wife. She said later they would practically growl at each other when passing on the stairs. In 1976, after she and a recuperated Roddy had resumed their relationship, the two were photographed eating lunch together at a bar in Mustique. Tony used the blurry picture as leverage to finally obtain a separation.

Margaret and Roddy's relationship continued throughout her separation, despite the disapproval of her sister and brother-in-law. Roddy, who'd by then completed a horticultural course and found his calling as a gardener, was brought out for events, in the hope that the public might come to accept him. But then he had to go and cut a record. And invest in a restaurant. And generally make a fool of himself. Basically, whatever Roddy did, it would invariably lead to bad press, with Margaret making a "twerp of herself" over him.

When Roddy eventually left her for a woman his own age, Margaret found herself alone yet again. She faced the situation with a stiff-upper-lip sort of realism: "I don't see myself ever marrying again. . . . As a member of the royal family, one is used as a figurehead and, being the sister of you-know-who, it would put her in a difficult position. Anyway, it would probably be too much of a bore!"

No Fairy-Tale Ending

Margaret never did remarry, and her middle age was marked by poor health. Drinking became her main vice, even after she received a diagnosis of alcoholic hepatitis in the late 1970s. In 1985 she had part of a lung removed but, according to the BBC, continued to smoke. She suffered a stroke in 1994 and another in 2000, followed by a ministroke; she lost vision in one eye and was confined to a wheelchair. She died on February 9, 2002, at the age of 71.

Throughout the 1980s and '90s, Margaret remained a favorite target for the British press. *Private Eye* always called her the "royal dwarf," owing to her tiny stature; even as a bedridden Margaret neared the end of her life, one tabloid declared, "She's spoilt and ill-mannered and over the years has drunk enough whisky to open a distillery."

As unfair and nasty as the press could be, Margaret didn't do much to dispel the public's negative perception of her. "One does feel rather sorry for her but she does so very little to help herself," wrote a palace insider. She was spoiled, even in middle age; a friend wrote of her in his diary, "She is, as we all know, tiresome, spoilt, idle and irritating; she has no direction, no overriding interest." Hapless and aimless, she did indeed drink her way through life. She could also be grumpy and ill-tempered, prone to pouts and sulking and occasional bouts of rudeness, none of which plays well to the public.

But Margaret could also be surprisingly kind. She could be counted on to remember birthdays and to send gifts. Her softer side made striking appearances, such as on a diplomatic trip to the tiny Polynesian island of Tuvalu. When her lady-in-waiting was practically eaten alive by insects, the princess gave her own bed to the unfortunate woman and tended the bites herself. She was also full of weird household tips, like how to make perfect scrambled eggs (add a raw egg at the final moment of cooking), and she wanted people around her to relax and "be normal." And though

Margaret may have been frivolous and boozy, she took her official duties very seriously—so much so that she capitulated to the will of the nation, didn't marry the man she wanted, and then stayed married to another whom she should have divorced years earlier.

Princess Margaret's life was certainly bizarre. She was never given anything to do, and so suffered the "spare's" fate of being purely ornamental. That left her more than enough latitude to get up to trouble, a situation compounded by being constantly hounded by paparazzi, a new breed of journalists more rabid and ubiquitous than their ancestors. Everything she did was in the spotlight in a way that would have been unimaginable to earlier generations of royals. And it made her a focal point for those in politics who wanted to curtail the monarchy—and its income. They couldn't attack the queen, on whose head the crown seems to sit as easily as those pillbox hats she wears. But they could attack her scandalous sister.

Margaret's life was recorded by a flock of unauthorized biographies, including *HRH the Princess Margaret: A Life Unfulfilled* and *Margaret: The Tragic Princess*. Even if the pages of such books are filled with speculation and gossip, they at least got the titles right.

Three Princesses Who Chucked Their Crowns for Love

Part of the tragedy of Princess Margaret's life is that she couldn't give it all up—the title, the family, the privilege—for the man she loved. But here are a few who did.

PRINCESS PATRICIA OF CONNAUGHT

The granddaughter of Queen Victoria, Patricia gave up her title when she married a commoner. Sort of. Though no longer allowed to call herself "princess," she was still a part of the British royal family, was invited to events, and stayed in the royal line of succession. But she was known as Lady Patricia Ramsey, wife of a naval commander, until her death in 1974.

PRINCESS UBOLRATANA RAJAKANYA

This Thai princess, the daughter of King Bhumhimbol Adulyadej, relinquished her royal title when she married an American commoner in 1972. The two met when they were studying at the Massachusetts Institute of Technology (she earned a degree in biochemistry). The marriage ended in 1998 after 26 years, and Ubolratana moved back to Thailand.

PRINCESS SAYAKO

The daughter of Japanese emperor Akihito, Sayako renounced her title and its privileges when she married a commoner in November 2005. Now simply Sayako Kuroda, she had to take driving lessons and learn how to shop at the supermarket. She also lost her royal allowance, though the sting of that loss was blunted by her $1.2 million dowry.

Madwomen

PRINCESSES WHO
WERE LIKELY MAD,
OR CLOSE TO IT

Anna of Saxony

The Princess Who Foamed at the Mouth

DECEMBER 23, 1544-DECEMBER 18, 1577
GERMANY, THE NETHERLANDS, TWO ROOMS
IN DRESDEN

I n 1561 William, Prince of Orange, was in the market for a wife. His first wife, a wealthy heiress, had died in 1558, and the prominent Dutch nobleman of the Spanish Empire was looking for another way to shore up his political influence.

Princess Anna of Saxony was an ideal candidate. Daughter of the late elector Maurice of Saxony, and niece of the reigning elector (a princely title of the Holy Roman Empire), she was well bred and well placed. True, she was no great beauty—she was "high colored" (excessively rosy cheeked), lame, and suffered a slight curvature of the spine. But what was that beside money and political connections?

Ahead of the couple's first meeting, one of Anna's ladies-in-waiting warned her aunt that if Anna didn't like William, there was no way she would play the dutiful princess and marry him: "The Fraulein will never be persuaded to do anything she is not inclined to." That was an understatement—Princess Anna of Saxony was a handful even then. It wasn't until after she married, however, that everyone found out just how difficult she could be.

CRAZY FOR YOU

Anna's childhood wasn't easy. At age 9 she lost her father, followed by her mother when she was 11. Raised by her aunt and uncle, the then-current elector of Saxony, Anna was encouraged to think that she was the center of the universe. But she was also an unloved child, forced to grow up in isolation and never forgiven for not being a boy. These circumstances aggravated her tendency to be cruel and self-absorbed. The family saw but one remedy for her unsavory behavior: marry her off early and make her someone else's problem.

Anna met William, then 28 and the acknowledged head of the Dutch nobility, at a wedding in his home region of Nassau. For 17-year-old Anna, it was love at first sight. Gone was the worry that she wouldn't be led to the altar, though it was replaced by another concern: Anna, single-minded and narcissistic, fell crazy in love. Within hours of his departure, she'd fired off three love letters to William. The flames of her hasty ardor were likely fanned by some of her relatives' objections to the match, her desperate need to claw at the affection she'd never really had, and the fact that she was absolutely insane.

William was busy with other things, so he just signed his name to the amorous replies penned by his brother and best friend, Louis. Despite using an epistolary surrogate, William *did* want to marry Anna—her position and wealth made the match exceptionally attractive. The two were wed in August 1561, during a weeklong bacchanal that included a jousting tournament and a public bedding (a charming custom in which bride and groom were conveyed to their chamber by jovial wedding guests, dumped into bed amid much ribald joking, and left to consummate the marriage while folks sniggered outside the door). The 5,500 guests drank 3,600 buckets of wine and 1,600 barrels of beer. At one point during the celebrations, William confided to Anna's aunt that he wanted his young bride to concern herself with dancing and French novels, not sewing and religious education. The electoress was shocked and prophesied that allowing Anna such freedom would prove her undoing.

Anna did come to a bad end, but it probably wasn't French novels and dancing that got her there. By 1565, whatever had been sweet in the couple's four-year marriage had completely soured. Everyone from aristocratic gossips to Antwerp housewives referred to Anna as William's "domestic curse." One biographer writing in the 1940s noted that "even the bitterest propagandists, who stopped at nothing to blacken William, could find no word to whiten his wife."

With twenty-first-century hindsight, it's pretty clear that Anna was mentally ill and that the vast amounts of alcohol she consumed, coupled with her social position, exacerbated the condition. She careened from melancholic weeping to reckless hilarity. She often threatened to kill herself and went without eating or speaking to anyone, shutting herself in her room and rocking back and forth. Or she'd go manic and tear off with her entourage of "lewd" friends to Spa, a town southeast of Liège. While there, she'd spend buckets of money she didn't have and then wail that her husband was trying to poison her when he demanded she come home. When she was home, she abused William's children from his previous marriage so much that he was forced to send them away.

Anna was a mean drunk. Once, while staying at a family castle during one of her last pregnancies, she raged against her hosts for trying to keep her from drinking wine. Even at a time when women routinely consumed alcohol during pregnancy, family members feared Anna's bouts of liquor-infused abandon would harm the fetus. Not that Anna seemed to care. She'd lost two children just days after their births, and though her third, a son, seemed likely to live, she was unable to express any affection for him. Still, despite her erratic behavior and inability to mother, Anna did her duty and gave William a respectable five children.

Anna was also bizarrely jealous. She loved to make scenes and was known to imply that William was involved in some sort of sordid, possibly sexual, relationship with his brother. One count recalled a disastrous evening during which Anna spent the entire meal abusing her husband for what she claimed was his social inferiority; once she finished that harangue, she started in on his sexual inadequacies. After such outbursts, Anna could be dramatically sorry, offering tearful apologies to her beleaguered husband, who by then knew better than to believe them.

By 1568, Anna's behavior had become intolerable. She seemed to genuinely hate William, who, to his credit, frequently tried to reconcile with her. Once, when she was living in grotesque extravagance in Cologne, a messenger arrived with a letter from him asking her to come home. In front of a crowd, she tore the note to pieces, stamped on it, and screamed that she'd sooner see him dead and buried than return.

After the birth of their last child, Anna broke with William completely. She took off with Johannes Rubens, a middle-aged lawyer who was married with children. The couple eventually shacked up outside Cologne in 1571. Though she tried to deny the affair, the evidence was rapidly growing—she was pregnant with her lover's child. Rubens confessed, causing Anna to pitch one of her trademark fits. She demanded that William kill both her and her lover, as was his right. Rubens, unsurprisingly, was not a fan of this idea; perhaps more surprisingly, neither was his wife, who pleaded for her wayward husband's life.

William declined to execute either of them. After all, beheading a princess of Saxony, mad though she was, was politically unpalatable. (For the history of art, too, this decision proved fortunate: Johannes Rubens would one day father Peter Paul Rubens, the Flemish baroque painter.) Johannes and his forgiving wife raised his daughter by Anna, likely sparing the child a lifetime of unhappiness.

Under Lock and Key

Anna, however, was not so lucky. William divorced her in 1571 and never set eyes on her again. The divorce was kept secret, and she was taken into custody by her family. Her manic behavior only intensified. She was never left alone and, by 1572, was treated to twice-weekly sermons from local preachers, in the hope that divine intervention might inspire her to step off her wicked path. It's a mark of the times that Anna was never perceived as anything other than willfully bad, guilty of a "stubborn, petrified malice." The treatment she received toward the end of her life mirrored that of other mentally ill individuals at that time: enforced isolation in abominable conditions, punctuated by frequent applications of religion.

In 1575, Anna was moved to her family home in Dresden. She was kept locked in two rooms with bricked-up windows; the door had only a small iron-gated opening for the delivery of food. Not surprisingly, her condition worsened. She complained of not being fed enough and drank huge quantities of olive oil for reasons known only to her. She was also tortured by hallucinations. She raved that people were trying to kill her, that she'd murdered her own children, that her daughters had been sexually involved with their father. She foamed at the mouth and talked gibberish "as if she were crazy." In 1576, she attacked a local man with knives, "raging and foolish as if she were possessed." She died in 1577, at the age of 33.

Sadly, some of Anna's children may have inherited their mother's wellspring of insanity, or perhaps they had been damaged by such a fraught upbringing. Emilia, William and Anna's youngest child, went the most spectacularly off the rails. She was arrested as a "madwoman," screamed at anyone near her, and attempted suicide several times before her death in 1629.

Three Mad Princesses (and One Who Probably Wasn't)

Anna of Saxony was by no means the only certifiable princess in European history. With consanguinity no barrier to marriage in the Continent's royal houses, inherited mental disorders were perpetuated, and the bizarre semipublic social positions into which unstable people were often thrust probably didn't help. But not all who were supposed to be mad really were. Madness, it seems, has its perks.

Princess Alexandra Amelie of Bavaria

The daughter of King Ludwig I of Bavaria, Princess Alexandra Amelie was the only one of her nine siblings who never married. Her father put off would-be suitors by claiming she was in fragile health. But her health wasn't the only thing fragile about Alexandra. At age 23, the pretty, dark-haired princess was found walking slowly, carefully, bow-leggedly down the corridors of the royal palace. When questioned by her worried parents, she claimed that as a little girl she had swallowed a full-size glass grand piano. The princess was worried that if she bumped into something, the piano inside her would shatter and leave her in bloody shreds.

Glass delusions were a frequent symptom of melancholy, the pre-psychology catchall diagnosis of mental illnesses that endured into the nineteenth century. Sufferers sometimes believed that part or even all of their bodies were made of the material. In the fourteenth century, for example, Charles VI of France thought he had glass internal organs, and to protect them he had iron ribs inserted into his clothes.

Alexandra's behavior was odd in other ways as well. She would only wear white and was obsessed with cleanliness; certain sights and smells disturbed her. Gossips claimed that she also believed she had a sofa in her head. In 1850, Alexandra was reportedly treated in a mental institution in Germany. She spent much of her adult life in a convent, where she was made an abbess, probably by virtue of her social station. She later had a career as a writer of children's stories. She died in 1875, at age 49.

Countess Elizabeth Bathory of Hungary

On December 29, 1610, Count George Thurzo, accompanied by an armed phalanx of soldiers, seized a small castle in northwest Hungary. Searching the grounds, they found the body of a young woman, recently dead and covered with bruises, rope burns, and cuts. In a dank dungeon, they found another woman, nearly dead from the festering wounds all over her body. And there were others, the count wrote to his wife in a hastily scrawled note on December 30, "that damned woman was keeping for torture."

"That damned woman" was Countess Elizabeth Bathory, princess of Hungary and one of the most powerful aristocrats in sixteenth-century Europe. A mass murderess, the story goes, she believed that bathing in the blood of young maidens would maintain her youth. This is probably just myth, but Elizabeth was undoubtedly cruel, sadistic, amoral, and insane.

The number of women and young girls she either killed or tortured—by beating, biting, burning, branding, cutting, and starving them, as well as forcing them to stand naked in freezing streams in the middle of winter—is unclear. Her servants, four people named as accomplices by an investigating commission, claimed they'd been party to between 36 and 50 murders. Later witnesses put the number as high as 650, though that figure is likely an exaggeration.

How Elizabeth could have killed so many women and gotten away with it for so long is mind-boggling. But at that time in Hungary, the feudal pact between the classes was lethally imbalanced. Masters had all the power and few obligations to their serfs. Where a serf could be executed for stealing, a member of the aristocracy could literally get away with murder, provided that the victim was of sufficiently low rank. Cruelty of the kind Elizabeth practiced on her servants was not unheard of—savage beatings for trivial or imagined offenses were the prerogative of the ruling class. What's more, Elizabeth was spectacularly powerful, second only to the king.

In public life, Elizabeth was a doting mother and a strong political force, even after the death of her husband, the reportedly cruel Count of Nadasdy. It appears that her murderous activities came to light only about 1609, when she began preying on noblewomen; in fact, most of the victims named in court testimonies were related to Elizabeth by blood or marriage. Though she had a reputation as a hard taskmistress, she enjoyed a steady supply of young noblewomen from poor families—years of war had left many families with more daughters than they could marry off.

Despite the stunning charges against her, not to mention the political factions who would have loved to see her executed, Elizabeth was never convicted of any crime. Three of her servants/accomplices were executed, as was a local woman accused of being a witch in Elizabeth's service. Elizabeth *was* punished, however, but it was her family, not a court, that decided to incarcerate her. She was locked in her bedchamber, the door bricked up, with only a small slot for delivering meals. She died on August 21, 1614.

MARIA I OF PORTUGAL

Queen Maria I of Portugal, whose madness was of a religious inclination, terrified the residents of her palace by moaning "Ai, Jesus, Jesus!" at all hours of the day and night.

But she wasn't always like that. Born in 1734, Maria inherited the throne from her father in 1777. Her first act was to kick out the marquis of Pomba, whom her father had allowed free rein to imprison and execute members of the nobility whenever he felt threatened. From then on, she was regarded as a wise queen. And even when faced with the deaths of five loved ones within three months, in 1788, she bore up with grace and strength. But in 1791, heredity caught up with her.

Maria came from a long line of anxious, twitchy, mentally ill royals. Her grandfather, Philip V of Spain, was tortured by the belief that he was being consumed by fire from within; he refused to cut his hair or toenails and claimed that his feet were different sizes. Her uncle, Ferdinand VI, refused to wash or shave, banged his head against the wall for hours, and refused all solid foods. And Maria's father was plagued by claustrophobia, the result of surviving a massive earthquake that destroyed his palace and killed more than 100,000 people. From an early age, Maria had what contemporaries termed a "gloomy temperament" and was "subject to nervous afflictions," anxiety attacks, and fears for her eternal soul.

With the death of Maria's confessor, a quiet man who could calm her fears, a new priest was appointed to safeguard her. A man of the cloth of the hellfire and damnation variety, he could not have been less suited to the task, only fueling Maria's anxieties that she and her loved ones were doomed. The revolution in not-too-distant France, which had stripped the Bourbon king of his powers, also did little to soothe her terror. In 1789, she banned the editor of the *Lisbon Gazette* from printing any more stories about the bloodshed abroad.

By October 1791, Maria was plagued by nightly panics

that kept her from sleeping; she complained of pains in her stomach and throat and refused to eat. Two months later, doctors were called to treat her worsening condition with a good bleeding. The experience only terrified the poor queen even more.

On February 2, 1792, Maria began howling during an opera performance. That week her foreign minister wrote to the Portuguese ambassador to England: "It is with great sadness that I inform you that Her Majesty is suffering from a melancholic affliction which has descended into insanity, into what is feared to be a total frenzy." The minister asked for Dr. Francis Willis, the famous Lincolnshire doctor who attended the unfortunate King George III of Britain during his bouts of insanity. Willis could claim success—he had "cured" the king at his private asylum after only a few months (though George III would go permanently mad in 1811). While waiting for Willis to arrive, court physicians treated Maria the only way they knew how: she was bled, forcibly dunked in waters at a therapeutic spa, and, because she refused medicine orally, held down and given enemas. When Willis arrived, he demanded full control over the queen's treatment, for which the Portuguese crown paid £20,000 (more than $1.5 million in today's currency). His brutal regimen was no more enlightened than that of the court doctors, although he did suggest a reprieve from the daily masses and religious pageantry that seemed to exacerbate her condition.

By this time Maria's son Prince João, a timid and uneducated ruler, had taken control of the country. While Maria sank into depression and madness, Portugal, burdened by João's cowardly leadership, fell prey to Napoleon Bonaparte. In November 1807, the French emperor's army marched into Lisbon. The royal family fled, with mad Maria bundled into a sedan chair and then forcibly dumped into the galley that rowed her to the flagship. Three months later, she and her family sailed into the harbor in Rio. Maria was packed off to a Carmelite convent, where she died in 1816.

Juana "la Loca"

Juana la Loca, or Joanna the Mad, was probably not really insane. But for those who wanted to control the future queen of Castile—that is, her husband, her father, and her son—it was convenient to let everyone believe that she was.

Born in 1479, Juana was the daughter of the monarchs known as the *Reyes Católicos*, Queen Isabella of Castile and King Fernando of Aragon, the powerful monarchs of two independent kingdoms. She was beautiful, with long auburn hair and clear blue eyes; conversant in Latin, French, and a host of Iberian languages; and clever, pious, and a stickler for formal court etiquette. In short, the perfect princess. In 1496, at age 16, she married Philip the Handsome, the 17-year-old duke of Flemish Burgundy, in a political union that brought together the Hapsburgs and her family, the Trastámaras.

Juana loved her husband, and he loved a lot of other women. Still, the couple produced six children in eight years, thus securing their own dynasty. In 1500, the unexpected deaths of three of Juana's siblings left her first in line for the Castile crown, and it was around this time that the seeds of her later "madness" were planted.

Despite being a princess, Juana had little money of her own; Philip held the purse strings, meaning that he controlled her household and, soon enough, her official affairs. When Juana seemed poised to rebel against his authority, Philip's courtiers began spreading gossip about her. Juana always had a mercurial, hysterical temperament, a fault her husband's courtiers exaggerated, claiming that she was insanely jealous, would agree to anything Philip said, and spent hours in the bath with her female Moorish slaves. But Queen Isabella, Juana's indomitable mother, was aware of Philip's power play and knew he did not have Spanish interests at heart. Though rumors of Juana's "ill health" were spreading, Isabella's last will reaffirmed her daughter's rights as successor and included directives to prevent Philip from stealing the Castilian crown.

Nevertheless, on Isabella's death in November 1504, Phillip did just that, proclaiming himself king of Castile. He then locked up his wife and drew up a document that would allow him to rule in her stead, forging her signature. He and his entourage continued to claim that "mad" Juana was unfit to rule. Two years later, when Philip died, Juana's father found it useful to keep up the pretense—he had his own designs on his late wife's kingdom.

On the surface, Juana's actions didn't help matters. Eight months pregnant at the time of Philip's death, she demanded that his body be buried in faraway Granada, at great personal and financial cost. The decision played right into the hands of her political rivals, making her mental state appear questionable and tallying with earlier claims that she loved her husband a bit too much. While the funeral procession was en route, rumors blossomed that Juana couldn't bear to be parted from Philip's decaying corpse, that she opened his coffin to kiss his rotting feet, that she believed he would be resurrected.

There is no evidence that Juana ever caressed her dead husband. And her decision to bury him in Granada was actually quite shrewd—Southern Spain was home to the only political faction that might be willing to back her. The trip got her away from her husband's Hapsburg relations and advisors, who were clamoring for her to surrender the throne. It also reinforced her right to rule Castile in the minds of those who witnessed the coffin-bearing pilgrimage through the country.

Unfortunately, the gambit didn't work. Her authority was already too far eroded, and Juana was easily outfoxed by her crafty father (not for nothing was he one of the models for Machiavelli's *Prince*). Under the guise of loving patriarch, Fernando made sure everyone believed Juana was toting around Philip's corpse because she was insane, and he began to assume control of her household, just as Philip had done early in their marriage. In 1507, he took over her government, and in 1509 Juana was permanently confined to the castle at

Tordesillas. When Fernando died in 1516, Juana's son Charles then kept up the fiction of his mother's madness.

Juana's behavior may not have always been normal, but neither were the circumstances in which she was forced to live. Ultimately her family's propaganda had done its job. Juana died at Tordesillas on April 12, 1555, and is still remembered as Juana la Loca, Spain's sad, mad queen.

Elisabeth of Austria

The Princess Who Wore
a Meat Mask

DECEMBER 24, 1837–SEPTEMBER 10, 1898
THE AUSTRIAN EMPIRE

I f Elisabeth, empress of Austria, ever told anyone she was busy washing her hair, chances are they believed her. For one thing, her hair was incredibly long. She wore it piled up in a braided crown, which had the effect of making her "head too big for the rest of her figure," according to one contemporary courtier. Washing this mass of to-the-floor auburn locks was like a military maneuver, requiring dozens of egg yolks and 20 bottles of the "best French brandy," according to her valet. She later added pressed onions and Peruvian balsam to the shampoo mix.

The nightly brushing took place over several hours and had its own rituals: a white cloth was laid over the floor, and the hairdresser was clothed entirely in white. After he'd brushed and arranged Elisabeth's hair, he gathered up the strands that had fallen out and counted them. If there were too many, the empress would "become disturbed." She saved them, marking the date that each one fell. Of course, micromanaging one's hair care makes sense when it's the *only* thing you're allowed any control over.

From Princess to Empress

Growing up in a sprawling Bavarian country home, Princess Elisabeth—or Sisi, as everyone called her—had a wild childhood. She stole fruit from neighbors' orchards and wrote treacly romantic poetry about nature and virtuous maidens. Sometimes she and her father would disguise themselves as peasants and perform a song-and-dance act outside beer gardens for pennies. And why not? It was her sister Helene who was being groomed for a grand match to Emperor Franz Josef of Austria, a cousin on their mother's side.

But it was beautiful, free-spirited Elisabeth, then 15 years old, who caught the eye of the handsome 23-year-old emperor. They met at a family reunion, and at a ball the next day, he requested every dance with her. It was just like one of the fairy tales Elisabeth loved to read, except it was happening to her and she was terrified. Within days, Franz Josef asked for her hand. She wept wildly in her mother's arms, crying that of course she loved him, but "if only he were not the emperor."

Elisabeth was hurriedly given an education in everything from history to etiquette. She was constantly surrounded by courtiers, dressmakers, teachers, doctors, lawyers, and ambassadors—overwhelming for anyone, let alone a high-strung girl who craved her freedom. On April 24, 1854, the two lovebirds married, and Elisabeth became empress of Austria and queen of Hungary. She cried like a child, and with good reason. The Austro-Hungarian Empire that she now ruled was a muddle of anarchists, abdications, and assassinations, not to mention stifling and sometimes bizarre court etiquette. Elisabeth was, by both temperament and education, ill-equipped to handle it.

She was certainly no match for her unsympathetic mother-in-law. When the imperial marriage was consummated two days after the wedding, Archduchess Sophia was the first to know. After the woman remarked on her daughter-in-law's "yellow teeth," Elisabeth would never open her mouth to smile and barely opened it to speak. Not that there was anyone to talk to anyway. Elisabeth was permitted to mingle with only a few families, and she had almost no friends. Moreover, her new fame meant that she couldn't so much as buy a pair of gloves at a shop without police protection. She chafed against it all; in time, her hatred of her mother-in-law would blossom into an obsession that lasted until the archduchess's death in 1872.

When Elisabeth became pregnant, any remaining freedom she'd enjoyed was wrenched away. In March 1855, at age 17, she gave birth to a girl, who was named Sophia *by* the archduchess *for* the archduchess. The girl was then taken away and placed under her grandmother's care. The imperial nursery was outfitted with staff chosen by the archduchess and had the added benefit of being located on the same floor as her apartments. But though Elisabeth later complained about being kept from her children, she probably didn't mind very much. Being relieved of the stresses of motherhood allowed her to spend more time on her favorite hobby: cultivating her beauty.

Fairest of Them All

If Elisabeth had been a character in a fairy tale, she would have been the one saying "Mirror, mirror on the wall." Her manic pursuit of physical perfection was classic image-disorder behavior. Unable to control most aspects of her life, she turned to the one thing she *could* manage: her appearance.

Along with the elaborate hair-care regimen, Elisabeth starved herself to preserve her tiny waist, which measured only about 18 inches, freakishly small even by the corseted standards of the day. She showed it off by having herself sewn into her riding clothes and wearing chamois leather undergarments to provide warmth without adding bulk. She insisted on weighing herself twice a day. If she exceeded her self-imposed limit of 110 pounds (on a 5-foot-8-inch frame), then she immediately put herself on a starvation diet of oranges, raw meat juice, and egg whites mixed with salt. During her pregnancies, she found her body disgusting and hated to be seen in public; after each birth, she would become obsessed with regaining her figure and followed a starvation diet and extreme exercise. By 1875 she was sleeping with hot towels wrapped around her waist to keep slim; though she was then 38 years old and mother of four children, her waist still measured no more than 20 inches. She remained rail thin, given to crash diets of, say, only grapes or milk and violet–flavored sorbet.

Throughout her life, Elisabeth exercised incessantly, walking for five or six hours a day, fencing, and riding horses. To keep her muscles supple, she had a Swedish masseur work on her with a special lotion of alcohol, glycerin, and "ox-gall" (cow bile, basically). She was also manic about cleanliness and hygiene. She had a bath installed in her dressing rooms so that she could plunge into cold water every morning. Later in life she frequently bathed in warm olive oil to keep her skin supple and soft. If she were near the coast, she'd have seawater brought in and warmed for her bath.

These punishing beauty and fitness routines became even more excessive under stress. When, at just 20 years old, she lost her daughter Sophia to the measles, Elisabeth refused to eat and seemed to be intentionally starving herself to death. She rallied after becoming pregnant for a third time in the hope that the child would be a son and she'd never have to deal with that baby business again. After Crown Prince Rudolph's birth in 1858, she threw herself right back into exercise. She had a gymnasium installed in her dressing room, complete with parallel bars and rings; the equipment was packed up and transported whenever she traveled.

As she grew older, Elisabeth's obsession with outdoor exercise and frequent crash diets began to take a toll on her skin, prompting her to go to radical measures to preserve it. Long before Lady Gaga donned meat as fashion, Elisabeth was sleeping in a silk face mask lined with raw veal as a remedy for freckles. Or she would coat her face in purified honey for several hours, following that up with a paste of fresh strawberries muddled with petroleum jelly. She traveled with a coterie of special Jersey cows, which she felt gave especially pure milk; she used their cream, mixed with a paste of lily bulbs, as a lotion. Of course, given that many cosmetics in the nineteenth century were made with lead and arsenic, she might've been better off.

UNHAPPILY EVER AFTER

Curiously, despite the attention lavished on her looks, Elisabeth bristled at anyone actually looking at her, hiding her face behind a leather fan or parasol. She seemed to see herself as a goddess whose beauty was not for mortal eyes, as if she feared people's gaze would somehow destroy it. This attitude tallied with her fascination with the Greek language, classical gods and heroes, writing and reciting poetry, and fairy tales. She also began to obsess over the idea of being the most beautiful woman in the world, collecting scrapbooks filled with pictures of women whom she considered her rivals. "Life will be worthless to me when I am no longer desirable," she's alleged to have said more than once.

Elizabeth's eccentricities affected several aspects of her personal life, but one of the most salient was the deterioration of her marriage. The emperor was infatuated with his young wife but was mystified by her, too. He was practical; she was romantic and prone to jealousy. He clung to etiquette; she was used to being with people like her mother, who kept her dogs on her lap during dinner, killing their fleas and depositing the dead insects on her plate. Ultimately, Franz Josef never understood his wife, and that deeply frustrated her. He also refused to acknowledge that the girl he'd married had blossomed into a clever young woman with a quick mind and sympathetic understanding of international politics. He frequently rebuffed her efforts to offer advice, disregarding what was often sound counsel.

As time went on, sex became a problem, too. Disgusted as she was by her body during pregnancy, Elisabeth was terrified of having more children. After Rudolf was born, she ended all intimate contact with her husband; abstinence also flattered her self-image as an unsullied goddess, desired but unattainable. By withholding sexual favors, though, she had to face the very real fear that Franz Josef would find another woman. And in 1860, her worst fears were realized: after being diagnosed with a venereal disease (likely gonorrhea), 23-year-old Elisabeth realized that her husband had been unfaithful. She took off traveling, the first of what would be a lifetime of trips to escape the Austrian court and Franz Josef, who bankrolled her peripatetic lifestyle without complaint.

The couple made up enough in 1867 for Elisabeth to become pregnant again, this time with Valerie, the only daughter she raised as she wished. She then spent the rest of her life keeping the emperor at arm's length. When Franz Josef began a long affair with an actress in 1885, Elisabeth not only promoted the match, she also seems to have orchestrated it by engineering frequent meetings. Her jealousy had clearly transmuted into something else.

From Mad to Worse

Elisabeth's obsession with her beauty was coupled with a deep persecution complex; as young as 22, she regularly complained of being surrounded by enemies. She wept often and would shut herself up in her room for days. She had a tendency toward hypochondria, which unfortunately was encouraged by her depression, unhealthy diet, and doctors.

Elisabeth's fragile state wasn't entirely unexpected—several of her close relatives also suffered from varying degrees of mental illness. King Ludwig II of Bavaria, one of her favorite cousins, lived a life of romantic isolation before allegedly turning dangerously paranoid and violent. She was aware that mental illness ran in the family and dwelled on the idea that she, too, would one day go insane. Even if she hadn't had a genetic propensity to madness, there was plenty in her life to drive a sane person batty. Along with constant political turmoil and increasing isolation, Elisabeth suffered personal tragedy. Her siblings and relatives were dying in increasingly awful ways (fire, firing squad, shipwreck), and in 1889 her estranged son killed himself and his 17-year-old mistress in a suicide pact. It's no wonder, then, that for her birthday one year, she asked for a Bengal tiger and, barring that, a fully operational lunatic asylum.

Elizabeth's response to the pressures of her life was flight, which exacerbated her problematic self-imposed isolation. One courtier remarked, "She has a mind diseased, and she leads such an isolated life that she only makes herself worse." But constant travel helped bring Elisabeth back to the person she thought she was. She could be brilliantly happy, especially when foxhunting in Ireland or swimming in the Greek islands. When away from court, she was charming, kind, solicitous, and loving to her children and husband. Perhaps that's why she pursued travel with almost as much fervor as she policed her own body.

Elisabeth's mother once wrote to her, "You don't know how to live or to make allowances for the exigencies of modern life. You belong to another age, the time of saints and martyrs. Don't give yourself too much the airs of the saint or break your heart imagining yourself to be a martyr." These words proved strangely prophetic. Elisabeth did become a martyr of sorts, emblematic of the dying European empires. While out on a walk in Geneva on September 10, 1898, she was stabbed through the heart by an Italian anarchist named Luigi Lucheni. She was 60 years old. Her murderer later said he had been looking for a crowned head to murder that day, and Elisabeth just happened to fit the bill. Adding insult to injury, Lucheni said, "She wasn't very beautiful. Quite old already."

Beware the Black Dwarf

Princess Catherine Radziwill, a disgraced member of Eastern European royalty (read about her on page 97), sometimes earned a living writing celebrity tell-alls about the aristrocrats of Europe, including a book titled *The Black Dwarf of Vienna and Other Weird Stories*. In this collection, the titular dwarf was a dreaded specter who appeared before every disaster that befell the Austrian royal family.

The dwarf was rumored to be a court fool in the employ of an Austrian emperor, but the emperor, for reasons unknown, executed the jolly man, condemning him to haunt the palace ever after. He was first seen "laughing sardonically" while wandering the halls of the Hofburg in Vienna in 1683, just before the city was besieged by the Turks. Only when the city was rescued by the Polish army did the dwarf disappear. He was practically a court fixture during the reign of the unhappy Maria Theresa, an empress who "hardly knew a quiet moment during the long years that she occupied her throne," according to Radziwill. He appeared the day the French queen and former Austrian princess Marie Antoinette mounted the scaffold to lose her head. On that occasion, he at least had the good grace to look "immeasurably sad."

The only time the Black Dwarf was ever seen outside the Hofburg halls was when he appeared to the ill-fated Empress Elisabeth and her lady-in-waiting at a hotel in Geneva. According to Radziwill: "He flitted before Elizabeth as she proceeded along the passage, but as she was to enter her apartments, he vanished, but not without having made her a sign of farewell, which was but too well understood a few hours later, when the dagger of Luchenni sent the Empress into eternity."

Charlotte of Belgium

The Princess Who
Scared the Pope

JUNE 7, 1840-JANUARY 19, 1927
MEXICO BOTH REAL AND IMAGINED

A polite princess—a polite anyone, really—knows not to stick her finger in the pope's hot chocolate. But when Princess Charlotte of Belgium burst in on His Holiness's breakfast at the Vatican, she was starving—she hadn't eaten more than a few bites in days, convinced that her enemies were trying to poison her. The pope's morning cocoa had to be safe, right? Surely no one would try to poison the pope . . .

Mexican Adventure

Charlotte wasn't always a crazed chocoholic. Life for the pretty, dark-haired princess began promisingly enough. She was born in 1840, the daughter of Leopold of Saxe-Coburg, King of the Belgians, and his second wife. Despite being named after Leopold's first (dead) wife (see "Death and the Victorian Age," page 221), nothing in her early years hinted at the tragedy to come. Serious and smart, little Charlotte started reading Plutarch at age 11 and was her father's favorite. At 16, she fell in love with Ferdinand Maximilian, the 24-year-old Hapsburg archduke and brother of Austrian emperor Franz Josef. Handsome (sort of) and passionate, he talked philosophy and religion with the fervor of a true believer. Against her father's wishes—he planned a match for her with the king of Portugal—she married Maximilian on July 27, 1857.

Unfortunately, Max's passions weren't limited to philosophy and religion. Charlotte tried to keep up the pretense of a happy marriage, but by 1859 she was no longer intimate with her unfaithful husband. Rumors began circulating that he'd given her a venereal disease, although later biographers suggest that Max, who preferred novelty and new experiences, was simply "unable to perform" with her.

In 1863, Napoleon III offered Maximilian the crown of Mexico, a country that had just spent decades embroiled in conflict and civil war. The republic was restored in 1860, but the reformist government under liberal Benito Juarez was broke and burdened with foreign debts. In 1861, on the pretense of trying to reclaim their lost money, France, Spain, and England invaded Mexico. After the latter two countries pulled out in April 1862, Napoleon III—craving the kind of empire his uncle had won—kept his troops in the capital. Maximilian was part of the French emperor's plan to solidify his claim in Latin America and form an alliance with Austria.

But from the moment Max marched into Mexico City in June 1864, it was clear the whole "Mexican empire" was an illusion. Most Mexicans did not want a foreign ruler; few cheered when the new emperor paraded through the city. They had good reason to be angry. On every corner of the squalid capital, people left maimed and poor by the last war were begging for food. No one working for the imperial government had been paid, and debts were mounting.

At first, Charlotte was keen to get to work. "This country is a vast field in need of cultivation," she wrote to her first cousin, Queen Victoria of Britain, adding that there was nothing else to do "but to till that field." But the hand at the plough was shaky—Maximilian was as bad a leader as he was a husband. He enacted several pieces of good legislation, but his policies lurched from overly liberal to overly conservative, and too often he listened to bad advice. Meanwhile, Benito Juarez was running a rebel government in Chihuahua, which the American government, among others, recognized as official in 1865. Napoleon III, facing increasing international and domestic pressure as well as the continued resistance of the Mexican rebels, was threatening to take his troops and go.

As the situation deteriorated, so, too, did Charlotte's mental stability. She'd tried to take an active interest in her imperial duties, touring the Yucatan and hosting charity events, but by 1865–66, she was wilting. She hated Mexico City and began to find it overwhelmingly dirty and dangerous. She suffered terrible headaches. A deep melancholia that she'd fallen into after her father died never truly dissipated. With the end of sexual relations with her husband, she no longer hoped to have a child; the Mexican public taunted her for being a "barren woman." At the same time, word reached her that the gardener's wife at her husband's Cuernavaca retreat was carrying his child. Just 26 years old, Charlotte sent increasingly incoherent letters to Maximilian that revealed a woman on the verge of a breakdown: "I think you should send [Queen] Victoria a decoration so you can get the Garter. God have mercy on our souls in Purgatory. I think it is going to snow."

But when Napoleon III gave the order to cut off all martial and financial support and reason demanded that Max abdicate, Charlotte sprang into action to defend her throne. In August 1866, she traveled alone to Europe to appeal directly to the French leader.

FIGHT POISON WITH THE POPE

The empress's mental state was questionable even before she left for Europe, but the strain of her critical mission proved overwhelming.

According to accounts, she was thin and haggard and seemed far from the serious but youthful princess who'd left Europe less than three years before.

The meeting with Napoleon III took place behind closed doors; later, Charlotte accused her hosts of trying to poison her. A second meeting went even worse, ending with Empress Eugenie pretending to faint to stop Charlotte's raving about the wrongs done to Mexico and the promises made by France. Then Charlotte went completely mad, seemingly undone by her failure to convince the French monarch to continue propping up the Mexican empire. She decided that duplicitous Napoleon was the Devil himself, out to destroy her and her husband. She became obsessed with the idea that the emperor's assassins were trying to poison her food and drink.

Throughout her European visit, Charlotte raved that her father, mother, and Prince Albert had all been poisoned; even now, she claimed, poisoners were trying to kill her, too. Some evenings she would eat only oranges and nuts, examining the peels and shells to make sure they were intact. She saw spies everywhere—while traveling in Italy, she was convinced that a peasant in a field had come to kill her on Napoleon's orders; an organ-grinder in the streets of Bozen was another of his murderers. Her entourage, who'd come with her from Mexico, became the objects of grave suspicion, and her periods of lucidity were fewer and farther between.

Just when it seemed as if Charlotte couldn't go any crazier, she did. On September 30, while in Rome, she ordered a carriage to drive her to the famous Trevi Fountain. Once there, she jumped down and gulped desperate handfuls of water, muttering, "Here, at least, it will not be poisoned. I was so thirsty." Then she ordered the carriage to take her to the Vatican, where she demanded an audience with Pius IX. Flushed and shaking, Charlotte begged him to protect her from Napoleon's assassins. Seeing a cup of hot chocolate on the table, she pounced on it, dipping her fingers in and licking them, wailing, "I'm starving! Everything they give me is poisoned!"

Charlotte refused to leave the pope's presence, spending hours ranting about the situation in Mexico. By midday, the storm seemed to have passed. At lunch she behaved almost normally, save her demand to eat off the same plate as her lady-in-waiting, and by the afternoon she was persuaded to return to her hotel. But upon noticing that her room keys were missing—they'd been taken with the intention of locking her in that night—she became hysterical and demanded to be returned to the safety of the Vatican. So at ten that night they all trooped back, where the patient pope ordered that the library be turned into a bedchamber. "Nothing is spared me in this life," he remarked wryly, "now a woman has to go mad in the Vatican." The next morning, after Charlotte passed a quiet night under the influence of serious sedatives, she refused to eat or drink anything that hadn't been prepared for His Holiness.

A regular madwoman was one thing, but a crazy empress was a much bigger diplomatic problem. Tongues were wagging, and it became clear that someone had to figure out how to extract Charlotte from her papal safe haven. One of the cardinals hit upon asking the mother superior of a local convent to invite Charlotte to visit the orphans in their care. A flattered Charlotte agreed, at first playing the role of the kind, charitable empress. But then she was shown the kitchens, where she commented on the delicious smell wafting out of the cooking pots. The nun showing her around offered her some of the ragout, using a knife that had a speck of dirt on it. Charlotte began screaming, "It's poison! Only God has saved me!" But she was still starving—she hadn't eaten since early that morning, and in her deranged state she thought that meat snatched directly from the boiling pot would be safe. The burns to her hand were so bad that she fainted while having them dressed.

The doctors could see that Charlotte was suffering from a "severe congestion of the brain," as they wrote to her husband, but what to do about it beyond a steady diet of "bromides" (sedatives) was unclear. The week between September 30, when Charlotte burst in on the pope, and October 6, when she was committed to the care of an imperial physician, was a long one. Her hotel was emptied of guests to minimize the risk that Charlotte would fly into another violent rage over "assassins" coming to kill her. In the mornings, she would direct a carriage to drive her to one of Rome's many fountains, where she'd fill a crystal jug and drink from a glass she'd taken from the papal rooms. She refused to eat anything that hadn't been prepared in front of her; her servants bought live chickens to be killed and trussed before her eyes and kept them tied to the legs of a gilded table in her royal suite. Her letters to Max careened from loving missives by a woman convinced she was dying to an embittered paranoiac convinced that her husband had been trying to murder her.

THE EMPIRE STRIKES OUT

Back in Mexico, Max was waking up to the fact that his empire was a hopeless cause. His wife was insane, French troops were leaving, and a bloody civil war was well under way. But rather than abdicate his throne, abandon his followers, and return to Europe in shame, he decided to stay. It would be an act of suicide.

The French left Mexico on February 5, 1867. With just 8,000 loyal soldiers against Juarez's roughly 40,000, Max waited out a siege at Santiago de Querétaro. The city fell on May 15, and Max and his generals were caught trying to escape. They were tried for treason and sentenced to death by firing squad. On June 19, 1867, Emperor Maximilian I of Mexico was executed by the new government of the country he'd tried to adopt.

Charlotte was never told about her husband's death; for the rest of her life, she was kept in Belgium by her family. Afraid of everyone and everything, she lived in a castle surrounded by a moat, physically and mentally cut off from the outside world. Although she did have lucid moments, Charlotte lived mostly in her own twilight world, never realizing that Max was dead. She waited for him to return, sometimes asking her servants why he was late for dinner. And every spring, she would walk down to the moat, step into a little boat anchored there, and proclaim, "Today we leave for Mexico."

Royal Hotline to Heaven

Charlotte of Belgium may have gotten an audience with the pope, but one princess claims her reach extends above even him. Princess Märtha Louise (b. 1971), the only daughter of King Harald and Queen Sonja of Norway and fourth in line to the throne, said she knew as a child that she could read people's feelings, that she was clairvoyant. It wasn't until her experiences with horses that she realized she could communicate with angels as well as the dead.

In 2007, she and Elizabeth Nordeng (a fellow spiritualist whom she met at a clairvoyance course) opened Astarte Education, an English-language school in Norway that aims to help individuals find their own "spiritual passwords," create miracles, and "get in touch with angels." Since then, the princess and Nordeng have written several books—best sellers in Norway—about their spiritual journey. They write, "There are an infinite number of angels all around us who want to help us in all circumstances and at all times. . . . They are there for us. They are real. They exist." The year it opened, the school offered a three-year course in angel spirituality at an annual cost of $4,150; it now offers workshops in angelic communication, too.

Märtha Louise's claims to contact extra-earthly beings didn't endear her to Norway's religious community—her father, after all, is nominally the head of the state church. In 2010, Norwegian bishop Laila Rikaasen Dahl told the local news, "We don't know enough about the status of the dead, but they belong to God and should be allowed to rest. We should remember the dead, not try to get in touch with them." Others warned the princess that trying to contact the dead was "unhealthy." The palace, however, is staying mum about the princess's hotline to heaven.

Franziska

The Amnesiac Who Became the Lost Romanov Princess

DECEMBER 16, 1896–FEBRUARY 12, 1984
THE RUSSIAN EMPIRE; MULTIPLE MENTAL
HOSPITALS; CHARLOTTESVILLE, VA.; AND
THE WORLD'S IMAGINATION

O n the night of February 17, 1920, a Polish factory worker named Franziska Schanzkowska slipped off a bridge in Berlin and plunged into the icy waters of the Landwehr Canal. She was, she admitted later, trying to kill herself. And in a way she succeeded.

When Schanzkowska was fished out of the frigid waters by police, she refused to speak. She had no identification and no money, only the clothes on her back. For lack of better options, the authorities brought her to a hospital.

Despite her dip in the canal, nothing appeared physically or mentally wrong with the young woman. They called her Fraulein Unbekannt, or "Miss Unknown"; she refused to say who she was and would speak only rarely. She was eventually transferred to Dalldorf, a state-run hospital for the mentally ill. There Miss Unknown kept to her bed, covered her face with blankets, and resisted having her photograph taken. She read constantly, especially newspapers and magazines. Such was Franziska's life for a year and a half—until the day she read about the Romanovs.

To Siberia and Back

Eighteen months before Franziska jumped into the canal, Anastasia Romanov, just a month past her seventeenth birthday, was executed in the basement of a Siberian mansion. She was the youngest daughter of Tsar Nicholas II of Russia, who had abdicated a year before in the face of the implacable Bolshevik army, communists demanding the destruction of the monarchy. Nicholas, his wife, and their children were placed under house arrest and later transferred to a residence in Ekaterinburg, Siberia. As the White Army—the anticommunists who supported the monarchy—inched closer to Ekaterinberg, the Bolsheviks started to panic.

On the night of July 17, 1918, the Romanov family, three of their servants, and their doctor were herded down to the building's basement, where they were shot, by order of communist revolutionary Vladimir Lenin. Empress Alexandra was killed before she could finish crossing herself, and those who survived the initial hail of bullets were stabbed to death with bayonets and beaten with rifle butts. Swiftly, brutally, and bloodily, a 304-year-old Russian dynasty was extinguished.

Two of the children's bodies were burned, and the remaining corpses of the tsar's family were sealed in a pit. The execution itself was hushed up—the Bolsheviks confirmed they'd executed the tsar on the pretext that he was going to try to escape but neglected to mention that they'd murdered the rest of the family as well. The information vacuum that followed allowed rumors to flourish that some of the Romanovs had survived. Within months of the execution, multiple imposters came forward claiming to be various members of the family. Most such impostors were dismissed out of hand, but other claims were not so easy to reject.

In 1921, the stories of Franziska Schanzkowska and Princess Anastasia collided.

Call Me Annie

During Franziska's nineteen months in the hospital, newspapers and magazines were her primary link to the outside world. One day, a chatty nurse showed her the October 23, 1921, issue of *Berliner Illustrirte Zeitung*, which featured a picture of three of the Russian princesses, accompanied by the dramatic speculation that Anastasia had survived the execution. The article announced, "To this day, it has not been possible to definitively establish if, during the course of the massacre, one of the Grand Duchesses, Anastasia, was not merely severely wounded and if she remained alive." Shortly after, Franziska declared that she was, in fact, Anastasia.

After dropping her bombshell, Franziska swore the staff and patients to secrecy. But her claim to be the lost Romanov princess couldn't be kept under wraps, and word soon got around (helped out the door by a fellow inmate). Before long, a continuous parade of curiosity seekers, Russian émigrés, former imperial officers, monarchists, and displaced minor nobility was lining up to see the supposed Romanov offspring. Most didn't believe her, but six months after making her claim, Franziska was adopted by two Russian émigrés, a baron and his wife. They'd never met the real Anastasia, but they were convinced that this woman was telling the truth.

And for good reason, or at least so it seemed. Franziska was about the same height as the murdered princess, had the same arresting blue-grey eyes, and even suffered from the same foot condition, *hallux valgus* (bunions). And when she was pulled from her watery would-be grave, reports noted that she was covered with lacerations and scars, including from a stab wound to her right foot that matched the triangular shape of the bayonets used by the Bolsheviks.

Other evidence soon surfaced. Franziska refused to speak Russian but could understand it and, according to a doctor, spoke it perfectly in her sleep. Under the influence of anesthesia, she raved in perfect English, the language of Anastasia's mother, and spoke French with a "perfect" accent. (Anastasia, like other princesses, had learned French from a young age.) Franziska could also recall intimate details of the Romanovs' family life, including nicknames Anastasia supposedly bestowed on obscure courtiers and military officials. Her imperial etiquette was impeccable. She convinced handwriting experts that she was the real deal (apparently having practiced copying Anastasia's signature from a signed photograph found in a book) and broke into genuine tears upon hearing an obscure waltz that had been played for the princess once upon a time. How could she have known all these things if she wasn't a true Romanov?

In 1922 Franziska, still living with the baron, didn't seem eager to press her claim to princesshood just yet, though she didn't disabuse anyone of the notion, either. When her hosts asked what they should call her, she told them to dispense with etiquette and just call her Fraulein Annie. Which was nice for them and handy for her, relieving her of the pressure to continually act like a princess. It also gave Franziska time to figure out exactly how best to become Anastasia.

At first, a string of happy coincidences, such as the foot deformity, tied Franziska to the deceased princess. But as time went on, three factors conspired to force her into perpetuating her claims: memory "lapses," a growing fear of being found out (Franziska was an unhinged woman with nothing to lose and a lot to gain), and the willingness of those who wanted so much to believe her.

As Anastasia, Franziska declared that the trauma of her family's execution, her beating at the hands of the Bolshevik soldiers, and her subsequent escape had resulted in huge memory gaps. She claimed to have been rescued by a man whom she variously described as a soldier she'd just met or a young guard who'd been friendly to her for weeks; he was either a peasant who'd raped her or a member of a fallen Polish noble family whom she'd married and whose child she'd borne (and then misplaced). She also maintained that her rescuer used some sort of device to alter the shape of her nose and mouth, thus explaining the differences in appearance between her and Anastasia. Most of her details were just as hazy, contradictory, and half formed. For example, she stated that she couldn't read German, tell time, or recognize numbers (despite being a devotee of solitaire). All such inconsistencies were assumed by her supporters to be evidence of the severe abuse she had suffered at the hands of the revolutionaries.

Growing increasingly afraid of being exposed, Franziska devoured everything about the Romanov family, ferreting away facts and information to dole out when questioned. Such details allowed her to endear herself to those people who wanted desperately to believe that Anastasia was alive, namely Romanov relatives. Aristocrats, too, yearned for the days before the Russian Revolution, which had completely destroyed their privileged way of life. Still other supporters hoped that if the imperial family did return to power, their loyalty and assistance to Anastasia would be rewarded. They all seemed to ignore moments when the pretend princess behaved strangely, such as the lapse in imperial etiquette she suffered when she ducked under the dinner table to wipe her nose.

Once people believed the outlandish story, it was difficult for them to stop. Committed to the idea that Anastasia still walked the earth, they were just as invested in the charade as Franziska was. Even evidence proving that she was lying couldn't dissuade them. In 1928, a dozen of the dead tsar's nearest relatives came together to assert that Anna Anderson (an alias Franziska used at hotels to avoid reporters in America) was not Anastasia. They stated, "Our sense of duty compels us to state that the story is only a fairy tale. The memory of our dear departed would be tarnished if we allowed this fantastic story to spread and gain any credence." But such statements didn't sway the true believers. Their belief alone was enough to confuse the general public, with its voracious appetite for stories about the fake Anastasia.

Franziska and her dogged supporters had another reason to stick to their guns despite the holes in her story: money. The tsar's considerable wealth hadn't disappeared with him; his stash of 2 million rubles (more than $20 million in today's money) was left to rot in a Berlin bank. In 1933 the bank issued shares of the remaining funds—totaling only about $105,000 in today's money—to seven Romanov heirs. Anastasia was not among them.

Franziska's lawyers filed a petition to stop the distribution of the inheritance, triggering a 37-year legal battle, the longest in German history, to prove that Franziska/Anna Anderson was Anastasia. The case staggered between rejection and appeal, and falsehoods abounded on both sides. When in 1961 the court finally decided that Franziska's claims were unfounded, her lawyers appealed and the case once again lurched forward. Franziska, however, never appeared in court, which only added an "aura of authenticity to her claim," according to one later biographer.

Nevertheless, the trials made a show of what were, by then, decades of conflicting accounts. People on both sides made up stories, gave inaccurate or contradictory testimony, and generally made a mess of things. Handwriting experts, accent specialists, psychologists, photographic analysts, and forensic investigators who claimed to be able to identify people by their ear shape all examined the evidence. The results were muddled. Some experts claimed that certain facts confirmed Franziska's story, but on the whole the evidence tended to discredit her. On February 17, 1970, the Western German Supreme Court handed down its verdict: the woman claiming to be Anastasia had not proved her case. Not that Franziska cared. By that time, she was in her seventies and frail, and she had long been pushed, prodded, coddled, and cajoled by people who believed her story.

Cat Lady

Franziska was also a little bit crazy. Perhaps unsurprisingly, given that her lifelong career as a royal impostor began with a suicide attempt. From the beginning, she always appeared to teeter on the edge of a nervous breakdown, careening from quiet happiness to tearful mania to dark depression. For someone who'd invented such an elaborate attention-grabbing story, she hated the spotlight and soon became paranoid, believing she was the victim of some vague conspiracy. Not long after moving in to the baron's home, Franziska's tantrums made her unwelcome; she spent the rest of the decade shuffling between hospitals and the homes of various supporters. Beginning in 1928, she lived in America with a wealthy cousin of (the real) Anastasia, Xenia Leeds, and then at the home of

Annie Burr Jennings, a Manhattan socialite happy to host the curiosity. After Franziska attacked the servants, ran naked onto the roof, threw a fit in a department store, and broke down after accidently stepping on and killing her pet parakeet, Jennings had her committed to the Four Winds rest home in upstate New York. Franziska left the sanitorium in 1931 for a psychiatric facility in Germany before resuming her peripatetic lifestyle, moving from guest room to guest room for the next 16 years while relying on the generosity of friends.

Franziska's first permanent home, a former barracks hut near the Black Forest in Germany, was purchased by one of her supporters in 1949. She boarded up the windows to keep out spies, erected a barbed wire fence, and procured four enormous wolfhounds to patrol the property. She became a hoarder, surrounded by cats and stacks of unopened mail. In 1960, she moved to a new prefab chalet, again provided by a supporter. In 1968, she was found inside unconscious, surrounded by her cats. That year, at the behest of a long time supporter, Franziska, now in her seventies, traveled to America. After her tourist visa expired, she married John Eacott Manahan, an eccentric history professor and gifted genealogist from Charlottesville, Virginia, who was more than twenty years her junior. To him, Franziska *was* the princess. He referred to himself as the "son-in-law of the tsar" and "grand duke in waiting." Franziska, now calling herself "Anastasia Manahan," still maintained that she was the lost princess. But as she slipped into dementia, her stories about the Russian imperial family became increasingly bizarre and contradictory. Some days, she even claimed that none of the Romanovs had been killed at all, that they'd all had body doubles who died in their places while the real family members escaped.

The couple lived in squalor for more than a decade, in the kind of house that had the neighbors calling officials about the rats, the garbage, the cats, the smell. They shared the home with more than 20 dogs and dozens of cats, who Franziska claimed were the reincarnations of Anastasia's dead relatives and friends. When the cats died, they were cremated in the fireplace. An overflowing tub of potatoes sat on the balcony to assuage Franziska's fear of being hungry in winter. Their car was stuffed with Styrofoam takeout containers; neither of them cooked.

When the couple came down with Rocky Mountain spotted fever in November 1983, it was clear Manahan could no longer care for his wife. She was committed to a psychiatric hospital for observation, only to be "freed" by her husband and then discovered three days later in their filthy station wagon next to an abandoned farmhouse. After that episode, Franziska was placed in a private nursing home. On January 28, 1984, she suffered a stroke; she died of pneumonia on February 12. Manahan would later claim she'd been murdered by KGB agents or possibly British intelligence operatives.

Ironically enough, it was her death certificate that gave Franziska the validation she'd been looking for all her life. Filled out by her husband, it lists her name as "Anastasia Nikolaievna Manahan" and gives her birth date as June 5/18, 1901 (that is, June 5 by the Julian calendar, which was used in Russia before the revolution, and June 18 by the Gregorian calendar) and her birthplace as Peterhof. Her parents are listed as Tsar Nicholas II and Alexandra of Hesse-Darmstadt; her occupation is given as "royalty." Manahan died in 1990.

IDENTITY CRISIS

Despite the court case, doubts and questions about the identity of Anastasia/ Anna/Franziska persisted until science was finally able to give the world a definitive answer. In 1994, using genetic evidence provided from intestinal surgery Franziska had undergone in 1979, scientists determined that she was definitely *not* a Romanov. Moreover, they were 98.5 percent sure that she *was* the Polish factory worker who'd gone missing in 1920. But even knowing who she really was, the questions remain. Why did she do it? And why did she keep up the pretense for the rest of her life?

The second question is the easier one to answer. Once she'd committed to being Anastasia, Franiziska was stuck with her story. She could never give up the assertion for fear of legal repercussions; she also had to be careful about when and how hard to press her claim for fear of being found out. From the moment she declared herself Anastasia, she lived in a kind of sad limbo, unable to return to being Franziska but not likely to ever convince the right people that she was the royal heir.

As for the first question, her initial decision was probably rooted in the same pressures that motivated her to attempt suicide early in life. As a factory worker, Franziska had it rough. It's hard to overstate just how difficult things were for people in Europe during the Great War; there was little food, little work, and little good news. Franziska had a particularly tragic history. After leaving Poland around 1916, she'd managed to find work, first as a maid, then as a waitress, and finally as a worker in a munitions factory. She met a young man, a soldier; they were engaged and she soon became pregnant. But before they were married, he was sent to the eastern front and died from combat wounds. It's likely that Franziska had an abortion. Then, she fainted at work one day and dropped the grenade she was working on. The bomb rolled into a line foreman and exploded, killing him. Franziska awoke in a pool of his blood.

After a nervous breakdown and a brief return to Poland to work in an agricultural field, Franziska eventually left her unsympathetic mother and wandered back to Berlin. She bore a triangular scar on her foot from another farmworker's attack with a farm tool. She found a room with a kind landlady and, it seems, began working as an occasional prostitute. By 1920 she had nothing to live for, and at age 23 she jumped into the freezing cold canal. It was this bizarre baptism that gave her a new life— she emerged first as Fraulein Unbekannt and then, to her lasting fame, the long-lost Romanov princess.

Other people have pretended to be lost royals—some have even pretended to be Anastasia—but none had the influence of Franziska. Her charade propelled the real princess Anastasia from a tragic footnote in a dark chapter of Russian history to being *the* story of the Bolshevik Revolution, inspiring a film starring Ingrid Bergman, a stage musical, and, strangely, a ballet. Even Franziska's death could not stop the flood of fables: in 1997, Fox Animation released a musical called *Anastasia* that took the bare bones of the Romanov story and outfitted them with a creepy sorcerer, a talking albino bat called Bartok, and Meg Ryan as the voice of the amnesiac princess.

It was a fairy tale about as true as Franziska's version of the grand duchess . . . but with a much happier ending.

Famous Last Words

In the end, death comes for us all, princess and pauper alike. But some princesses went out a bit more stylishly, a bit more heroically, a bit more *dramatically* than others. Rani Lakshmibai of Jhansi died fighting the British; Queen Durgavati killed herself after she was wounded in battle rather than be captured by her enemies. Others died as they lived: Anne Boleyn, witty and clever to the end, joked with her executioner that he'd have an easy job chopping off her head because her neck was so thin. All these memorable women passed out of this life and into legend.

MARIE ANTOINETTE:
THE PRINCESS WHO ASKED FOR PARDON (SORT OF)

Marie Antoinette, the lovely, extravagant, too fashionable, and much-maligned victim of the French Revolution, mounted the scaffold to her death on October 16, 1793, with the distinguished bearing of the princess she was. Though whether that bearing was courage and strength or hauteur and arrogance depended on who is telling the story.

Either way, most accounts agree that the Austrian princess and French queen's last words were, "Pardon me, sir, I did not mean to do it." She wasn't, however, talking about all her profligate spending (the porcelain cups in the shape of breasts, the little cottage where she and her friends liked to dress up as shepherdesses, all those Versailles parties) or what the frenzied revolutionaries felt was her evil influence on her weak and by-then 9-months-dead husband, Louis XVI. She was apologizing to the executioner, whose foot she'd just trod on.

ELISABETH OF HESSE AND BY RHINE:
THE PRINCESS WHO DIED SINGING

Elisabeth was the granddaughter of Britain's redoubtable Queen Victoria and a well-loved society beauty in her youth. She married in 1894, but the union was short-lived: her husband, Sergei, was killed by a bomb tossed by a member of the Socialist Revolutionary Party in February 1905; Elisabeth saw his blasted remains lying in the snow. A devout believer in Russian Orthodoxy, Elisabeth forgave her husband's murderer, prayed for him, and even petitioned the court to commute his death sentence. Afterward, Elisabeth became a vegetarian and a nun, divesting herself completely of her vast fortune, even selling off her wedding ring, to build a convent.

But the man who killed her husband wasn't alone in his hatred of blue bloods, and by 1917 the Bolshevik movement had gained an unstoppable momentum. Being even faintly royal was tantamount to a death sentence, and in 1918 Elisabeth was arrested on the orders of Lenin; she'd been offered the opportunity to flee Russia but chose instead to remain with her order. For several months, Elisabeth was shuttled from town to town, under the brutal hands and ruthless eyes of the Red Army guard.

The Bolsheviks, having heard about the tsar's assassination, decided that the rest of the family needed to die as well. On the night of July 17, 1918, the same day the tsar and his family were killed (see "Franziska," page 273), Elisabeth and several other members of the Russian imperial family were woken by Red Army guards and bundled into the back of a cart.

According to one of the assassins, a soldier named Ryabov, her murderers chose an abandoned half-flooded mine shaft some 65 feet deep outside a small village in the Russian countryside for their evil deed. Ryabov recalled that the princess and the others were thrown down the shaft in the hopes that they would drown or die in the fall; they didn't, so their executioners tossed a hand grenade after them. Incredibly, the victims were still alive, so the soldiers tossed in another grenade. "And what do you think—from beneath the ground we heard singing! I was seized with horror. They were singing the prayer: 'Lord, save your people!'" recalled Ryabov. "We had no more grenades, yet it was impossible to leave the deed unfinished. We decided to fill the shaft with dry brushwood and set it alight. Their hymns still rose up through the thick smoke for some time yet."

About three months later, White Army soldiers, the anti-Bolshevik forces, discovered the bodies in the mine. Elisabeth's horrible death and divine life inspired the Russian Orthodox church to canonize her in 1981 and declare her a martyr in 1992 (after, notably, the fall of the Communist regime that killed her).

Noor Inayat Khan:
The Resistance princess who died with "Liberté" on her lips

Princess Noor Inayat Khan, heroine of World War II, deserves a whole chapter, a whole book to herself. The daughter of an Indian father and American mother, Noor was a descendent of Indian Tipu Sultan, the eighteenth-century "Tiger of Mysore" who held off the British East India Company with the first military rockets ever used. Though gentle—before World War II, she was a harpist, a children's book writer, and a Muslim Sufi pacifist—she clearly inherited some of Tipu's martial strength.

In 1940, Noor joined the Women's Auxiliary Air Force and trained to be a wireless operator. Two years later, Britain's Special Operations Executive (SOE) deployed her to Nazi-occupied France as a wireless operator, armed only with a false passport and a pistol, codenamed "Madeleine." At 29 years old, she was the first female wireless operator in occupied France. By the summer of 1943, as the Gestapo ferreted out cell after cell, she was doing the work of six operators and virtually running Resistance communications.

Noor was betrayed by a contact and, after three months on the run, was caught by the Gestapo. She fought like a tiger and tried to escape, climbing out a bathroom window, but she was caught. Regarded by the Germans as uncooperative and dangerous, she spent 10 months in solitary confinement in chains, beaten, starved, tortured, and condemned to "*Nacht und Nebel*" (Night and Fog), the code reserved for people who were to be disappeared. But she never talked. Noor was executed by the Nazis on September 13, 1944, at Dachau prison camp, shot through the back of the head. Her last word was "*Liberté.*"

Noor was posthumously awarded Britain's George Cross, making her one of only three women from the SOE to receive the honor, and France's Croix de Guerre for her bravery. It took a years-long campaign and the concerted effort of many people, but in 2012, Princess Anne unveiled a bronze bust of the spy princess that now graces a London park.

Selected Bibliography

Alfhild

Davidson, Hilda Ellis, commentary, and Peter Fisher, translation. *Saxo Grammaticus: The History of the Danes, Books I–IX, Vol. II Commentary.* Woodbridge, UK: D. S. Brewer, 1980.

Grammaticus, Saxo. *The Danish History, Books I–IX.* http://tinyurl.com/c3ryzv3 (accessed May 15, 2013).

Sawyer, Birgit, and Peter Hayes Sawyer. *Medieval Scandinavia: From Conversion to Reformation, Circa 800–1500.* Minneapolis: University of Minnesota Press, 1993.

Pingyang

Cawthorne, Nigel. *Daughter of Heaven: The True Story of the Only Woman to Become Emperor of China.* Oxford: Oneworld, 2007.

Lewis, Mark Edward. *China's Cosmopolitan Empire: The Tang Dynasty.* Cambridge, Mass.: The Belknap Press of Harvard University Press, 2009.

Peterson, Barbara Bennett, et al., eds. *Notable Women of China: Shang Dynasty to the Early Twentieth Century.* Armonk, N.Y.: M.E. Sharpe, 2000.

Walker, Hugh Dyson. *East Asia: A New History.* Bloomington, IN: AuthorHouse, 2012.

Seven Warrior Queens of Antiquity

Cassius, Dion. *Dio's Roman History.* Trans. Earnest Cary and Herbert Baldwin Foster. Cambridge, Mass.: Loeb Classical Library, 1925.

"Herotodus: Queen Tomyris of the Massagetai and the Defeat of the Persians under Cyrus." Internet Ancient History Sourcebook. http://tinyurl.com/bnuw5h9 (accessed May 15, 2013).

Jones, David E. *Women Warriors: A History.* Washington, D.C.: Brassey's, 1997.

Plutarch. "Pyrrhus." *Parallel Lives.* Trans. John Dryden. Internet Classics Archive. http://tinyurl.com/5r7ejr (accessed Jun 4, 2013).

Schwarz-Bart, Simone, and Andre Schwarz-Bart. *In Praise of Black Women.* Vol. 1, *Ancient African Queens.* Trans. Rose-Myriam Rejouis and Val Vinokurov. Madison: University of Wisconsin Press, 2001.

Skinner, Patricia. "'Halt! Be Men': Sikelgaita of Salerno, Gender and the Norman Conquest of Southern Italy." *Gender and History* 12, no. 3 (Nov 2000): 622–41.

Olga of Kiev

Sherman, Heidi. "Grand Princess Olga: Pagan Vengeance and Sainthood in Kievan

Rus." *World History Connected* 7, no. 1 (Feb 2010).

Zenkovsky, Serge A. "Epics and Stories from the Chronicles." Part A in *Medieval Russia's Epics, Chronicles, and Tales*. New York: Meridian, 1974.

Khutulun

Polo, Marco. *The Travels of Marco Polo: The Complete Yule-Cordier Edition*, vol. 2. New York: Dover, 2012.

Weatherford, Jack. *The Secret History of the Mongol Queens: How the Daughters of Genghis Khan Rescued His Empire*. New York: Crown Publishers, 2010.

———. "The Wrestler Princess." Roundtable (blog), *Lapham's Quarterly*, Sep 3, 2010. http://tinyurl.com/bqjvdyq (accessed May 15, 2013).

Lakshmibai

Kincaid, C. A. "Lakshmibai Rani of Jhansi." *Journal of the Royal Asiatic Society*, 75, nos. 1–2 (Jan 1943): 100–104.

Lebra-Chapman, Joyce. *The Rani of Jhansi: A Study in Female Heroism in India*. Honolulu: University of Hawaii Press, 1986.

Mukherjee, Rudrangshu. "The Reluctant Rebel: Rani Lakshmibai of Jhansi." *Manushi*, no. 87 (1995): 6–10.

Hatshepsut

Brown, Chip. "Hatshepsut." *National Geographic*, Apr 2009.

"Egypt's Golden Empire." PBS interactive website. Mar 15, 2006. http://tinyurl.com/2lmqnd (accessed May 15, 2013).

Tyldesley, Joyce. *Hatshepsut: The Female Pharaoh*. London: Viking, 1996.

———. "Hatshepsut and Tuthmosis: A Royal Feud?" BBC History, Feb 17, 2011. http://tinyurl.com/7xvfpyb (accessed May 15, 2013).

Wilford, John Noble. "Tooth May Have Solved Mummy Mystery." *New York Times*, Jun 27, 2007.

A Family Affair

Dobbs, David. "The Risks and Rewards of Royal Incest." *National Geographic*, Sep 2010.

Wu Zetian

Anderson, Mary M. *Hidden Power: The Palace Eunuchs of Imperial China*. Buffalo, N.Y.: Prometheus Books, 1990.

Barrett, T. H. *The Woman Who Discovered Printing*. New Haven, Conn.: Yale University Press, 2008.

Clements, Jonathan. *Wu: The Chinese Empress Who Schemed, Seduced, and Murdered*

Her Way to Become a Living God. Stroud, UK: Sutton Publishing, 2007.

Dash, Mike. "The Demonization of Empress Wu." Past Imperfect (blog), *Smithsonian*, Aug 10, 2012. http://tinyurl.com/bv79xlg (accessed May 15, 2013).

Wei's Way

Clements, Jonathan. *Wu: The Chinese Empress Who Schemed, Seduced, and Murdered Her Way to Become a Living God*. Stroud, UK: Sutton Publishing, 2007.

Njinga

Heywood, Linda M., and John K. Thornton. *Central Africans, Atlantic Creoles, and the Foundation of the Americas, 1585–1660*. New York: Cambridge University Press, 2007.

Jones, David E. *Women Warriors: A History*. Washington, D.C.: Brassey's, 1997.

Miller, Joseph C. *Kings and Kinsmen: Early Mbundu States in Angola*. Oxford: Clarendon Press, 1976.

———. "Nzinga of Matamba in a New Perspective." *Journal of African History* 16, no. 2 (1975), 201–16.

Orchardson-Mazrui, Elizabeth. *Nzinga, the Warrior Queen*. Nairobi: Jomo Kenyatta Foundation, 2006.

Schwarz-Bart, Simone, and Andre Schwarz-Bart. *In Praise of Black Women*. Vol. 1, *Ancient African Queens*. Trans. Rose-Myriam Rejouis and Val Vinokurov. Madison: University of Wisconsin Press, 2001.

Sweetman, David. *Queen Nzinga: The Woman Who Saved Her People*. London: Longman, 1971.

Thornton, John. "Legitimacy and Political Power: Queen Njinga, 1624–1663." *Journal of African History* 32, no. 1 (1991): 25–40.

Justa Honoria Grata

Bury, J. B. "Justa Grata Honoria." *Journal of Roman Studies* 9 (1919): 1–13.

Gordon, Colin Douglas. *The Age of Attila: Fifth-Century Byzantium and the Barbarians*. Ann Arbor: University of Michigan Press, 1960.

Jenkins, Philip. *Jesus Wars: How Four Patriarchs, Three Queens, and Two Emperors Decided What Christians Would Believe for the Next 1,500 Years*. New York: HarperOne, 2010.

Oost, Stewart Irvin. *Galla Placidia Augusta: A Biographical Essay*. Chicago: University of Chicago Press, 1968.

Isabella of France

Castor, Helen. *She-Wolves: The Women Who Ruled England Before Elizabeth*. London: Faber, 2010.

The Sorceress Princesses

Davis, J. *Duke Humphrey: A Sidelight on Lancastrian England*. Ed. Mary P. Lucy. Ilfracombe, UK: Arthur H. Stockwell, 1973.

Gregory, Philippa, David Baldwin, and Michael Jones. *The Women of the Cousins' War*. New York: Simon & Schuster, 2011.

Mantel, Hilary. "Anne Boleyn: Witch, Bitch, Temptress, Feminist." *The Guardian*, May 11, 2012.

Vickers, Kenneth Hotham. *Humphrey, Duke of Gloucester: A Biography*. London: A. Constable, 1907.

Roxolana

Clot, André. *Suleiman the Magnificent: The Main, His Life, His Epoch*. London: Saqi Books, 2005.

Peirce, Leslie P. *The Imperial Harem: Women and Sovereignty in the Ottoman Empire*. New York: Oxford University Press, 1993.

Yermolenko, Galina I., ed. *Roxolana in European Literature, History and Culture*. Farnham, UK: Ashgate, 2010.

———. "Roxolana: 'The Greatest Empresse of the East.'" *The Muslim World* 95, no. 2 (Apr 2005): 231–48.

Catherine Radziwill

"Ex-Princess Held at Ellis Island." *New York Times*, Apr 30, 1917.

Ferrant, Leda. *The Princess from St. Petersburg*. Lewes, UK: Book Guild, 2000.

"Princess Radziwill Held as Hotel Beat." *New York Times*, Dec 14, 1921.

Roberts, Brian. *Cecil Rhodes and the Princess*. London: Hamish Hamilton, 1969.

Thomas, Antony. *Rhodes: The Race for Africa*. London: Penguin, 1997.

Stephanie von Hohenlohe

Hohenlohe, Franz. *Steph, the Fabulous Princess*. London: New English Library, 1976.

Roosevelt, Franklin Delano. *Memorandum regarding Princess Stephanie von Hohenlohe Waldenburg, with aliases*. Oct 28, 1941. Franklin D. Roosevelt Presidential Library and Museum, Hyde Park, New York.

Schad, Martha. *Hitler's Spy Princess*. Stroud, UK: Sutton Publishing, 2004.

Wilson, Jim. *Nazi Princess: Hitler, Lord Rothermere, and Princess Stephanie von Hohenlohe*. Gloucestershire, UK: History Press, 2011.

Lucrezia

Bellonci, Maria. *Lucrezia Borgia*. London: Phoenix, 2002.

Bradford, Sarah. *Lucrezia Borgia: Life, Love and Death in Renaissance Italy*. New York: Viking, 2004.

Gregorovius, Ferdinand. *Lucretia Borgia: According to Original Documents and Correspondence of Her Day*. Trans. John Leslie Garner. New York: Benjamin Blom, 1904.

Shankland, Hugh. *The Prettiest Love Letters in the World: Letters between Lucrezia Borgia and Pietro Bembo*. London: Collins Harvill, 1987.

Malinche

Cutter, Martha J. "Malinche's Legacy: Translation, Betrayal, and Interlingualism on Chicano/a Literature." *Arizona Quarterly: A Journal of American Literature, Culture and Theory* 66, no. 1 (Spring 2010): 1–33.

Cypess, Sandra Messinger. *La Malinche in Mexican Literature from History to Myth*. Austin: University of Texas Press, 1991.

Thompson, Maris Wistar. "La Malinche: Various Perspectives." In *Selected Essays from the International Conference on Word and World of Discovery, 1992*, ed. Gerald M. Garmon. Carrolton: West Georgia International Conference, 1994.

Townsend, Camilla. *Malintzin's Choices: An Indian Woman in the Conquest of Mexico*. Albuquerque: University of New Mexico Press, 2006.

The War Booty Princess

Maund, Kari. *Princess Nest of Wales: Seductress of the English*. Stroud, UK: Tempus, 2007.

Sophia Dorothea

Herman, Eleanor. *Sex with Kings: 500 Years of Adultery, Power, Rivalry and Revenge*. New York: William Morrow, 2004.

———. *Sex with the Queen: 900 Years of Vile Kings, Virile Lovers, and Passionate Politics*. New York: William Morrow, 2006.

Van der Kiste, John. *The Georgian Princesses*. Stroud, UK: Sutton Publishing, 2000.

Williams, Robert Folkstone. *Memoirs of Sophia Dorothea, consort of George I, chiefly from the secret archives of Hanover, Brunswick, Berlin, and Vienna. . . .* London: H. Colburn, 1845.

Marriage or Insane Asylum?

Marengo. "Princess Louise of Belgium: 'Eve After The Fall of Man.'" The Royal Articles, May 19, 2009. http://tinyurl.com/banvev7 (accessed May 15, 2013).

"Princess Louise of Belgium Elopes." *New York Times*. Feb 1, 1897.

"Princess Louise of Belgium Insane." *New York Times*. Jan 6, 1902.

"Princess Louise, Long a Court Exile, Dies." *New York Times*. Mar 2, 1924.

"Sister Asks Judicial Council For Estate of Louise of Belgium." *New York Times*. Mar 12, 1912.

"$300,000 for Princess: Louise of Belgium Settles Her Troubles With Creditors." *New York Times*. Jan 18, 1914.

Sarah Winnemucca

Canfield, Gae Whitney. *Sarah Winnemucca of the Northern Paiutes*. Norman: University of Oklahoma Press, 1983.

Hopkins, Sarah Winnemucca. *Life Among the Piutes: Their Wrongs and Their Claims*. Ed. Mrs. Horace Mann. Boston: Cupples, Upham, 1883.

Lape, Noreen Groover. "'I Would Rather Be with My People, but Not to Live with Them as They Live': Cultural Liminality and Double Consciousness in Sarah Winnemucca Hopkins's *Life Among the Piutes: Their Wrongs and Claims*." *American Indian Quarterly* 22, no. 3 (Summer 1998): 259–79.

McClure, Andrew S. "Sarah Winnemucca: [Post]Indian Princess and Voice of the Paiutes." *MELUS* 24, no. 2 (Summer 1999): 29–51.

Senier, Siobhan. *Voices of American Indian Assimilation and Resistance: Helen Hunt Jackson, Sarah Winnemucca, and Victoria Howard*. Norman: University of Oklahoma Press, 2001.

Sneider, Leah. "Gender, Literacy, and Sovereignty in Winnemucca's *Life Among the Piutes*." *American Indian Quarterly* 36, no. 3 (Summer 2012): 257–87.

Sorisio, Carolyn. "Playing the Indian Princess? Sarah Winnemucca's Newspaper Career and Performance of American Indian Identities." *Studies in American Indian Literatures* 23, no. 1 (Spring 2011): 1–37.

Stewart, Patricia. "Sarah Winnemucca: Paiute Princess." *Nevada Magazine*, 1978.

Sofka Dolgorouky

Skipwith, Sofka. *Sofka: The Autobiography of a Princess*. London: Hart-Davis, 1968.

Zinovieff, Sofka. *Red Princess: A Revolutionary Life*. London: Granta Books, 2007.

Christina

Buckley, Veronica. *Christina of Sweden*. London: Harper Perennial, 2004.

Jones, David E. *Women Warriors: A History*. Washington, D.C.: Brassey's, 1997.

Thomas, Henry, and Dana Lee Thomas. *Living Biographies of Famous Women*. London: W. H. Allen, 1959.

Caraboo

Gutch, John Matthew. *Caraboo: A narrative of a singular imposition, practised upon the* benevolence of a lady residing in the vicinity of the city of Bristol. . . . London: Baldwin, Cradock and Joy, 1817.

Raison, Jennifer, and Michael Goldie. *Caraboo: The Servant Girl Princess: The Real Story of the Grand Hoax*. Gloucestershire, UK: Windrush Press, 1994.

Wells, John. *Princess Caraboo: Her True Story*. London: Pan Books, 1994.

Six Ways to Fake Princesshood

Bloch, Hannah. "Mummy Not So Dearest." *Time*, Apr 23, 2001.

Brodie, Neil. "Persian Mummy." Trafficking Culture, Aug 12, 2012. http://tinyurl.com/a38np7j (accessed May 15, 2013).

Burton, Sarah. *Impostors: Six Kinds of Liar*. London and New York: Viking, 2000.

Danilevski, Grigory Petrovich. *The Princess Tarakanova: A Dark Chapter of Russian History*. Trans. Ida de Mouchanoff. London: Swan Sonnenschein, 1891.

Grigoriadis, Vanessa. "Her Royal Lie-ess." Intelligencer (blog), *New York*, May 21, 2005. http://tinyurl.com/at7gdlv (accessed May 15, 2013).

Khan, Aamer Ahmed. "Burial for Pakistan's Fake Mummy." BBC News, Aug 5, 2005. http://tinyurl.com/aelytlv (accessed May 15, 2013).

Martinez, Jose. "Fake Princess Antoinette Millard Drops $1.1 Million Lawsuit against Michael Eigen New Directions." *New York Daily News*, Mar 26, 2010.

"Mysterious Mummy 'Princess' Examined in Pakistan." Al Bawaba, Oct 26, 2000. http://tinyurl.com/a8fyy5n (accessed May 15, 2013).

"The Mystery of the Persian Mummy." *BBC Horizon*, BBC Two, Sep 20, 2001. Transcript available online at http://tinyurl.com/ax6q9 (accessed May 15, 2013).

Naqvi, Abbas. "Fake 'Mummy' Still Awaits Burial." BBC News, Jan 24, 2008. http://tinyurl.com/aac9l6r (accessed May 15, 2013).

Romey, Kristin M., and Mark Rose. "Special Report: Saga of the Persian Princess," *Archeology* 54, no. 1 (Jan/Feb 2001).

Saulny, Susan. "Officials Cite Big Spending of a Princess Who Wasn't." *New York Times*, May 8, 2004.

Serres, Olivia Wilmot. *The Princess of Cumberland's Statement to the English Nation, as to her application to ministers. . . .* London: Redford & Robins, 1822.

Shapiro, Harriet. "Dressmaking Was Not Beneath India's Princess Sumair—Now Only Her Prices Are Untouchable." *People*, May 5, 1980.

Sheppard, Eugenia. "Designing Princess Flouts Custom." *Palm Beach Daily News*, Nov 27, 1979.

Wasserstein, Bernard. "Collaborators and Renegades in Occupied Shanghai." *History Today* 48, no. 9 (1998): 20.

———. *Secret War in Shanghai: Treachery, Subversion and Collaboration in the Second World War*. London: Profile Books, 1999.

Charlotte of Prussia

Connolly, Kate. "Sex parties, bloody duels, and blackmail: Life at court of last German emperor." *The Guardian*, Sep 2, 2010.

Van der Kiste, John. *Charlotte and Feodora: A troubled Mother-Daughter Relationship in Imperial Germany*. Seattle, Wash.: Amazon Media, 2012.

Clara Ward

"American Girls Who Married Titles: Clara Ward Becomes Princess Chimay." *The Pittsburgh Press*, Jun 13, 1915.

"American Who Thrilled Europe with Her Loves: End of a Whirlwind Career." *Evening Telegraph*, Jan 4, 1917.

Amory, Cleveland. *Who Killed Society?* New York: Harper, 1960.

Cabot, James L. "Lumberman's Daughter Married a Prince." *Ludington Daily News*, Mar 1, 2003.

"The Chimay Scandal." *Lincolnshire Echo*, Aug 3, 1897.

"Clara Ward Left by Angry Husband." *The Pittsburgh Press*, Jun 19, 1910.

Henrickson, Wilma Wood, ed. *Detroit Perspectives: Crossroads and Turning Points*. Detroit: Wayne State University Press, 1991.

"Hooting a Princess: The Gipsy and His Royal Wife: Hissed in a Paris Theatre." *The Evening Post*, Apr 5, 1902.

Passante, Anna. "Clara Ward: Paparazzi Princess." *Bay View Compass*, Aug 1, 2010.

"The Princess de Chimay." *Evening Telegraph*. Jan 23, 1897.

"A Princess with Conneaut Connections." *Star Beacon*, Apr 1, 2012.

The Dollar Princesses

Brandon, Ruth. *The Dollar Princesses*. London: Weidenfield and Nicolson, 1980.

Kahan, Sylvia. *Music's Modern Muse: A Life of Winnaretta Singer, Princesse de Polignac*. Rochester, N.Y.: University of Rochester Press, 2003.

Sebba, Anne. "Hearts and Hearths." *History Today* 57, no. 9 (2007): 2.

"What Happened to Gladys Deacon, Duchess of Marlborough?" BBC News, Feb 17, 2011. http://tinyurl.com/b3b8m8w (accessed May 15, 2013).

Gloria von Thurn und Taxis

Colacello, Bob. "The Conversion of Gloria TNT." *Vanity Fair*, Jun 2006.

———. "Let Them Eat Lobster!" *Vanity Fair*, Sep 1986.

Fesperman, Dan. "The Party Over, Bavarian Princess Hosts a Most Unusual Yard Sale." *The Baltimore Sun*, Oct 10, 1993.

Melikian, Souran. "Death and Taxes Squeeze Thurn und Taxis Estate: The Growing Cost of Keeping Art." *New York Times*, Jul 22, 1992.

Petkanas, Christopher. "Icon of the Decade: the 1980s: Gloria von Thurn und

Taxis." *W*, Nov 2012.

"Princess Gloria von Thurn und Taxis." *Bloomberg Businessweek*, Jun 16, 2002.

Rockwell, John. "A Princess Tightens Her High-Fashion Belt." *New York Times*, Oct 14, 1993.

Silva, Horacio. "The Talk: Gloria in Extremis." *T Magazine*, Dec 4, 2008.

Stockem, Stefani. "A New Bang for 'TNT': Princess Gloria's New York Tea Party." Spiegel Online, Oct. 9, 2008. http://tinyurl.com/cdoxmk4 (accessed May 15, 2013).

"West Wing." Thurn und Taxis Family Website. http://tinyurl.com/bnge6ts (accessed May 15, 2013).

Princess Excess

Pettifer, Hannah. "Thai Princess Clears Shelves During 8-hour, $40,000 UK Antique Shopping Spree." NBC News, Oct 8, 2012. http://tinyurl.com/d28xpxf (accessed May 15, 2013).

Rayner, Gordon. "WikiLeaks cables: Thailand's Royal Pet." *Daily Telegraph*, Feb 5, 2011.

Rice, Tamara Talbot. *Elizabeth, Empress of Russia*. New York: Praeger, 1970.

Shaw, Adrian. "Epic bail: Saudi princess caught doing a runner from hotel at 3:30 am . . . with 60 servants in tow." *The Mirror*, Jun 5, 2012.

Wilson, Peter H. "Women and Imperial Politics: The Württemberg Consorts 1674–1757." In *Queenship in Europe, 1660–1815: The Role of the Consort*, ed. Clarissa Campbell Orr, 221–51. Cambridge, UK: Cambridge University Press, 2004.

Caroline of Brunswick-Wolfenbüttel

Holme, Thea. *Caroline: A Biography of Caroline of Brunswick*. New York: Atheneum, 1980.

Melville, Lewis [Lewis Saul Benjamin]. *An Injured Queen: Caroline of Brunswick*. London: Hutchinson, 1912.

Plowden, Alison. *Caroline and Charlotte: Regency Scandals, 1795–1821*. Stroud, UK: History Press, 2005.

Richardson, Joanna. *The Disastrous Marriage: A Study of George IV and Caroline of Brunswick*. London: Cape, 1960.

Van der Kiste, John. *The Georgian Princesses*. Stroud, UK: Sutton Publishing, 2000.

Pauline Bonaparte

Fleischman, Hector. *Pauline Bonaparte and her lovers, as revealed by contemporary witnesses, by her own love-letters, and by the anti-Napoleonic pamphleteers*. London: John Lane, 1914.

Fraser, Flora. *Pauline Bonaparte: Venus of Empire*. New York: Alfred Knopf, 2009.

Kühn, Joachim, and Walter Henry Johnson. *Pauline Bonaparte: Napoleon's Attendant Star*. London: Hutchinson, 1937.

Ortzen, Len. *Imperial Venus: The Story of Pauline Bonaparte-Borghese*. London: Constable, 1974.

Margaret

Dempster, Nigel. *H.R.H. the Princess Margaret: A Life Unfulfilled*. Bath, UK: Chivers Press, 1981.

Heald, Tim. *Princess Margaret: A Life Unravelled*. London: Weidenfeld & Nicolson, 2007.

Lawrence, Will. "Revisiting the Riddle of Baker Street." *The Daily Telegraph*, Feb 15, 2008.

Anna of Saxony

Midelfort, H. C. Erik. *Mad Princes of Renaissance Germany*. Charlottesville: University of Virginia Press, 1994.

Wedgwood, C. V. *William the Silent, William of Nassau, Prince of Orange, 1533–1584*. London: Jonathan Cape, 1944.

Three Mad Princesses (and One Who Probably Wasn't)

Aram, Bethany. *Juana the Mad: Sovereignty and Dynasty in Renaissance Europe*. Baltimore: Johns Hopkins University Press, 2005.

Fox, Julia. *Sister Queens: The Noble, Tragic Lives of Katherine of Aragon and Juana, Queen of Castile*. New York: Ballantine, 2011.

Levy, Deborah, and Kate Bland, producers. "The Glass Piano." BBC Radio 3, Dec 2011.

Midelfort, H. C. Erik. *Mad Princes of Renaissance Germany*. Charlottesville: University of Virginia Press, 1994.

Poeta, Salvatore. "The Hispanic and Luso-Brazilian World: From Mad Queen to Martyred Saint: The Case of Juana la Loca Revisited in History and Art on the Occasion of the 450th Anniversary of Her Death." *Hispania* 90, no. 1 (Mar 2007): 165–72.

Roberts, Jenifer. "Portugal's Mad Queen." *History Today* 57, no. 12 (2007): 32.

Thorne, Tony. *Countess Dracula: The Life and Times of the Blood Countess, Elisabeth Báthory*. London: Bloomsbury, 1997.

Elisabeth of Austria

Haslip, Joan. *The Lonely Empress: A Biography of Elizabeth of Austria*. London: Phoenix Press, 2000.

Sinclair, Andrew. *Death by Fame: A Life of Elisabeth, Empress of Austria*. London: Constable, 1998.

Beware the Black Dwarf

Radziwill, Catherine. *The Black Dwarf of Vienna and Other Weird Stories*. London: William Rider and Son, 1916.

Charlotte of Belgium

Haslip, Joan. *Imperial Adventurer: Emperor Maximilian of Mexico*. London: Weidenfeld & Nicholson, 1971.

Ibsen, Kristine. *Maximilian, Mexico, and the Invention of Empire*. Nashville, Tenn.: Vanderbilt University Press, 2010.

Reiss, Ben. "Death by Firing Squad." *History Today* 57, no. 1 (2007): 2.

Royal Hotline to Heaven

Astarte Education website. http://tinyurl.com/mjmkxrz (accessed Jun 5, 2013).

"Norway princess 'talks to angels.'" BBC News, Jul 25, 2007. http://tinyurl.com/lamg7d7 (accessed Jun 5, 2013).

"Norway's princess moving to London with family." The Local, Apr 27, 2012. http://tinyurl.com/n24dh6v (accessed Jun 5, 2013).

"Princess Märtha Louise celebrates 40th birthday." Norway.com, Sep 22, 2011. http://tinyurl.com/kc3syt3 (accessed Jun 5, 2013).

"Princess upsets Norway's bishops." Views and News from Norway, Sep 14, 2010. http://tinyurl.com/22n6ps8 (accessed Jun 5, 2013).

Franziska

King, Greg, and Penny Wilson. *The Resurrection of the Romanovs: Anastasia, Anna Anderson, and the World's Greatest Royal Mystery*. Hoboken: Wiley, 2011.

Tucker, William O., Jr. "Jack & Anna: Remembering the Czar of Charlottesville Eccentrics." *The Hook*, no. 627 (Jul 5, 2007).

Famous Last Words

Fraser, Antonia. *Marie Antoinette: The Journey*. London: Phoenix, 2001.

"Noor Anayat Khan: The Princess who Became a Spy." *The Independent*, Feb 20, 2006. http://tinyurl.com/2ejarkw (accessed Jun 5, 2013).

Olsoufieff, Alexandra. "Palace Personalities: HIH Grand Duchess Elisabeth Feodorovna." Trans. Rob Moshein. Alexander Palace Time Machine. http://tinyurl.com/kq5y8zz (accessed Jun 5, 2013).

Serfes, Archimandrite Nektarios, comp. "Murder of the Grand Duchess Elizabeth." Archimandrite Nektarios Serfes personal website. http://tinyurl.com/mmauaao (accessed Jun 5, 2013).

Index

abdication, 241
Ahmose, Queen, 52
Albert, Prince, 203, 269
Alexander VI, Pope (Rodrigo Borgia),
    114–15, 117
Alexandra Amelie, 250–51
Alf, 16–17, 18
Alfhild, 15–19
Al-Sudairi, Maha, 208
Amenhotep II, 55
Amina of Zaria, 31
Anastasia, 281
Anderson, Anna (Franziska Schanzkow-
    ska), 11, 277–78
Anle, Princess, 64–65
Anna of Saxony, 11, 245–49
Arachidamia, 26
Armstrong-Jones, Antony, 236–37
Attila the Hun, 75, 77–78
Augusta, Empress, 97–98, 99
Austen, Jane, 217
Aztec (Jennings), 125

Baker, Mary. *See* Caraboo (Mary Baker)
Bathory, Elizabeth, 251–52
Behind the Veil of the Russian Court
    (Vasili; Radziwill), 103
Benedict XVI, 205
Bergman, Ingrid, 281
Berlin Society (Vasili; Radziwill), 98, 99
Bernhard III, 184, 186
Bhumibol Adulyadej, 209, 241
*Black Dwarf of Vienna and Other Weird
    Stories, The* (Radziwill), 103, 265
Bobrinsky, Sophy, 145
Boleyn, Anne, 89–91, 282
Bonaparte, Napoleon, 223, 225, 227,
    228–30
Bonaparte, Pauline, 223–31
Borghese, Alessandra, 203
Borghese, Camillo, 227–28, 230
Borgia, Cesare, 113, 115, 116, 117–18,
    119
Borgia, Lucrezia, 113–19
Borgia, Rodrigo (Pope Alexander VI),
    114–15, 117
Boudicca, 27
British East India Company (EIC),
    42–44, 46

Calixtus III, Pope, 114
Canova, Antonio, 223–24
Caraboo (Mary Baker), 11, 162–69
Caroline of Brunswick-Wolfenbüttel,
    213–20
Caselato, Abano, 194–95
Cates, Phoebe, 169
Catherine of Aragon, 90
Catherine the Great, 145, 170, 171
Charaman-Chimay, Joseph de, 190, 191
Charles II, 57
Charles VI, 250
Charlotte (daughter of George IV), 215,
    218, 221–22
Charlotte, Queen, 171
Charlotte of Belgium, 266–71
Charlotte of Prussia, 182–87
Christina of Sweden, 155–61
Churchill, Winston, 197, 235
Cinderella Ate My Daughter (Orenstein),
    9–10
Cobham, Eleanor, 86–88
Constantine VII, 36
Constantinius III, 76
Cortés, Hernan, 121–23, 124, 125
Cortés, Martín, 123, 125
Cyrus the Great, 28

Dahl, Laila Rikaasen, 272
Deacon, Gladys, 197–98
Descartes, René, 157
Despenser, Hugh, 81–82, 83
Devall, William, 172–73
Diana, Princess, 10
Díaz del Castillo, Bernal, 121–22, 124
Dolgorouky, Sofka, 144–51
Dollar Princesses, 196–99
Douglas, Lady, 216–17
Dumas, Thomas, 228
Durgavati, Queen, 30–31, 282

Edward II, 79–84
Edward III, 82–83, 84

Edward IV, 89
Edward VIII, 107, 234
Elisabeth of Austria, 258–64, 265
Elisabeth of Hesse and by Rhine, 283
Elizabeth, Empress, 170
Elizabeth I (England), 90, 158
Elizabeth I (Russia), 207
Elizabeth II, 233, 234, 235
Este, Alfonso d', 116–17
Este, Ercole d', 117
Eugenie, Empress, 269
Eugenius, 76–77

Faure, Jean-Baptiste, 199
Feodora, 184, 186, 187
Ferdinand Maximilian (Maximilian I), 202, 267–68, 270
Ferdinand VI, 253
Fernando of Aragon, 255, 256–57
Fitzherbert, Maria, 214, 215
Franz Josef, 259, 262–63, 267
Fu Hao, 25–26

Galla Placidia Augusta, 76
Gaozong, Emperor, 59, 60–61
Gaozu, Emperor, 23–24
Garbo, Greta, 161
Gaveston, Piers, 79–80
Genghis Khan, 38, 40
George Augustus (George II), 128, 133
George III, 171, 173, 174, 186, 216, 217, 218, 222, 254
George IV ("Prinney"), 213–16, 217–18, 219, 220, 221
George Louis (George I), 127–29, 130, 132
George VI, 234
Gesta Danorum (Deeds of the Danes), 16, 19
Gray, Catherine Willis, 196–97
Guiscard, Robert "the Weasel", 29–30
Gutch, John Matthews, 167–68

Harald, King, 272
Hatshepsut, 51–55
Hayes, Rutherford, 141
Henry I (Wales), 126
Henry IV, 85–86

Henry V, 86, 88
Henry VI, 86, 89
Henry VI, Part 2 (Shakespeare), 88
Henry VIII, 89–91
Henry XXX Reuss, 186
Herodotus, 28
Hitler, Adolf, 105–6, 107, 108
Hohenlohe, Stephanie von, 105–9
Hoover, J. Edgar, 108, 109
Hopkins, Sarah Winnemucca, 11, 136–43
Hugo, Victor, 119
Humphrey, duke of Gloucester, 86, 87–88
Hyacinthus, 77

Igor, 32–33, 35
imposters, 170–81
incest, royal, 56–57, 60
Isabella of Castile, 255
Isabella of France, 79–84
It Really Happened (Radziwill), 104

Jacquetta of Luxembourg, 88–89
Jameson Raid, 99–100, 101, 103
Janczy, Rigo, 191–92, 193–94
Jaramillo, Juan, 123–24
Jennings, Annie Burr, 278–79
Jerome, Jennie, 197
Joan of Navarre, 85–86
John Paul II, 204–5
Johnson, Lyndon B., 109
Josephine, Empress, 225, 228–29, 230
Jourdemayne, Margery, 87
Juana la Loca, 255–57
Juarez, Benito, 267–68
Justa Honoria Grata, 75–78

Kamehameha III, King, 56
Khan, Noor Inayat, 284
Khubilai Khan, 38
Khutulun, 37–40
Komnena, Anna, 29
Konigsmarck, Christopher von, 129–32
Kotze, Leberecht von, 184–85
Kuroda, Sayako, 241

Lakshmibai, Rani, 41–47, 282

last words, 282–85
Leclerc, Victor Emmanuel, 224, 225, 226
Leeds, Xenia, 278
Lenin, Vladimir, 274, 283
Leopold II, 134, 135, 190
Leopold of Saxe-Coburg-Saalfield, 221, 267
Licinia Eudoxia, 78
Life among the Piutes (Hopkins), 137
Li Yuan, 21–22, 23–24
Llewellyn, Roddy, 238
Louise Marie Amélie, 134–35
Louis VII, 117
Louis XVI, 282
Louverture, Toussaint, 225–26
Lucheni, Luigi, 264, 265
Ludwig I, 250
Ludwig II, 263

Malinche, 120–25
Manahan, John Eacott, 279–80
Manu, Bithur. *See* Lakshmibai, Rani
Marco Polo, 38–39
Margaret (England), 232–40
Maria Eleonora, 156–57
Maria I of Portugal, 253–54
Maria Theresa, 265
Marie Antoinette, 265, 282
Märtha Louise, 272
Mattachich, Geza, 134–35
Mazarin, Jules, 160, 161
Mbandi, 66, 68, 69
Middleton, Kate, 10
Millard, Antoinette Lisa (Lisa Walker), 177–78
Moctezuma, 122–23
Montezuma's Daughter (Haggard), 125
Mortimer, Roger, 82–83, 84
Mustafa, Prince, 95–96

Nahi'ena'ena, Princess, 56
Napoleon III, 267–68, 269
Nest of Wales, 126
Nicholas II, Tsar, 99, 274
Njinga of Ndongo, 66–71
Nordeng, Elizabeth, 272

Olga of Kiev, 32–36
Olive of Cumberland (Olivia Serres), 173–75
Olivier, Laurence, 147, 149
Orenstein, Peggy, 9–10
Our Etiquette (Thurn und Taxis), 204

Pasha, Ibrahim, 92, 94, 95
Pasha, Rüstem, 95, 96
Persian Princess, 178–81
Peter III, 170
Philip of Saxe-Coburg-Gotha, 134–35
Philip the Handsome, 255–56
Philip V, 253
Pingyang, 20–24
Pius IX, 269–70
Platen, Clara Elizabeth von, 131
Plutarch, 26
Puccini, Giacomo, 40
Pyrrhus of Epirus, 26

Qaidu Khan, 38, 40

Radziwill, Catherine, 97–104, 265
Rajakanya, Ubolratana, 241
Ramsey, Patricia, 241
Rhodes, Cecil, 99–102
Richard II, 85
Richard III, 89
Rinehart, William, 138–39
Riurik, 35
Romanov, Anastasia, 274
Roosevelt, Franklin, 108
Rothermere, Lord, 106, 108
Roxolana, 92–96
Royal Marriages Act (1772), 235
Rubens, Johannes, 248
Ryabov, 283–84
Ryan, Meg, 281
Rzewuska, Ekaterina Adamevna. *See* Radziwill, Catherine

Sade, Marquis de, 70
Sally of the Northern Paiute people. *See* Winnemucca, Sarah (Hopkins)
Saxo Grammaticus, 16, 17, 18–19
Schanzkowska, Franziska (Anna Anderson), 11, 273–81

Schlulenberg, Melusine von der, 129, 130
Scholfield, Lemuel, 108–9
Serres, Olivia (née Wilmot), 173–75
Seymour, Jane, 90
Sforza, Giovanni, 115, 118
Sigismund I, 94
Sikelgaita, 29–30
Simpson, Wallis, 107, 234, 235
Singer, Winnaretta, 198–99
Singh, Rajkumari Sumair Apjit, 175–76
Skipwith, Grey, 147–48
Skipwith, Sofka. See Dolgorouky, Sofka
Sonja, Queen, 272
Sophia, Archduchess, 260
Sophia Dorothea, 10–11, 127–33
Sousa, Anna de. See Njinga of Ndongo
Srirasmi, 208–9
Stravinsky, Igor, 198
Suleiman, 92, 93, 94, 95, 96
Sumaire, 175–76
Susanna Caroline Matilda (Sarah Wilson), 171–73

Taiping, Princess, 64–65
Taizong, Emperor, 24, 60
Tales of Bygone Years, The (Russian Primary Chronicle), 33, 35
Tang dynasty, 23–24, 59–60, 62, 64–65
Tarakanova, 170–71
Theodosius I, 76
Theodosius II, 77
Thurn und Taxis, Gloria von, 200–205
Thurn und Taxis, Johannes von, 200–202, 203
Thurn und Taxis, Marie Auguste, 206
Tomyris, 28
Toulouse-Lautrec, Henri de, 193
Townsend, Peter, 234–36, 237
"Turandot" (Pétis de la Croix), 40
Turandot (Puccini), 40
Turandotte (Gozzi), 40
Tutankhamun, 57
Tuthmosis III, 52, 54–55

Valentinian III, 75–76, 77–78
Vasili, Paul, 97, 103
Vernon, Caroline, 172

Victoria, Queen, 46–47, 183, 185, 222, 268, 283
Viktoria Elisabeth Auguste Charlotte, 182–87

Walker, Lisa. See Millard, Antoinette Lisa (Lisa Walker)
Wang, Empress, 59, 61
Ward, Clara (Princesse de Caraman-Chimay), 11, 188–95, 197
Washington, George, 196
Wei, Empress, 64
Wilde, Oscar, 199
Wilhelm I, Kaiser, 97, 183
Wilhelm II, 184, 192
William, Prince, 10
William Austin (Willikin), 216–17
William II, 126
William of Orange, 245–48
Wilmot, Olive, 173, 174
Wilson, Sarah. See Susanna Caroline Matilda (Sarah Wilson)
Winnemucca, Sarah (Hopkins), 11, 136–43
witchcraft, 85–91
Woodville, Elizabeth, 89
Woolf, Virginia, 199
Worrall, Samuel and Elizabeth, 163–66, 168
Wu, Empress, 11
Wu Zetian, 58–64

Yangdi, 21–22, 23

Zhou dynasty, 62
Zinovieff, Leo, 146–47

Acknowledgments

This book could not have been written without the work of the many historians who dedicated themselves to telling a story about a princess. Their tremendous work made my job that much easier; for a list of some of the sources consulted, please see the bibliography. And really, please do—there are some great reads in there.

The British Library and its excellent staff—big shout out to the Humanities I Reading Room and the café—were very helpful in making sure my research went smoothly. That such a place exists, where you can examine original copies of John Matthew Gutch's 1817 pamphlet on Princess Caraboo's exploits in the English countryside, mildly pornographic pictures of Princess Nest making out with Henry I, and Princess Catherine Radziwill's entire catalogue, is a gift.

I'd very much like to thank the fine folks at Quirk Books, especially Jason Rekulak, whose brilliant idea was the genesis of the book, and editor Rick Chillot, who is the reason why it makes sense. And a big thanks to the wonderful folks at *Mental Floss* magazine, past and present, who got me working on great stories like the history of toilet paper and how food shaped the course of human evolution.

My friends and family (McRobbies, Eides, and London), who have had to listen to countless stories about this one princess who ran away with a gypsy or that other princess who murdered her rivals in that astounding grisly fashion, thank you. To my Mom, Anita Corbitt, thanks for never calling me your "little princess" and for being generally amazing, and to my step-dad, Joel Corbitt, thanks for marrying my mom. To my glorious, wonderful, adorable, clever little boy, Austin Thomas Rodriguez McRobbie, you are the best reason for me to leave the library.

And of course, I'd like to thank the one without whom this book would be a lot slimmer (to the point of nonexistence): my cat, Norgus. Just kidding, kitty, you're a jerk. The person really responsible for making the following pages happen is Christopher Austin McRobbie, my own Prince Charming—thanks for all those mornings you let me sleep in.

*And they all lived
happily ever after?*

NOT EXACTLY.

For more princesses behaving badly—
plus an exclusive interview with author
Linda Rodriguez McRobbie—
visit quirkbooks.com/
princessesbehavingbadly